Battlegrou

YPRES 1914

THE MENIN ROAD

Battleground series:

Battleground Europe

YPRES 1914

THE MENIN ROAD

Nigel Cave
and Jack Sheldon

Series Editor
Nigel Cave

Pen & Sword
MILITARY

First published in Great Britain in 2019 by
Pen & Sword Military
An imprint of
Pen & Sword Books Ltd
47 Church Street
Barnsley
South Yorkshire   S70 2AS

ISBN 978 178159 200 7

Typeset in Times New Roman by Chic Graphics

Printed and bound in England by
CPI Group (UK) Ltd., Croydon, CR0 4YY

Pen & Sword Books Ltd incorporates the imprints of Pen & Sword
Airworld, Archaeology, Atlas, Aviation, Battleground, Discovery,
Family History, Fiction, History, Maritime, Military, Military Classics,
Politics, Select, Social History, True Crime, Frontline Books, Leo
Cooper, Remember When, Seaforth Publishing, The Praetorian Press,
Wharncliffe Local History, Wharncliffe Transport,
Wharncliffe True Crime and White Owl.

For a complete list of Pen & Sword titles please contact
PEN & SWORD BOOKS LIMITED
47 Church Street, Barnsley, South Yorkshire, S70 2AS, England
E-mail: enquiries@pen-and-sword.co.uk
Website: www.pen-and-sword.co.uk

CONTENTS

Series Editor's Introduction

A project that was first considered several years ago has finally come to an end: three *Battleground Europe* books about a battle that lasted more or less a month and which marked the end of open warfare on the Western Front. There would be no return to such operations for more than three years. Splitting the battle into three books has in many ways proved to be a useful exercise in both understanding the battle and opening up the possibilities for further study.

It is often not appreciated enough that the intention of the Allies, urged on by Joffre, was to carry out offensive actions almost up to the end of October. Higher command decisions, therefore, have to be seen in this light. One such, for example, was Capper's controversial action in holding the Kruiseke Salient rather than falling back to the next defensible line, where in fact it finally ended up in the middle of November. British popular perception has First Ypres as a defensive battle, in which the line was held by the skin of the BEF's teeth, epitomised by the charge of the 2/Worcesters on 31 October at Geluvelt and the repulsing of the Prussian Guard on 11 November. The reality is somewhat different; in particular the role of the French is usually much understated.

The battle was a shining example of inter-allied cooperation, with each of the components playing an effective role and working closely with each other. Examples include the French intervention to bolster the Belgian army along the Yser and the despatching of reinforcements by Dubois and Foch to provide crucial support for the rapidly shrinking part of the line held by the BEF. The long term impact on the relationship between Foch and Haig was, I suggest, considerable: Foch proved to be an entirely reliable ally, in contrast to Lanzerac, who was largely responsible for poisoning military relations between the British and the French in the first months of the war.

Not enough attention, it seems to me, has been paid to a number of other factors, for example: the depth of command capability at all levels in the BEF, given the extent of casualties amongst the officers, from divisional commanders downwards; the ability to break up battalions and redeploy them rapidly, yet still leaving them effective; the crucial role of the BEF's cavalry; the effective deployment of engineering resources; surprisingly good logistical support; even the (political?)

courage of the King of the Belgians to allow the inundation of a good deal of his country. It would be a long time before the allies had the ability or the goodwill to act so closely in harmony again.

On the German side, in addition to the desperate use of undertrained troops, there was an inability to force decisive action, most notably exemplified by the split major attacks on the 10th (largely against the French, to the north) and 11 November. If these attacks had been combined on the 10th, as was the original intention, then there is a very good chance that they would have broken through.

At the end of it all, any dispassionate observer would have to say that both Haig and Foch (and d'Urbal, for that matter) had conducted operations under very difficult conditions in a professional, skilful manner. The same could not be said for the Germans.

Nigel Cave
Ratcliffe College, November 2018

List of Maps

8

9

Introduction

The *Menin Road 1914* is the last of the three books in this series on the First Battle of Ypres to be published. Below we give a brief account of the developing campaign of 1914 in the west that culminated in the desperate fighting that was broadly centred around Ypres. A fuller background section is to be found in *Messines 1914*.

In the main narrative we use spellings found in the British Official History 1914, Volume II; and German time has been altered to that used by the British.

Ypres 1914 was a battle that the British tend to think of as theirs; in fact to the north it involved the whole of the remainder of the Belgian field army and a very substantial contribution by the French. By the end of the battle the latter were holding far more of the Ypres 'line' than were the British. Nevertheless, this book – as do the others – concentrates on the British and German fighting, although we do make frequent references to (and make acknowledgement of) the vital contribution of, in this case, the French.

It is no easy task to summarise the beginnings of the Flanders campaign; the best modern description is to be found in Ian Beckett's *Ypres: The First Battle 1914*; whilst Jack Sheldon's *The German Army at Ypres 1914*, published subsequently, gives a full overview of the German fighting in western Belgium in October and November 1914. *The British Official History 1914*, Volume II and its accompanying case of maps, despite being almost ninety years old, is still a masterpiece of condensation of a very complex battleground; the availability of many more records, official and unofficial, along with considerable academic study over the last fifty years in particular, inevitably presents areas where correction and reinterpretation have been necessary.

IV Corps was the first British formation in the area covered by this book. Its opponents were units and formations of the newly raised German XXVII Reserve Corps from Saxony and Württemberg. IV Corps was formed on 9 October 1914, under the command of Lieutenant General Rawlinson. It comprised 7th Division (Major General Capper), formed mainly from troops that had been garrisoning various parts of the Empire and

Major General T Capper.

10

made up from remaining regular troops in the UK, and the weak 3rd (Cavalry) Division (Major General Byng). After landing at Zeebrugge on 7 October, it was preparing to engage in operations around Antwerp, which still held out against the Germans and containing within its fortified zone the bulk of the Belgian field army.

About the same time the rest of the BEF was moving from the Aisne to Flanders. The background to the move to Flanders is discussed in more detail in *Langemarck 1914* in this trilogy. On 10 October, the Antwerp defences formally surrendered. Belgian troops withdrew, with some difficulty, heading back to a defensive line based on the Yser. IV Corps made

Major General Julian Byng.

its way west towards Ypres, where it arrived about 15 October. The day afterwards, I Corps (Lieutenant General Sir Douglas Haig) began its move to the north from the Aisne, where it had seen considerable action the preceding month. It was the last formation of the BEF to leave the area, and assembled around Hazebrouck on 17 and 18 October.

In very broad terms, the allied concept was to continue to push east from north of Arras and then to swing southwards, taking the Germans on their open flank; such an idea had not escaped the German staff, engaged in similar planning. By 15 October the BEF was spread from approximately west of La Bassée in the south to the Belgian frontier in the north, with II Corps to the south and III Corps to the north of the line; and with Allenby's Cavalry Corps acting as a screen up to the area of Ypres.

Lieutenant General Sir Douglas Haig.

A new German Fourth Army (Generaloberst Duke Albrecht of Württemberg) was formed at the time that Antwerp fell, with instructions to press westwards, bypassing Lille to the north, prior to swinging southwards, with its right flank west of St Omer. To the south, the German Sixth Army (Generaloberst Crown Prince Rupprecht of Bavaria) captured Lille on 12 October, but on 14 October was instructed to limit the push westwards until the Fourth Army's attack began to take effect.

Crown Prince Rupprecht of Bavaria.

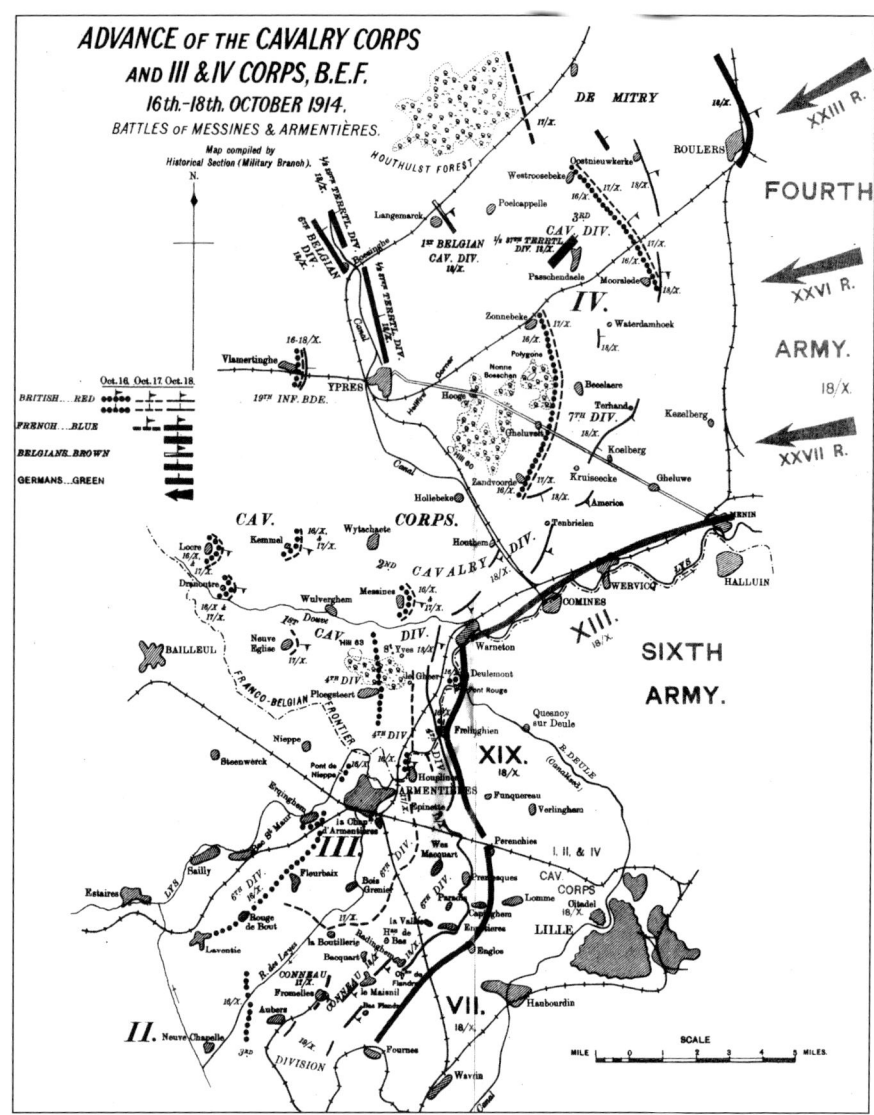

Situation of the BEF in Flanders 16-18 October 1914.

The Germans, meanwhile, were advancing on the withdrawing Belgian field army, which was supported by some French forces. They then launched a major attack against the Belgians and the French, the Battle of the Yser, commencing on 18 October, a ferociously fought battle, that finally was literally swamped by the inundation of the ground to the west of the canalised river, which had taken full effect by 30 October.

I and IV Corps were to form the northern part of the BEF's attack against the Germans; by the time I Corps was fully in position and ready to advance, on 20 October, the Germans were equally engaged, which led to the encounter battle described in *Langemarck*. From the point of view of providing a coherent narrative and of the three areas into which this trilogy of books has divided the Ypres 1914 battlefield, *Langemarck* is the easiest to understand and to follow at battalion level. The Menin Road is the most difficult because, by the end of proceedings, much of the BEF's efforts at Ypres were concentrated on a front from Polygon Wood to Hill 60. Troops from the 1st, 2nd and 3rd Divisions, as well as of the 1st

Duke of Württemberg.

and 3rd Cavalry Divisions, were all fighting within this small area of front, a maximum of six miles in length. Great lengths of the old British line were by then held by two French corps – IX Corps to the north, holding the line from Broodseinde to Langemarck and beyond towards Zonnebeke; and XVI Corps to the south, from Hill 60 to west of Messines.

Almost the whole of this line – though further to the east (it originally extended further to the north, well up towards Passchendaele) – was held on 19 October by Capper's 7th Division, though at that time it lay further to the east, with the easternmost point forming a sharp salient before Kruiseecke. Then it formed a front of eight miles held by this one reasonably complete division, which had not faced any but minor engagements before it moved to Ypres (about 15 October) after its abortive mission to assist in the defence of Antwerp.

It is difficult to extract and present a comprehensive history, a task that the British Official History (BOH) tackles manfully. Even the wonderfully detailed, practically day by day, maps, produced in a separate case to accompany Volume II of the 1914 account, can only provide a snapshot of a particular time (usually, but not exclusively, the evening) on a particular day, so frenetic did things become on an almost daily basis. Unit war diaries – even higher formation diaries – are often very short and singularly uninformative (and some were lost in the fighting). A lot of the detail of what went on was extracted subsequently by interviews and written testimony from a wide range of officers of all levels of rank. It is not uncommon to find in the battalion and brigade files at the National Archives narrative accounts provided by such people. On at least one occasion a battalion was so badly damaged that

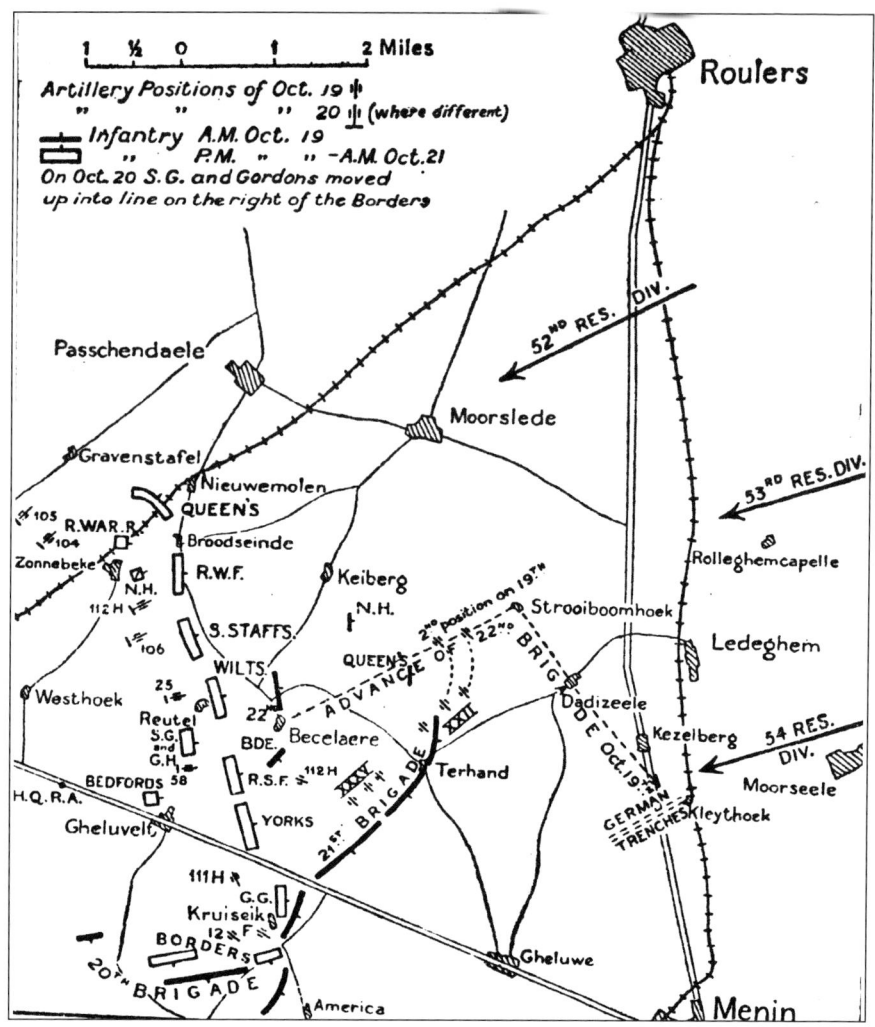

The Advance on Menin and the line held by the 7th Division, 19-20 October.

their part in a particular action had to await the repatriation of their officers from prisoner of war camps. Not one officer of 1/Wilts remained after heavy fighting near Polygon Wood on 24 October 1914, when all of them became casualties, the majority taken prisoner. This is an extreme case, but it gives a good indicator of the problem of trying to reconstruct what happened in a particular instance.

On the German side, no such official attempt was made. The focus of the series *Der Weltkrieg* was always on the corps level and above, reflecting the sheer scale of operations conducted by that army. A

14

plethora of post war regimental (i.e. equivalent to the British brigade level) histories, many of which contain personal accounts, partially fill the gap, as does the fact that the archives of Württemberg and Bavaria survive largely intact. Nevertheless, there is no equivalent in Germany to the huge holdings of documents at the National Archives or Imperial War Museum, so reconstructions of events from the perspective of the attackers can be problematic. In the case of the Menin Road this is especially so because the war diary and all supporting documentation of one of the Württemberg regiments primarily involved was lost during the battle for Gheluvelt.

During the intense fighting British units in particular became hopelessly entangled and mixed up: the author of the 7th Division's history, a highly experienced writer of such accounts, notes of the fighting on 24 October: '…the admixture of units from the Gheluvelt crossroads northwards was really remarkable; 5, 21 and 22 Brigades being almost inextricably intermingled'. These three brigades came from two different divisions (1st and 7th) and, at that time, two different Corps (I and IV). At the end of his description of fighting on the same day at the crossroads east of Gheluvelt, he adds a heartfelt footnote:

It is typical of the difficulty of putting together an accurate story of these days of unending and complicated fighting that this incident is given as having occurred on different days and at different times in three separate [war] diaries. What fixes it as the 24th are the messages reporting casualties given as appendices to the Divisional [7th] diary. But the discrepancies in the fragmentary and disjointed stories which do duty for materials for history are certainly hard to reconcile.

It is evident, therefore, that the best that can be attempted in a book of this nature is to seek to provide a series of overviews from the attackers' perspective and then to cover a number of particular incidents in more detail to give some idea of what the men on both sides endured and achieved in these Flanders fields during the late autumn of 1914. The aim is to illustrate some of the most professional performances by the BEF of the war by men of all ranks and to give some idea of the problems faced by poorly trained and equipped soldiers of the German Fourth Army. Three areas, i.e. Polygon Wood, the Menin Road and Kruiseecke, have been rather arbitrarily selected for more particular examination, but they are by no means exclusive to each other. Fighting in the area around Klein Zillebeke falls within the remit of *Messines 1914*; the area was then – and is now, though less so – heavily wooded, which makes it difficult to follow the action on the ground today – and difficult to understand for the men who were fighting at the time. Fortunately this covers a part of Belgium that is still largely one of fields and woods, though major improvements in roads – notably the A19 motorway and the expansion of the Menin Road itself – have cut up the battlefield, as has the inevitable housing, industrial, recreational and other developments.

Chapter One

20–29 October 1914

North of Polygon Wood to north of Gheluvelt.
Advancing on the extreme left of the German Fourth Army and allocated
the most direct approach to Ypres was XXVII Reserve Corps. This
formation, comprising 53rd and 54th Reserve Divisions, was drawn from
Saxony and Württemberg. Of its ten regiments (infantry and artillery), six
were from Saxony and four from Württemberg. It also had the services
of two jäger battalions at this early stage of the war: Reserve Jäger 25
from Dresden and Reserve Jäger 26 from Freiburg
in Saxony. As far as its state of training and
preparation was concerned, this was as lamentable
as that which obtained in the other corps, indeed it
appears that Reserve Jäger 26 spent most of its
training time on the drill square learning a set of
completely useless drill manoeuvres more
appropriate to the battlefields of the eighteenth,
rather than the twentieth, century. The Corps
Commander was the Minister of War for Saxony,
General der Infanterie Adolph von Carlowitz.
Although Carlowitz was a career officer and a

General Adolph von Carlowitz.

member of the Great General Staff, he had had no experience of command
at either divisional or corps level and during these early battles it showed.

On **20 October** the General, members of his staff and other
subordinate commanders were assembled at Moorslede for an orders
group, during which Carlowitz made an extraordinary pronouncement
(see Map 1, page 12).

> *The advance is to continue via Dadizeele, Terhand, Becelaere
> and Gheluvelt. Once that place is captured, it is to be continued
> on to Ypres. The line Poperinghe – Dickebusch is to be secured.
> Orders group tonight in the town hall at Ypres.*

Given that the British army was manning delaying and defensive
positions from Passchendaele to Gheluvelt long before XXVII Reserve

Corps even appeared in view, this order was completely unrealistic and reflects poorly on the corps commander's judgement.

In the absence of brigade headquarters in the reserve divisions and to simplify command and control, 53rd Reserve Division was split into two columns on 20 October. Generalleutnant Bierling, the divisional artillery commander, commanded Reserve Infantry Regiments 242 and 244 in an advance towards Dadizeele and Generalleutnant von Criegern, commanding Reserve Infantry Regiments 241 and 243, moved on the line Waterdam – Zonnebeke, despite the best efforts of delaying parties all over the battlefield. No sooner had Bierling's advance guard closed up on Dadizeele than there were indications that the column was about to be attacked. Shaking out

Oberst Kurt von Holleben, commanding RIR 243.

quickly into hastily selected defensive positions, Reserve Infantry Regiment 242 dug in feverishly near to Strooiboom, just over one kilometre to the northwest of Dadizeele. In the event there was no attack and the German formations pressed on. 54th Reserve Division was soon involved in heavy fighting near the Molenhoek area and although 53rd Reserve Division was not involved directly, its movement was certainly affected. Very soon its units were crowded together in the pouring rain astride the Dadizeele-Terhand road, prevented from advancing due to concentrations of artillery fire forward of its positions.

Having been stalled for a long time as the battle raged in and around Becelaere, and just as thoughts were turning to halting for what was left of the night, elements of Reserve Infantry Regiment 243, which had pushed on further forward than the remainder, came under fire. Reacting with commendable swiftness, despite the general confusion, Criegen's column deployed into attack formation and, with Reserve Infantry Regiment 241 right and Reserve Infantry Regiment 243 left, with one battalion of Reserve Infantry Regiment 241 under command, it advanced towards the Keiberg – Waterdam area. It was an extremely difficult operation, as Unteroffizier Siegfried Brase of Reserve Infantry Regiment 241 later pointed out.

This was a risky endeavour because we knew absolutely nothing about the strength or location of the enemy. We opened fire on the enemy at a range of 500 – 600 metres ... and began to work our way forward in short bounds, just as we had practised on the

18

Oberst von Holleben, commanding RIR 243, issuing orders on 20 October.

training area ... The enemy infantry were not alone. To their rear a supporting battery fired four swift salvos. Each time this happened, shrapnel balls whistled past our ears. I myself suddenly received an extraordinarily heavy blow. It felt as though half of me had been blown away. I looked down, but I was still in one piece ... but a spade, which I had bent over and was using as a rifle rest, was swept away by an ugly fist-sized fragment of the jacket of a shell, as though by an iron broom.

Meanwhile General der Infanterie von Schäfer's 54th Reserve Division, which comprised Reserve Infantry Regiments 245,

General der Infanterie von Schafer, commanding 54th Reserve Division.

19

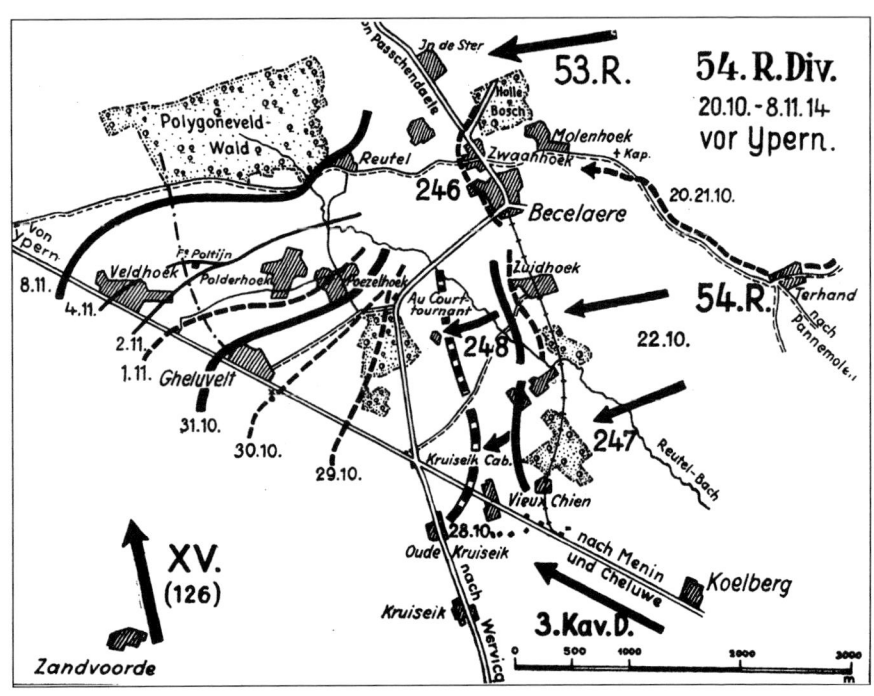

The Advance of 54th Reserve Division along the Menin Road, 20 October – 8 November.

246, 247 and 248, had advanced past Terhand by the afternoon of 20 October and were moving through awkward close country towards Becelaere. With 2nd Battalion Reserve Infantry Regiment 246 in the lead, contact was made about 300 metres west of Terhand, even though the distance to Becelaere was over two kilometres. Troops began to pile up in every piece of cover in and around Terhand, as each attempt by the advance guard to push forward was greeted by concentrated British small arms and artillery fire. Despite this, the advance continued, use being made by Reserve Infantry Regiments 245 and 246 of all available covered approaches. Eventually, by evening, the guns had been redeployed, heavy fire was coming down on the Becelaere road and soon there was a close quarter battle raging in the eastern part of the village. British rifle and machine gun fire was being poured in from all directions so that, although numbers eventually told and slow progress was made, it was at huge cost to the attacking Württembergers who, moving from one building to another, cleared their costly way to the last of the British positions.

It was not just the leading elements that were badly hit. The reserve companies of Reserve Infantry Regiment 245 were engaged so heavily from concealed positions in the direction of Reutel that they were almost annihilated, their bodies being littered all over the approaches to the village. All this took momentum from the attack and British artillery fire, directed at Becelaere once it became known that that place had fallen, blunted the attack further. There were numerous attempts, gallantly led, to press forward, but it was no use. For the time being all the impetus had gone from the advance of XXVII Reserve Corps and, one by one, then by sections, the companies began to fall back into the cover of the burning village of Becelaere, taking cover or digging in for protection against harassing fire. There would be no more advancing that day, though some men from Reserve Infantry Regiment 248 did manage to link up at Koelenberg with 1st Battalion Bavarian Reserve Infantry Regiment 1 of 1st Bavarian Reserve Division, which was operating with 3rd Cavalry Division and which was in great need of the newly-arrived support.

Meanwhile, on the 7th Division front, just before 11 am on 20 October, in line with Field Marshal French's strategy of offensive

FM Sir John French, second left.

21

operations by I and IV Corps, a reconnaissance in force from 20 Brigade, accompanied by the divisional cyclists and cavalry (Northumberland Hussars) and a battery of artillery, was pushed down the Menin Road towards Gheluwe. The left flank was covered by the advance of a strong flanking group, two battalions and some artillery from 20 Brigade, which first cleared Becelaere and then advanced along the Terhand spur. Good progress had been made until, about midday, the situation of 3rd (Cavalry) Division around Passchendaele and of 22 Brigade, east of Zonnebeke, threatened IV Corps' left flank. The movement was halted, 20 Brigade returning to its line without difficulty; the two battalions from 21 (Guards) Brigade, 2/Wiltshires (Wilts) and 2/Scots Fusiliers (RSF) faced a more difficult task, in particular 2/Wilts, which suffered some sixty casualties before getting back to its former positions north of Reutel.

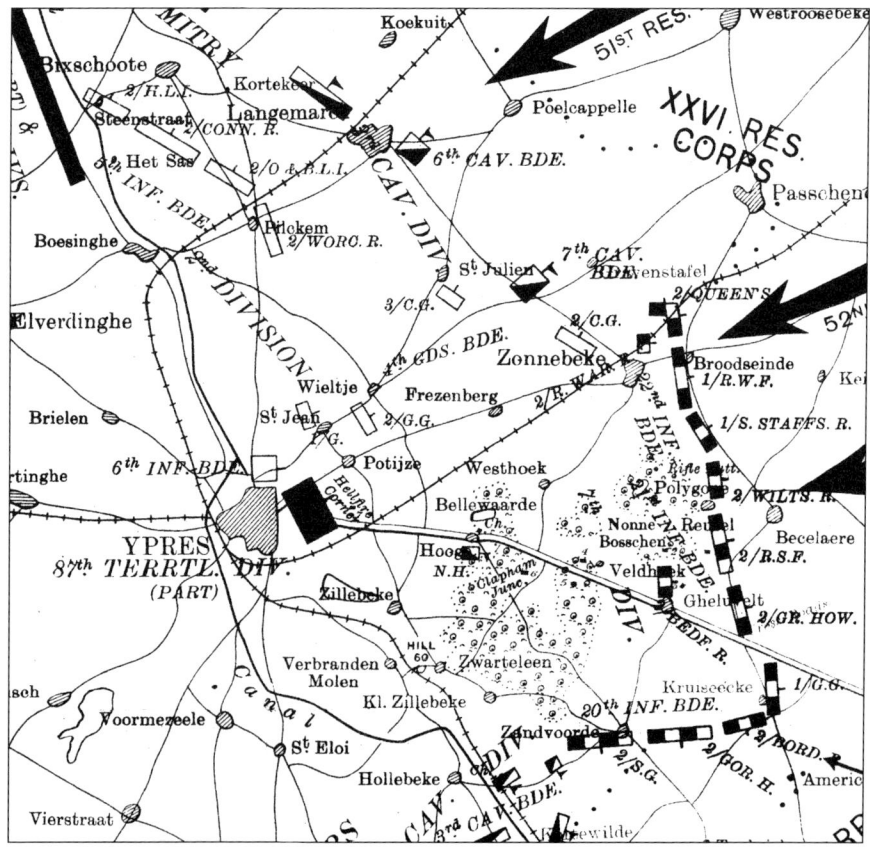

The Situation of the 2nd and 7th divisions on the evening of 20 October.

The situation on the left deteriorated further, mainly because of the enforced withdrawal of the French cavalry on IV Corps' left; as the day progressed, 20 Brigade came under increasing pressure but it was nothing that it could not handle. However, 21 (Guards) Brigade was attacked at about 4 pm, by German troops of 54th Reserve Division coming from the direction of Becelaere. This attack was focussed on 2/Wilts and 2/RSF respectively, well to the east of Polygon Wood and south of Reutel. These attacks were hit in flank by the machine guns of 2/Green Howards (Yorks) east of Gheluvelt; and by some very effective shelling by XXXV Battery, catching the advancing Germans as they came over the ridge. Attempts by the enemy to advance south of the Menin Road were all seen off, largely by the artillery – some guns, firing at a range of 1400 yards, had fuses set to clear the crest and 'just catch the German infantry'.

Up to this point the 7th Division had been holding a front of eight miles and yet had engaged in an advance; the British knew nothing about the strength of the German forces opposite, nor of their intention to launch a major attack. It was certainly hardly in a position to be able to withstand a huge attack; however, the situation was alleviated by the arrival of I Corps (Lieutenant General Sir Douglas Haig) on the left flank, and in particular the 2nd Division (Major General Charles Monro), its new immediate neighbour. It was planned that I Corps would launch an attack on 21 October, striking east

Major General Charles Monro.

beyond Passchendaele, in co-operation with French troops on its left; that was not to happen – or, rather, it never got very far.

The entire battlefield on the German side was one great chaotic scene. The rain poured down, adding to the difficulties and soaking men, who were destined to go hungry, as the rationing system failed and the roads and villages were jammed with all manner of vehicles, equipment and marching men. It was poor preparation for a resumption of the attacks, yet that was the precise thrust of the orders which filtered down to the units in the early hours of **21 October**. Speed was of the essence, despite stiff British opposition but, nevertheless, it was mid-afternoon before sufficient order had been restored to permit a resumption of the general advance westwards. That had not prevented isolated attempts being made by 3rd Battalion Reserve Infantry Regiment 247, which had spent the night at a farmstead near Zwaanhoek, on the road to Passchendaele and about 500 metres north of Becelaere. The same efforts were made by elements of the Saxon 53rd Reserve Division, which took advantage of a misty morning to press on at about 8.00 am. They were soon locked into fire fights with British units and their isolated attacks stalled. XXVII Reserve Corps deployed its final reserves from Reserve Infantry Regiment 247 to reinforce the attack; but by then it was too late and it was not until well into the afternoon that a properly constituted advance on Reutel could be launched by 2nd and 3rd Battalions Reserve Infantry Regiment 247. Once more there were heavy losses caused by fire from well concealed British positions. Encouraged by the almost suicidal bravery of their company and battalion officers, the German troops strove to get forward, but their inexperience and poor fieldcraft and tactics counted against them. They were simply unable to use effective fire and manoeuvre and were picked off in huge numbers by skilled British defenders. Even when some progress had been made south of Reutel, the only outcome was that the flank so presented to the British defenders of Reutel enabled them to cause total havoc in the German ranks. The attack was a complete bloody fiasco and, as soon as it went dark, there was nothing else for it but for those who had survived to pull back to their start lines, painfully aware that poorly prepared and supported attacks against the BEF were simply suicidal. Such were the losses that it was never possible to discover precisely how many there had been that day, but there was great concern that the right flank of 54th Reserve Division was now so weak that immediate reinforcement from 53rd Reserve Division was a top priority.

As has been noted, on **21 October** the Germans launched major and continuous attacks along the whole front of the 7th Division; that on 22 Brigade has been covered in *Langemarck*. On the left of 21 Brigade, 2/Wilts fought the massed attacks to a standstill. 2/RSF, on the right, were equally successful, as the 7th Division's history records:

Here the left company, C, had only about a 200 yards' field of fire, but others were more fortunate. The line was heavily bombarded from about 6.30 am, and during the hours of darkness there had been several attacks. As the morning wore on these continued, the Germans seeking persistently to find a gap in the line. With a long and thinly held front, and in country as yet little damaged by war, so that buildings, hedges and woods provided excellent cover, it was impossible to keep every approach under effective fire, and about noon Germans managed to penetrate between the Yorks' and the Fusiliers' right company, D, whose trenches were in front of Poezelhoek hamlet. They pushed a machine gun up into the gap, and its enfilade fire forced D back to the Chateau grounds.

24

The Germans then tried to press on against B Company in the centre, but some of A reinforced B and by their aid this attack was stopped. C, north of the Reutelbeek, was also attacked in great force, but it also held on and punished the enemy severely, an attempt to outflank its line being checked by effective cross fire from a section near the bridge of the Reutelbeek. Thus, despite the loss of D's trenches, the Scots Fusiliers had no reason to be dissatisfied; whilst against the Yorkshires [on the right of 2/RSF] *the Germans were even less successful, though severely pressed, they beat off all efforts to turn its left.*

To give an indication of how unhelpful the War Diaries of this period can be, that of 2/Yorks merely states: 'Artillery fire continued soon after day break, increasing in force towards midday. Enemy made an unsuccessful attack on the left flank of our position. A few casualties caused by shrapnel.' And that is it. However, rather more eloquently, a Battalion diarist on that day wrote:

Early this day we saw masses of the enemy who offered very fine targets for our machine gunners, who were not slow to take full advantage of them; all companies poured in a very heavy independent rifle fire, and the enemy recoiled with many casualties. Apparently he had been massing for an attack, but the fierce fire poured into his troops made him withdraw and alter his plans.

All this belies the fact that units (and even split units) of the division were being pushed around to act as military 'firemen', seeking to shore up a defence here or suppress an advance there. (This was a precursor of 'puttying up', when units from different brigades and even divisions were formed into *ad hoc* groups to deal with particular sections or parts of the line, something that is first noticed on 21 October.) When that particular emergency was either resolved or failed to materialise, they were then sent scurrying off to another part of this over-extended line, which was still eight miles long at the end of the day. Indeed, the 2nd Division was gradually being sucked in to this defensive fighting, with battalions on its right assisting 22 Brigade as the latter withdrew its line back, under the German pressure, from Broodseinde to the western fringes of Zonnebeke.

Reserve Infantry Regiment 242, having arrived from Terhand during the afternoon of 21 October, sent its 1st and 3rd Battalions towards Zuidhoek, about two kilometres west southwest of Terhand. It did

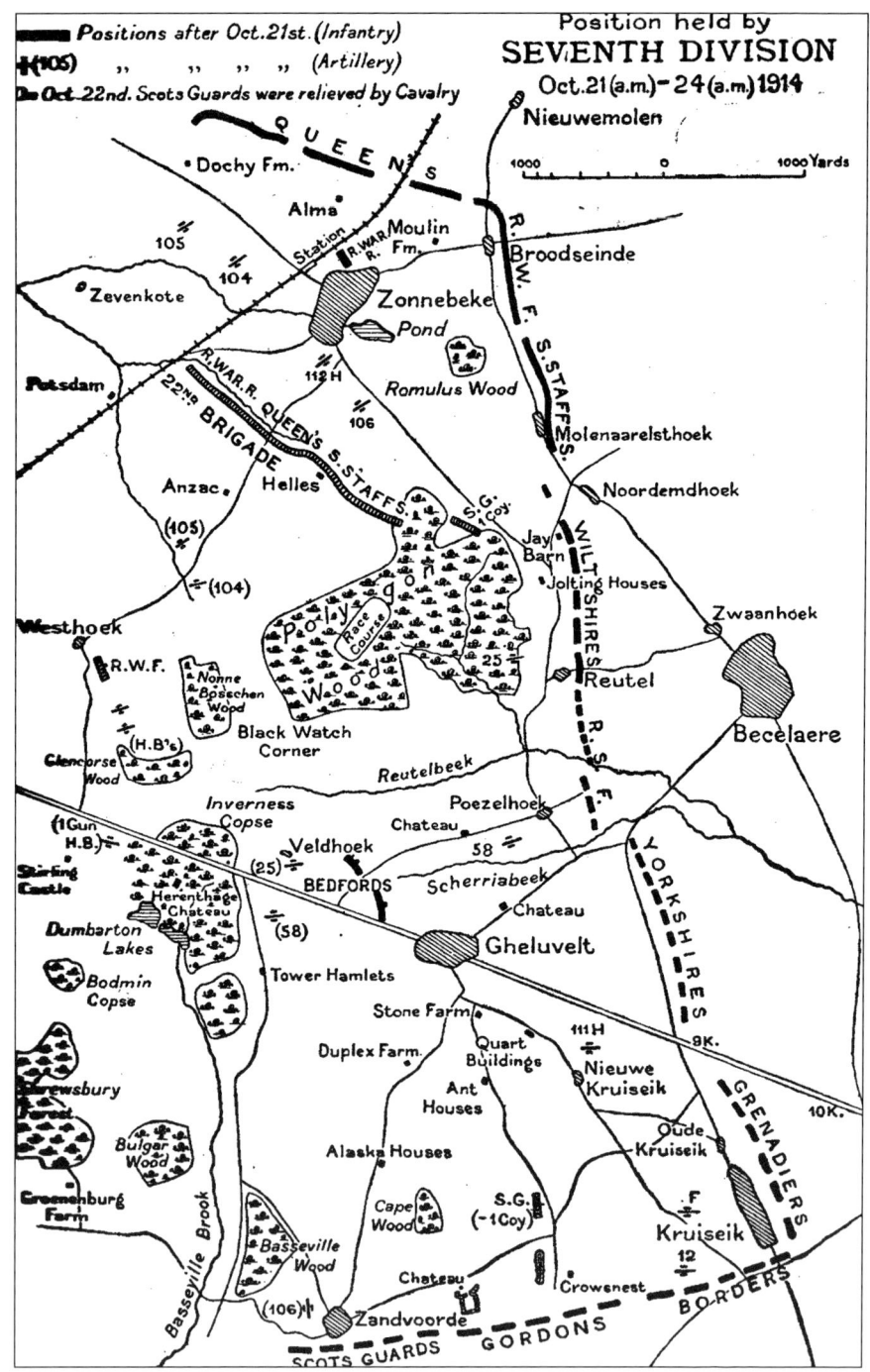

Positions held by the 7th Division, 21-24 October.

succeed in capturing a small hill from which the British withdrew but, as soon as an attempt was made to continue, heavy British small arms fire from completely concealed positions stopped this in its tracks and there was no alternative but to dig in amongst the sugar beet. It was yet another dispiriting day, made even worse by the lack of hot food and drinks and, as day broke on 22 October after another night of cold drizzle, with nothing but the remnants of iron rations and food taken from the dead to sustain them. The front line troops were in no condition to maintain the advance, even though XXVII Reserve Corps, pressured by Fourth Army, was still insisting that the offensive be continued. Generalleutnant von Reinhardt, the newly appointed commander of 107 Reserve Brigade of 54th Reserve Division, felt that this was asking too much, that there might be a British

Generalleutnant von Rheinhardt, 107 Reserve Infantry Brigade. He was killed in action near Becelaere on 22 October.

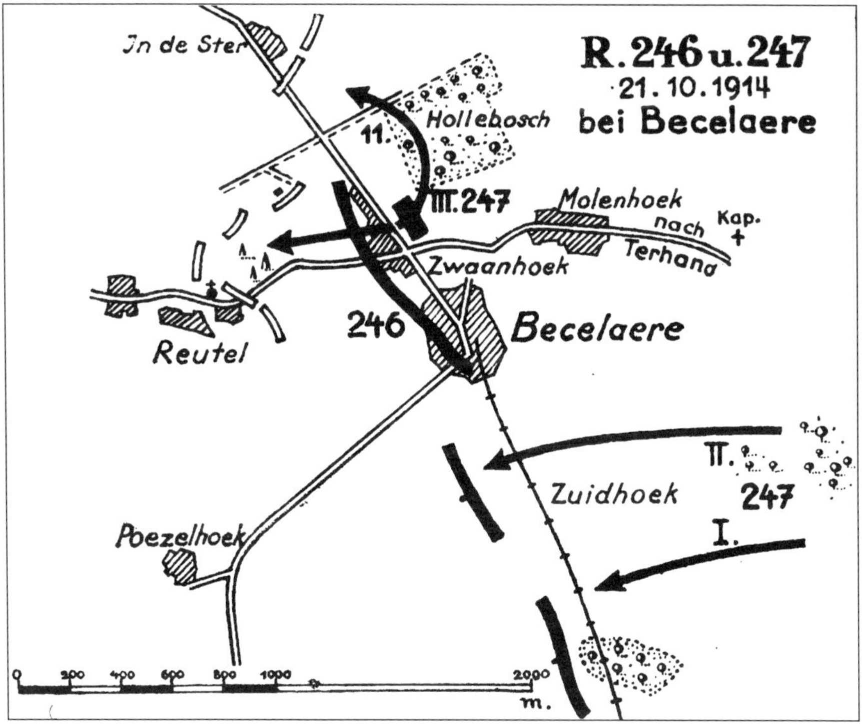

surprise attack and ordered that the western edge of Terhand be put into a state of defence.

Situation of the 54th Reserve Division, 21 October.

However, Reinhardt was overruled and 54th Reserve Division set to work to attack south of Becelaere, towards Vieux Chien and Oude Kruiseecke. Oberst von Bendler, commander of Reserve Infantry Regiment 247, was ordered to attack on a two battalion frontage with, in reserve, all the men who could be made available from Reserve Infantry Regiment 248. For once the quartermasters got hot food forward, where it was devoured by the waiting troops, ravenously hungry after forty-eight hours with virtually nothing to eat or drink. Meanwhile, from 2.00 pm, heavy German guns began to pound the objective and the road to Gheluvelt and several sections of field guns were deployed so as to provide close observed fire for the attacking infantry. With a light screening force in the lead, 1st Battalion Reserve Infantry Regiment 247 deployed to the left, with 2nd Battalion on the right and set out; most of the movement being by company columns for ease of command and control.

Naturally there was a British reaction, but shrapnel fire did not prevent Reserve Infantry Regiment 247 from reaching the area of the Reutelbeek and the woods north of Vieux Chien largely untouched. The minute they broke cover, however, they came under accurate fire and began to suffer serious losses. Once more it was a case of the British pinning them down with accurate fire from a series of well placed mutually supporting fire positions near Oude Kruiseecke. This situation persisted well into the night, with the British infantry firing periodically to trick their raw opponents into wasting large amounts of ammunition. Not only did they succeed but the ensuing confusion caused several friendly fire incidents, including one where two adjacent companies fired at one another in the dark for an extended period of time. This general inexperience and nervous behaviour, compounded by hunger, lack of sleep, artillery firing short and bad weather – which was replicated all along the Fourth Army front – led to panicky withdrawals from places won at great cost earlier. Instructions were given personal weapons, apart from those of sentries, were to be unloaded at night and that only officers and senior NCOs could give the order to open fire.

The offensive to take the line of the Menin Road and open the way to Ypres was stuttering; it finally stalled for forty eight hours when, later that night, Generalleutnant von Reinhardt was shot through the head whilst visiting forward positions and killed instantly. He had been an inspirational figure and his loss was keenly felt when, two days later, the assault on Reutel and Polygon Wood, defended by the 7th Division, was re-launched.

On **22 October** French instructed the 7th Division to hold its positions whilst I Corps was to press forward; something which the latter failed to do, facing increasing pressure as it did, particularly on its left, which had been left exposed by the withdrawal of French troops to the canal line. By and large this was a quiet day for the 7th Division, except for problems created by a large gap of several hundred yards between 22 and 21 (Guards) Brigades. This was partly filled by the reserve company of 2/Wilts and then by the Northumberland Hussars and the divisional cyclists. Capper actually had a battalion in reserve, 2/Scots Guards, having been able to withdraw it at Zandvoorde. The day that followed for them is a good example of what happened to so many British battalions (or, as the days passed and casualties mounted alarmingly, shadows of battalions) during this battle.

On the 21st, 2/Scots Guards were at Zandvoorde; at 8 am a company was ordered forward to support 2/Gordon Highlanders (Gordons), to the right of Kruiseecke; in due course, this particular emergency having been contained, the same company (RF – ie Right Flank Company) was sent to Hollebeke, where it held a mile of front with two other Scots Guards' companies on the left. The company had to dig trenches under shellfire. In mid afternoon two platoons of RF Company were sent to assist the cavalry to stabilise the situation at Hollebeke Chateau. The battalion was relieved at night – which covers a fairly considerable time span – and then marched 'most of the night' to Veldhoek, where it arrived at 5 am. At 8 am the battalion was ordered up to the north east corner of Polygon Wood, in the process covering 'a mile over shell swept country, which they were fortunate to accomplish without casualties, except 'seven men wounded in F Company'. There they had to entrench, in thick wood, in support of the forward battalions; there they stayed, except for RF (again!) and G Companies, ordered back across the same shell swept ground to [20] Brigade Headquarters and then took up position once more between Zandvoorde and Kruiseecke, i.e. the southern part of the 7th Division's line, whilst the other two companies remained in support of the northern part of the divisional line. Thus, after a busy previous day, with barely three hours' rest, very dangerous approaches to the lines and moving around considerable distances over difficult ground, the Battalion found itself split in two, with at least one company (the poor old RF) commanded by only a lieutenant. Many others were to be in the same situation during First Ypres. [In case of confusion about terms such as 'RF Company', the Scots Guards' history details all in a footnote: 'A and D of the 1st Battalion are known as Right and Left Flank companies, and in the 2nd Battalion E and H Companies are similarly known'; one can only hazard an educated guess as to why this might be so.]

The 21 (Guards) Brigade had a hard day, especially towards the north of its position. The German artillery was now more accurate, destroying trenches, burying men and rendering rifles useless as they became covered in sandy mud. It was difficult to supply ammunition; as the reserve trenches were pulverized and because of the lack of communication trenches, it had to be carried across the open, with the inevitable results for many of the bearers. However,

When the Germans attempted to advance from the woods where they had massed they were met by such a storm of fire from guns and rifles that their dead were literally piled up in heaps. Nothing could have exceeded the determination and gallantry with which these new levies came on, but for all their resolution they were unable to establish themselves within 400 yards of the Wiltshires.

They were equally unsuccessful against 2/RSF, who even attempted a moderately successful counter attack in the late afternoon to recapture their trenches, ultimately failing to do so when the Germans were reinforced, but still managing to get back into Poezelhoek and to bring back thirty prisoners. The fighting and the shelling took its toll, as one officer wrote:

It is very difficult to differentiate between day and night. With only occasional lulls the terrific din of fighting went on without ceasing. Shells, guns and rifles all going at once made one's recollections of the Boer fire seem like crackers at a picnic. And all the time the Boche coming on, rows and rows of cannon fodder; four or five to one, perhaps more, but as we were in good trenches we had only slight losses at first.

Meals 'were uncertain and scrappy' and men could consider themselves lucky if they had got 'biscuits or hard chocolate in their pockets'; 'an occasional hot meal was an incident of note. To wash or shave was out of the question for the majority of officers and men and the strain on all ranks was enormous.'

Pressure continued against 21 (Guards) Brigade on **23 October**. Once more an attempt was made to recapture 2/RSF's lost position of the 21st (this time with the aid of a company of 2/Bedfords, a regiment who was soon to belie the nickname of 'The Peacemakers' and its unofficial motto of, 'Thou Shalt Not Kill', a consequence of a long period of service in the past when it did not fire a shot in anger). This

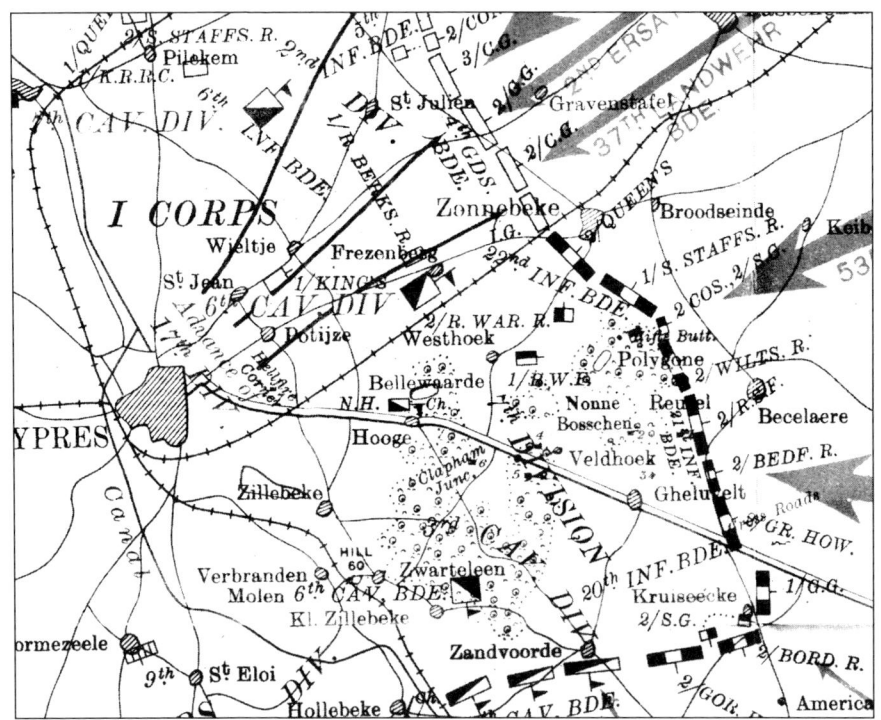

Situation of the 2nd and 7th Divisions, evening of 23 October.

failed and the Germans counter attacked in the morning, in particular against the Wilts and the Yorks. By this stage the trenches in many places had disappeared and the men were lying out in the open. Destruction of nearby houses in the rear had the consequence of destroying the wells as well, thus making the supply of water extremely problematic. The staunchness of 2/Yorks was noted in the Brigade War Diary: 'The tenacity of this battalion was most remarkable; though subjected to heavy artillery fire and constant infantry attacks, it held on stoutly and never wavered'. But this was all desperate stuff and the men in the line were becoming ever more exhausted.

During the night of the 23rd, the 2nd Division was relieved. The intention was for I Corps to sidestep to its right whilst fresh French troops came up to pursue the offensive that Foch, commanding French troops in the north, and French planned to continue; I Corps would provide the British element for this attack, once the 1st Division had been relieved from around Langemarck. The statement that the French were always one corps and one day too late in their enveloping attacks of late 1914 might equally apply to the Germans. 7th Division was dreadfully over extended but, just at the apposite moment, the 2nd Division was moved into reserve to its rear.

In the early hours of **24 October**, heavy German artillery fire was directed against both places then, at exactly 6.00 am, the assaulting troops, Reserve Infantry Regiment 244, 53rd Reserve Division and Reserve Infantry Regiment 246, 54th Reserve Division, climbed out of their slit trenches and began to advance on a cold, wet, misty morning. Reserve Infantry Regiment 244 chose to advance deeply echeloned against the British 21 Brigade, with its 2nd Battalion in the lead, 3rd Battalion in support and 1st Battalion in reserve under the direct control of the commander. Once again the old pattern was repeated and, as soon as the leading troops were spotted by the defence, heavy fire was brought down. This caused some casualties, but did not prevent the attack from being pressed home. The British positions were rushed at great cost and soon fighting was hand to hand all along this sector.

Major Baumann, 1st Battalion RIR 246, died of wounds received on 21 October 1914 on 15 November.

As has been mentioned, there were serious German casualties but, for once, the British forward positions were assaulted in great strength and overrun. Two platoons of 2nd Wilts had been overwhelmed by around 7.00am, then the forward companies of Reserve Infantry Regiment 244 rolled up the entire front line. Thirteen British officers and well in excess of five hundred other prisoners were captured near Reutel itself, but the energy of the attack was soon spent. The German assault force did push on towards the edge of Polygon Wood and drove back a company of 2nd Battalion Royal Scots Fusiliers that had been rushed forward. However Reserve Infantry Regiment 246 was caught in vicious cross fire and lost half its remaining strength. There was a confused intermingling of units and sub units and, just when it appeared nothing else could happen to make the situation worse, some German field guns brought down fire on their own men as they advanced west of Reutel. Spotting this, the British defenders brought down large amounts of shrapnel fire, taking a deadly toll; Major General Capper, sent the last of his reserves, the Northumberland Hussars, into Polygon Wood. This was the first significant deployment of a British territorial unit on the Western Front.

The battle continued to rage at the edge of Polygon Wood, but once a properly organised counter-attack by 2nd Battalion Highland Light

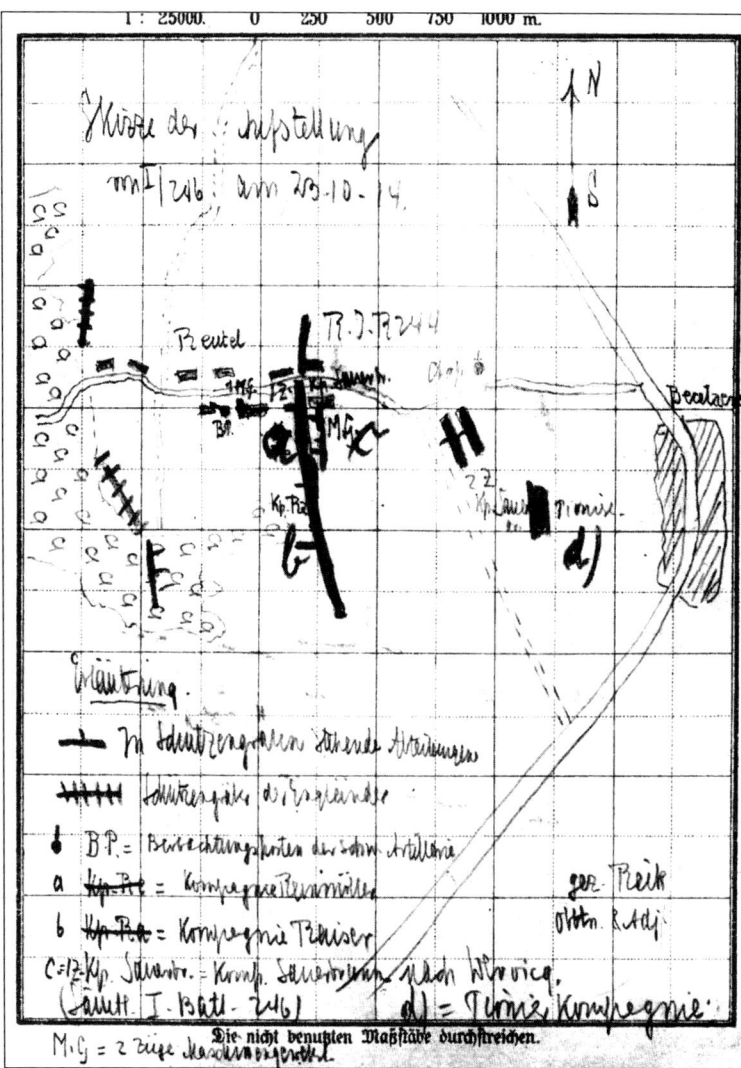

The situation of RIR 244 east of Reutel on 23 October. A sketch map from a field notebook.

Infantry and 2nd Battalion Worcestershire Regiment was launched, the defenders began to prevail. Oberst Straube, commanding Reserve Infantry Regiment 246, felt that only possible decision was to withdraw the survivors and rally them in a small area of old British trenches on a small knoll two hundred metres east of the wood. Oberleutnant von Criegern, on his own initiative, secured an additional position just to the south, and took under command all the men left on their feet from 3rd

Battalion. Nevertheless, the Germans were extremely vulnerable to a counter-attack at that moment, so it was very fortunate that severe losses on the British side ruled out any such action. Elsewhere within the space of this terrible day Reserve Infantry Regiment 244 had gone from a strength of fifty seven officers and 2,629 other ranks to a mere six officers, seventy seven NCOs and 671 other ranks.

Hardly any ground had been gained in return for these losses and, worse, because on the right the remaining troops had had to fall back, the position of Reserve Infantry Regiment 246 was in considerable danger. Desperate efforts were made to rally all the stragglers from Reserve Infantry Regiment 244 and many were used to reinforce the local lines. However, pressure continued to build from the area of Polderhoek Chateau. This increased and eventually, orders or no orders, the survivors of Reserve Infantry Regiment 246 began to leave their exposed temporary positions and pull back all the way to the Reutelbeek.

Polderhoek Chateau under German occupation.

Although seriously disappointing, the development came as no surprise. By evening Major Holtzhausen, commanding officer 3rd Battalion Reserve Infantry Regiment 246, had fallen and a further sixteen officers, eighteen offizierstellvertreters and 1,800 other ranks were casualties. With seventy percent of its fighting strength gone and the survivors mentally and physically exhausted, for the time being Reserve Infantry Regiment 246 was effectively finished as a viable formation.

Major Holtzhausen, 3rd Battalion RIR 246, killed in action at Reutel.

From the British perspective, **24 October** opened, at 5 am, with the removal of Germans who had infiltrated the position through a gap in the line during the night, on the left flank of 2/RSF; forty prisoners were taken. The ferocious German artillery fire, which began at about 5.30 am, undid any work done in restoring trenches and jammed rifles as a consequence of the sandy soil that the shells threw into the air. It was followed by a series of assaults, one soon after the bombardment opened and two others at about 7 am and 8 am. Communications between Brigade HQ and the firing line were soon destroyed and thus information about what was going on was hard to establish, though it was clear that there were problems in front of Polygon Wood – 2/RSF saying that the Germans had entered Polygon Wood and were threatening the left flank, against which they formed a north facing line with every man available. The problem seemed to be with 2/Wilts.

What exactly happened to 2/Wilts, assaulted by Reserve Infantry Regiment 244, is largely a matter of conjecture; not one of its officers (apart from the quartermaster, who was not in the line) survived to tell the story until some were repatriated from PoW camps. 2/Wilts held a position on Reutel Spur, parallel and to the east of Polygon Wood. On the right flank, a company of 2/RSF was forced to give some ground, exacerbating the dangers of the two hundred yards gap that already existed between them; whilst on the left, the two companies of 2/Scots Guards, forming the bridge between 22 and 21 (Guards) Brigade, were also driven back early in the morning. The platoons of 2/Wilts covering the southern edge of Reutel were overwhelmed, effectively surrounded, at about 8 am. The Germans then massed in Reutel, on the Wilts' right flank and possibly also to their rear, and simply rolled the position up from right to left whilst the defenders were trying to deal with a simultaneous frontal attack. 450 men, wounded and unwounded, were taken, leaving the QM, the sergeant major and 172 men to answer the roll call the next day, about fifty percent of whom had not been in the line at the time of the attack. Similarly, F Company of the Scots Guards, to the left, were reduced to a small platoon – their trenches had been blown in by the German bombardment and many of the men buried. Most of

Captain the Master of Kinnaird.

them were taken prisoner, it would seem, as recorded deaths are few. Amongst them was Captain the Master of Kinnaird, whose burial place, puzzlingly enough, is in Godezonne Farm Cemetery, near Kemmel, and about ten miles south east of where he was killed. He is the only identified 1914 casualty in this small cemetery. He was moved here in 1925.

Brigadier General Watts (21 Brigade) informed Capper that the Wilts and Scots Fusiliers were in serious trouble and that Germans were in Polygon Wood, though in the latter case this did not necessarily mean complete disaster because, although Germans had infiltrated the wood, the British positions to the east were still sound; and such parties had been successfully removed before. 22 Brigade reacted by sending into Polygon Wood 2/Warwicks and a company of 1/South Staffs, attacking from the north. Meanwhile the Northumberland Hussars moved to clear the wood from the south west and to cover 2/RSF's left.

> *There was not a moment to lose. A hurried gallop up the Menin Road and an advance in open order across the usual sticky turnip field, brought us to the forefront of the battle. Too far, in fact, for a raking fire from a machine gun played havoc in the ranks and was responsible for most of the casualties.*

The wood was cleared south of the racecourse by the Hussars and in the event only three men of the regiment were killed. But it had been a close thing and it had needed the assistance of some French cavalry to assist in driving the Germans out. From the north, the troops of 22 Brigade removed the immediate threat, if not all of the Germans: but at a cost. 2/Warwicks lost its CO, Lieutenant Colonel Loring, and suffered almost 300 hundred casualties in the action. The situation was still very fraught,

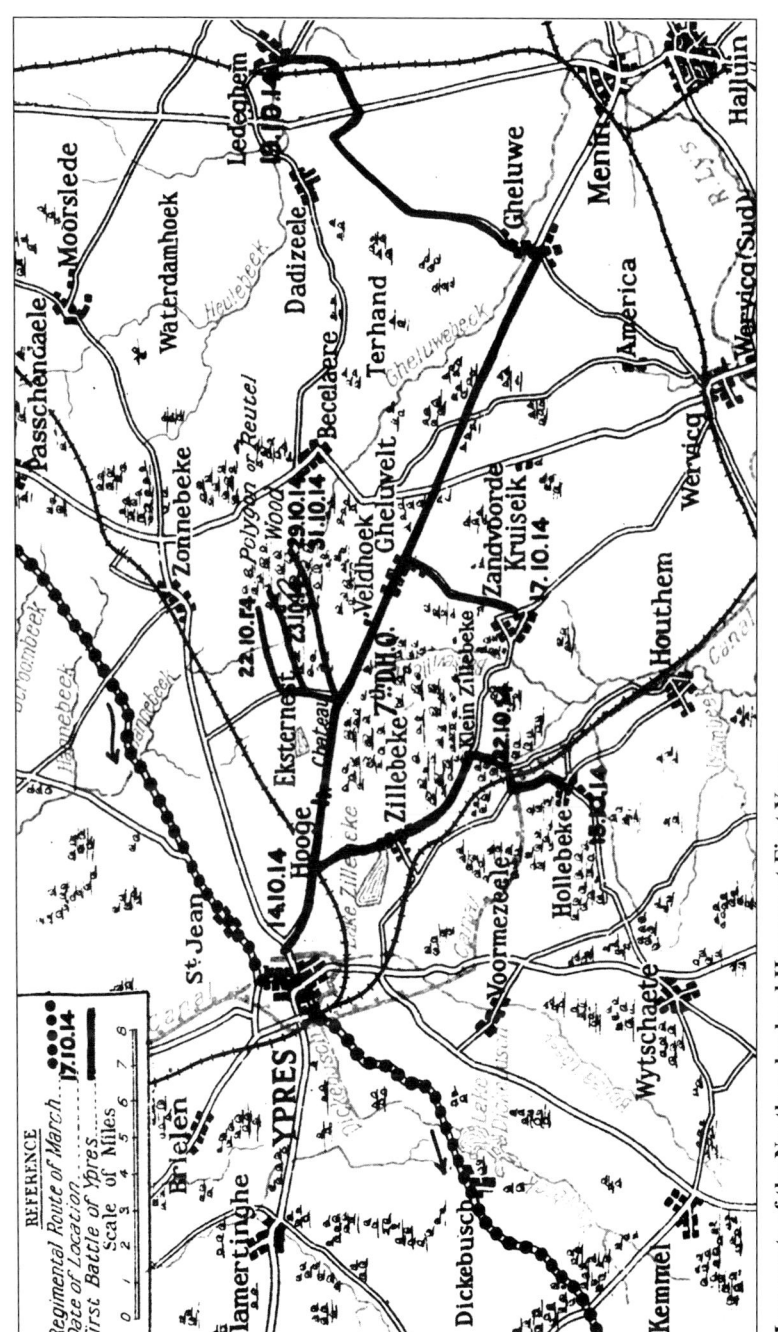

Movements of the Northumberland Hussars at First Ypres.

Germans continued to infiltrate into the wood and matters had to be resolved, especially in the light of what was planned for the 2nd Division that day.

At a conference held at Capper's HQ (five kilometres from Ypres on the Menin Road, near Clapham Junction) at 6.30 am, orders were received from Haig (GOC I Corps) that the 2nd Division was to relieve the 7th Division's line between Poezelhoek and Zonnebeke; 6 Brigade (Fanshawe) to relieve the 22nd and 5 Brigade (Haking) to relieve the 21st, beginning at 11 am. 4 Brigade (Scott-Kerr) was to be in reserve around Eskernest/Westhoek. The idea was to launch an attack, moving through 21 and 22 Brigades' lines, commencing at 12.30 pm. This was to fall in with a French offensive that was to take place on the left. It was a plan that was effectively to be stillborn because of the events already taking place on 21 Brigade's front.

Relieved by the French during the night, 5 Brigade's bivouac lines were around what was then called Halte but soon became known as Hell Fire Corner. The last battalion to arrive, held back to cover the withdrawal of the guns, were 2/Worcs, who came into the lines at 8 am, under the happy delusion that they were to have three days of rest and regular food. By 8.20 am, in 2/Worcs case without breakfast, they and the rest of 5 Brigade were on the move, instructed now to clear the Germans out of Polygon Wood before the attack could proceed.

The counter attack was not easy to arrange. There was no exact knowledge of the situation in Polygon Wood on its further side, or of the numbers or location of British troops in it. Orders were therefore given to 2/Worcs and 2/HLI, the two forward battalions, that bayonets only were to be used in making the move through to the wood's eastern edges and the start line of the proposed attack proper.

Polygon Wood in 1914 was a thick wood of pine trees, with dense undergrowth of beech and chestnut. So dense was the undergrowth that from the start it was difficult for the companies to keep formation. The ordered line was broken by the thickets; touch with the HLI was lost, and it became clear that they had not kept pace. The disorganisation became serious, although no enemy had yet been met, until Major Hankey [the acting CO of 2/Worcs] eventually called a halt and ordered the companies to fall back out of the wood.

When the Battalion was again assembled, Major Hankey reformed the disordered line. Then, taking post with his Adjutant in the centre of the line, he ordered all to keep direction by him and led the Battalion again into the wood. The HLI had likewise reorganised, but in the subsequent advance their left flank lost distance and eventually followed behind the right flank of the Worcestershire, who now pressed resolutely forward.

Suddenly in the dense wood the advancing platoons encountered the leading troops of the enemy [men from RIR 244]. *A swift and murderous fight ensued at close quarters; and the struggle grew more and more desperate as reinforcements for each side forced their way through bushes and brambles into the fight. At one point a party of Worcesters charged, cheering. The cheer echoed all through the wood and was taken up all along the line. Everywhere the men of the Regiment plunged with the bayonet and the Germans gave way. Back through the wood they were driven, and after them, in a long, ragged line came the Worcesters, shooting and stabbing, hunting out the broken enemy from behind trees and bushes and cheering fiercely as they charged forward. For over half a mile the pursuit continued. Then, as the wood began to thin and daylight showed between the trees, sharp bursts of fire from the edge of the open ground brought the advance to a stop. The fierce cheering which had demoralised the enemy's infantry in the wood had also served to warn the German reserves on the far side, and on the edge of the wood the Battalion met a storm of shrapnel and machine gun bullets. The companies took up the best position they could on the eastern edge of the wood and dug in.* [Contact was established with 20 Brigade and the HLI extended the line.] *A detachment...became separated in the wood and eventually took up position still further to the right, near Polderhoek Chateau, where they organised a defensive position with some remnants of 2/Warwicks and of other regiments who were still holding their ground.*

The fight had not been without a stiff cost; the initial casualty return of about eighty casualties was later amended to 200, including six wounded officers, one of whom, Second Lieutenant CM Pope, subsequently died of his wounds. The line established had 2/Worcs on the left, 2/HLI in the centre and a mixed company of Worcs, Warwicks and 2/Queen's – the latter two from 22 Brigade – on the right.

The clearing of Polygon Wood had been altogether confusing. The 7th Division history observes in a footnote:

The precise relation between these different counter attacks seems to defy all efforts at elucidation. Presumably the Warwickshires coming from Zonnebeke cleared the NE portion of the wood, the

Yeomanry [Hussars] *coming from Hooge cleared the southern borders, and the two battalions of 5 Brigade, coming up rather late, swept through the wood from SW to NE, going right across the race course. The company of 1/South Staffs seems to have joined in with this attack, in the course of which it captured a house in a clearing held by sixty Germans but lost its commander, Captain J Dunlop.*

The poor Dunlop family lost two sons in a very short period of time: Julian Dunlop has no known grave; his brother, Frederick, was killed on 8 November and is buried in Royal Irish Graveyard Cemetery, Laventie; yet another brother, Kenneth, was killed during the battle of Loos and is buried at Vermelles, whilst a fourth brother, William, was severely wounded in April 1915; a fifth survived the war relatively uscathed.

6 Brigade, meanwhile, had a rather curious approach march. When the Brigade set off from St Julien it comprised only the HQ and 1/King's Liverpool (King's); at Frezenberg it collected 1/Berks; whilst 2/South Staffs (arriving at midday) and 1/King's Royal Rifle Corps (KRRC) – arriving only at 7 pm – made their way independently. The Brigade was ordered to advance in conjunction with the French on the left and in support of 22 Brigade, then holding an almost north south line between west of Zonnebeke and Polygon Wood. The objective was the ground from Noordemdhoek to the six kilometres stone, just south of Broodseinde.

1/Berks was on the left, south of Zonnebeke; and 1/King's was on the right, having established contact with the troops from 5 Brigade and the Scots Guards on the eastern edge of Polygon Wood. The attack commenced at 3.30 pm. Because of the failure of 4 (Guards) Brigade to move any further forward than the positions reached by 5 Brigade, the King's had to cover the right flank, which meant putting almost the whole of the battalion into the attacking line.

All went well until they reached the western outskirts of the village [Molenaarelsthoek]. *The houses had, however, been well prepared for defence by the Germans, who had loopholed all buildings, in some of which they had mounted machine guns. A Company* [left flank] *was the first to be brought to a standstill by a perfect hurricane of bullets from the loop-holed houses. Casualties now became numerous but, not to be denied, the King's men charged the houses and cleared the Germans from them. With the exception of about half a dozen houses on the eastern side of the village, Molenaarelsthoek was in the hands of the 1ˢᵗ King's, but it was from these buildings that the heaviest machine gun fire came. Twice they were charged by the two platoons of D Company* [to the right of the attack] *under Second Lieutenant Denny, without success, the gallant young subaltern falling mortally wounded, and eventually the platoons fell back into a hastily dug trench in which, for the time being, they took shelter.*

By dusk 6 Brigade's had mainly achieved their objectives, with the 1/King's line bent back at the 5 km stone to connect up with 5 Brigade in Polygon Wood. The Berks suffered fifty-three casualties, including five officers, all wounded. 1/King's lost their CO, Lieutenant Colonel Bannatyne, killed shot through the heart, near A Company's forward positions. In addition, two other officers were wounded and twenty-four (or twenty-seven) ORs were killed, wounded and missing – depending on whose figures you use. At the end of the day there was one odd feature of the new line:

[1/Berks] *had a strange experience in finding that at one point a trench full of the enemy's troops was only six yards distant, though the British and German troops were separated by a hedge. During the following day the Berks captured this trench, along with one officer and seventy men; those of the enemy who tried to escape were shot down.*

It should not be thought that all was quiet elsewhere on the 7th Division's line on the 24th. To the east of Gheluvelt there had also been heavy fighting, with seemingly an endless sequence of German attacks. At one stage a breakthrough threatened the boundary between 20 Brigade – 2/Green Howards and 21 (Guards) Brigade (1/Grenadiers). A counter attack by 4 Company (Major Colby) of the Grenadiers was ordered.

Great difficulties were added to its task by the tobacco drying grounds – ready made entanglements on which the men's packs and accoutrements caught while the German machine guns were practically enfilading them.

The Grenadiers' history notes that only one company officer escaped unscathed; Colby and Lieutenant Antrobus were killed. Somewhat alarmingly, the history says that a hundred men of the company were also killed. The CWGC registers only half a dozen, so this figure is very much exaggerated, even allowing for errors and misreporting that might have worked their way into the Commission's system. The divisional history's

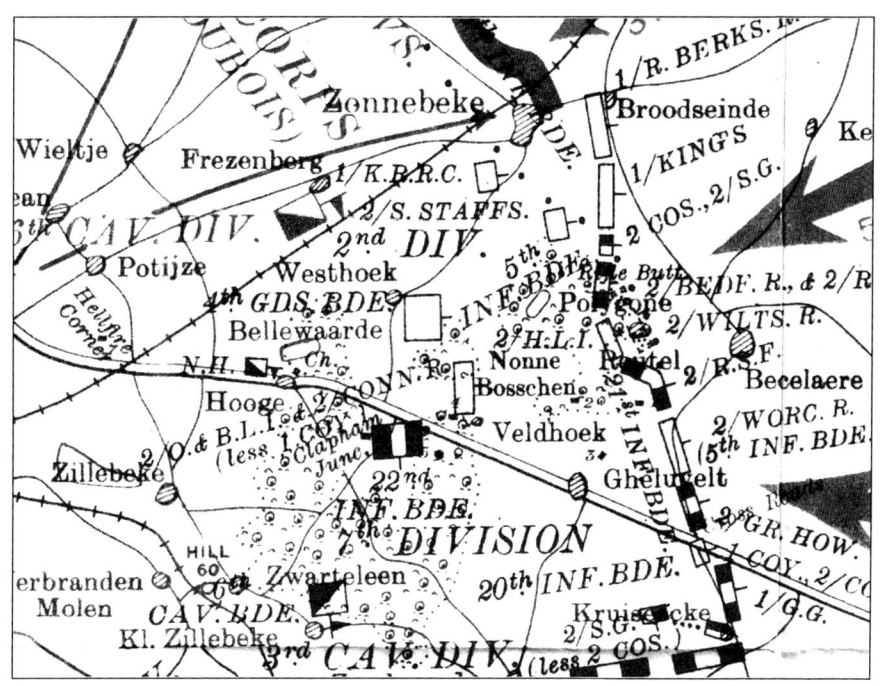

Situation from Kruiseecke to Broodseinde, evening of 24 October.

report of a hundred wounded seems altogether more likely. Whatever the truth, the company was reduced to one officer and eighty effectives.

By the end of the day, apart from the position that had been held by 2/Wilts, the line of the 7th Division had held, though about 1,500 casualties had been inflicted upon it. The 7th had lost about a quarter of its infantry in the few days it had seen action at Ypres. On a positive note, relieved by French troops from their positions centred on Langemarck, where they had been engaged in heavy fighting for three days, the 1st Division had finally got into their reserve positions east and south of Ypres by about 8 am on the 24th.

The 24th had also been a difficult day for the Franco-Belgian forces to the north; the Germans managed to cross the Yser south of Nieuport; but they failed to get their artillery across. Albrecht's Fourth Army concentrated its efforts there. The commander ordered his troops from the Menin Road to Bixschoote 'to maintain and strengthen their positions and to take every opportunity of seizing important points on their immediate front'; in the north 'where a decision seemed imminent' he directed that the attack should be continued.

Over the next days the action to the north of the Menin Road, in particular north and east of Polygon Wood, was associated with the

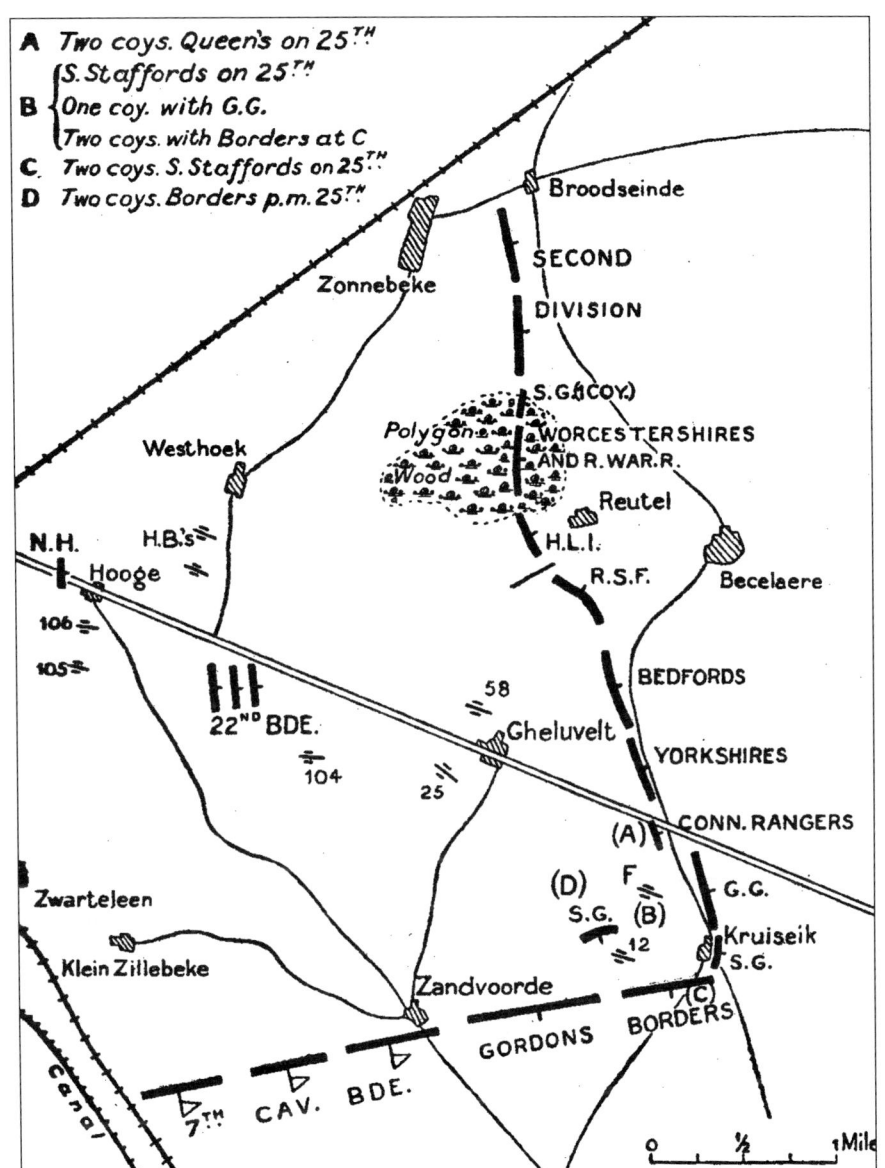

A Two coys. Queen's on 25TH
    (S. Staffords on 25TH
B { One coy. with G.G.
    Two coys. with Borders at C
C Two coys. S. Staffords on 25TH
D Two coys. Borders p.m. 25TH

Broodseinde

SECOND
DIVISION

Zonnebeke

S.G.(COY)
Polygon
Wood WORCESTERSHIRES
AND R. WAR. R.

Westhoek

Reutel

N.H.   H.B.'s   H.L.I.

Hooge   R.S.F.   Becelaere

106
105   BEDFORDS

58

22ND BDE.   Gheluvelt   YORKSHIRES

104   25

(A)   CONN. RANGERS

Zwarteleen   (D)   F   G.G.
     S.G. (B)

Klein Zillebeke   12   Kruiseik
     S.G.

Zandvoorde   (C)

GORDONS   BORDERS

7TH CAV. BDE.

Canal

0   ½   1 Mile

The 7th Division's situation, 25 October.

continued attempts by the French, with British help where possible, to continue an offensive against the Germans – an offensive that was not finally abandoned until 30 October. This fact is often forgotten; it has become obscured in the popular memory of Ypres as a desperate defensive battle – which, of course, it became. But an understanding of

43

offensive intentions by the allies, so far into the Battle of Ypres, needs to be kept in mind when assessing what lay behind the thinking of allied commanders during this long drawn out engagement. On the **25th** the British line was pushed forward somewhat: on the left 6 Brigade got across the Becelaere road and over the ridge; and on the right 4 Brigade, whilst not particularly successful, had managed to establish a line on the western slopes of the Reutel Spur, the Irish Guards ending up about 200 yards from the edge of Reutel.

Men of Field Artillery Regiment 80 bathing in a pond at Oude Kruiseeke.

Kruiseecke

It is doubtful if many visitors ever visit this part of the Ypres battlefield; there are no CWGC cemeteries, and few memorials and not a sign that this was such a hard fought over area in October 1914. Once more, the early days of the major fighting here involved the 7th Division. 19 October marked the end of the division's attempts to exploit east down the Menin Road, with the exception of a reconnaissance in strength on the 20th; events to the north ensured that this would be the last time that the BEF set foot on the soil beyond Kruiseecke for almost four years.

This small village formed the point of a very sharp, right angled salient in the 7th Division's line. For several days the most intense action was to the north and 20 Brigade (Ruggles-Brise, until earlier that year Commandant of the School of Musketry at Hythe and, along with WN Congreve, largely responsible for the rapid fire capability of the British infantry) had a relatively easy time, although it had a very long front and was often called upon to use its reserve on other parts of the divisional line.

For much of the time its main problem was from snipers and machine guns – particularly those in America. Occasionally German thrusts on the north side of the Menin Road meant that battalions on the Brigade's left flank got tied into the fighting – such as happened on 24 October.

The position was a useful one from the British perspective – it had good views to the south and east. The artillery, in particular F Battery and 12 Battery, provided both effective and imaginative support to a line that was based on a forward slope position – fine for observation, extremely difficult to maintain in the face of a determined onslaught. Thus, although the salient was never under very serious threat, it was subject to probing attacks and artillery fire and it would be quite wrong to give the impression that it was a 'quiet' part of the front. The defenders were also considerably over extended.

The arrival of the 2nd Division and the taking over of the line of 22 Brigade by 5 and 6 Brigades, who were ordered to participate in French attempts on the left to push forward, meant that what was left of the battered brigade was now available to act as a reserve for its sister brigades in the division.

At Kruiseecke, the night of **24/25 October** was very active, with the Germans laying down almost continuous rifle fire – one officer commented that it was like 'sheets of lead going over our heads all night'. Small probing attacks caused no great problems and 12 Battery RFA moved three guns into the open. At dawn on the 25th these opened fire at close range and destroyed machine gun positions in houses nearby.

As night fell it became apparent that the Germans had intentions on the salient. At various times during the night, D Company of the Queen's came forward to reinforce 2/Yorks; D Company of 1/South Staffs reinforced 1/Grenadiers. G Company of the Scots Guards held the 'point' position, with the battalion's other two companies behind it in support. Two more companies of 1/South Staffs came next, having relieved two of 2/Border Regiment (2/Borders), and on the right were 2/Gordons, whose right hand neighbours came from the 3rd (Cavalry) Division.

The position was not covered by a continuous line and there were many gaps – for example, when men of the South Staffs moved up to the line they collected a number of German prisoners, men who had infiltrated the line. Considerable controversy has been caused by the positioning of the trenches that did exist – i.e. on a forward slope, narrow and with minimal cover. For this Rawlinson, IV Corps' commander, has taken some blame. In fact, Capper himself seems to have determined the design of the line, based on observations on the conduct of the Russo-Japanese war of 1904-1905 – thus: forward slopes; overhead cover of planks and earth – fine for shrapnel, dangerous with HE shells; and narrow trenches. There were also criticisms of the lack of field works; but communication trenches were practically impossible, given the location of many of the forward positions and the incessant German fire. Whilst considerable efforts were made to improve, for example, the barbed wire defences, lack of wire and the difficulty of constructing such fortifications effectively in sandy soil – and under fire – meant that these were, indeed, inadequate at best and non-existent at worst.

By evening on **24 October**, throughout the length of the XXVII Reserve Corps front all the impetus seemed to have been lost. However that situation was completely unacceptable to the German higher headquarters so, even though there was a lack of strength to mount a really major offensive effort, nevertheless poorly planned small scale actions, launched with very inadequate reconnaissance and indifferent fire support, continued to be mounted against the highly skilled British infantry, which took a severe toll of the attackers' numbers. One such attack was conducted towards Kruiseecke on 25 October, the objective being defended by 20 Brigade

All the British defending units were well below their normal strength and, as has been mentioned, the physical defences were also in a very poor state because of all the gunfire. There were no communication trenches between the isolated positions and there was no barbed wire. Nevertheless, situated as it was on rising ground and clearly defended in some strength, the German army regarded it with respect and devoted considerable time to the preparations to attack it. Reserve Infantry Regiment 242, which participated in the final assault, was also heavily involved in a series of small scale preliminary actions that cost it a great many casualties. The preparations paid off, however. Following what was for once an effective bombardment, 20 Brigade's positions were stormed to the accompaniment of drums and trumpets.

In the event, the Germans failed to capture Kruiseecke on the **25th**. They did manage to penetrate the Grenadiers' right flank, pushing through on the Scots Guards' left trench but failing to dislodge completely Captain Paynter's G Company, even though they had a force of Germans to their rear. Two companies of Scots Guards under Major Fraser moved up to reinforce the position, aiming to clear the village from the south. An attempt to take the lost trench resulted in forty men, including Major Fraser, becoming casualties and was unsuccessful. Elsewhere, however, a scissors movement resulted in the capture of seven officers and some 200 men (other reports say five officers and 187 men) from Reserve Infantry Regiments 233 and 242. LF Company, after handing over their prisoners,

Then returned to the front to complete their brilliant success by retaking the lost trench. It proved to be full of dead and wounded Germans [and, indeed, British, both sides mostly killed or wounded by bayonet]*, but it was found necessary to re-dig it and most of the other trenches which the two companies now occupied. This allowed the relief of Captain Paynter's men, who, though repeatedly attacked, had held on tenaciously, repulsing not only direct attacks, but the more insidious attempts by the enemy to represent themselves as friends.*

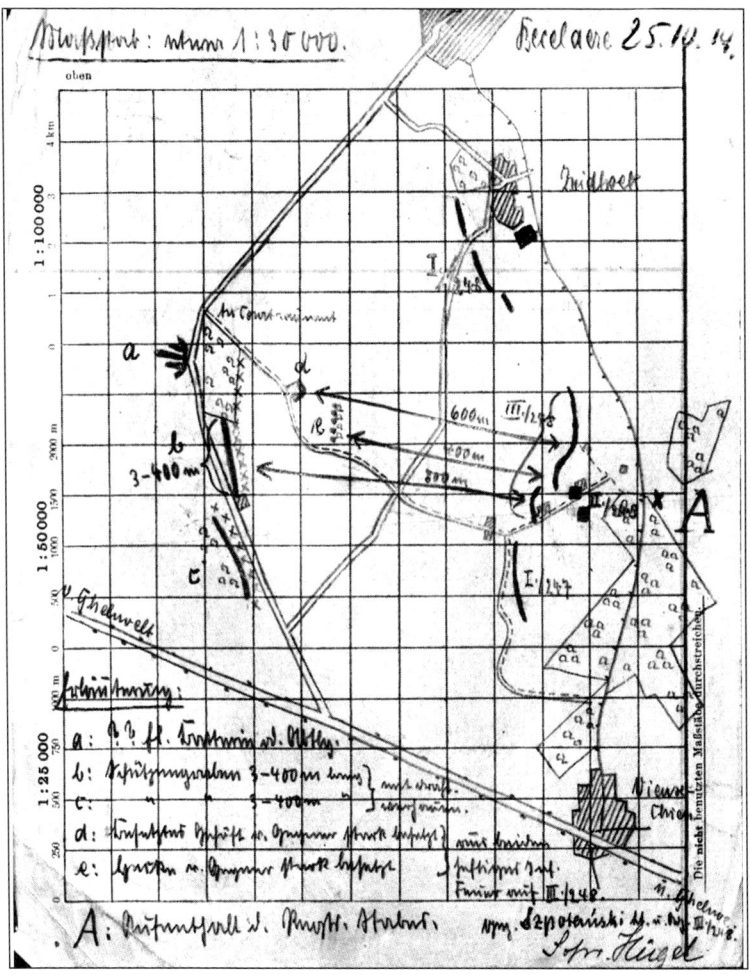

Situation of RIR 247 north of Vieux Chien (and the Menin Road), 25 October. The indicated lines of attack run along and parallel with the A19 motorway.

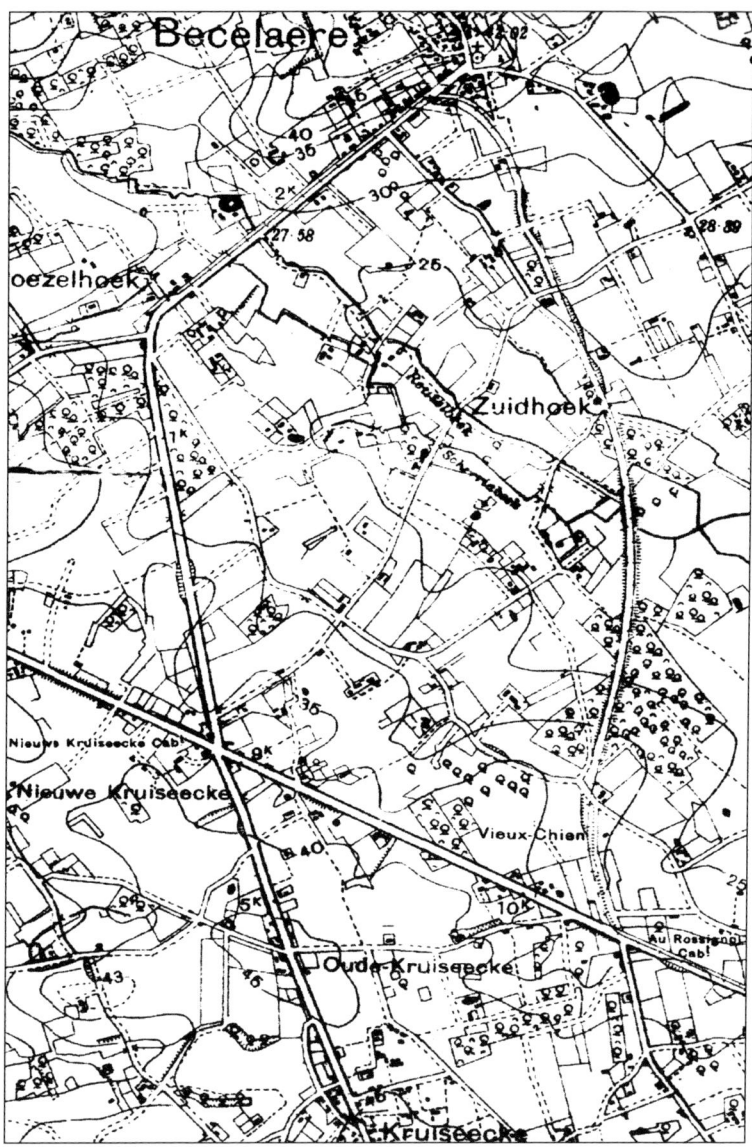

Approximately the same area extracted from a contemporary map.

Elsewhere along this part of the front the German attacks had been beaten off, if at a cost, 'so that once again morning [26th] found the line of the sorely tried 20 Brigade still intact, though all ranks were almost exhausted'.

To the north, the Belgian army was also coming close to exhaustion. Since 15 October, 9,145 of their wounded had been evacuated, with another thousand in local hospitals; the Germans managed to move

48

artillery across the Yser and active consideration was being given to a withdrawal to the line of the Dixmude railway embankment and to prepare for the inundation by the sea of the ground to the east of it.

Finally, exploiting the exhaustion of the British garrison, following almost twenty-four hours of continuous hard fighting, Kruiseecke was captured and several hundred British prisoners were taken.

26 October.

The German bombardment recommenced that morning; trenches were blown in and many men were buried. The British guns were shelled out of their positions and had to relocate to new ones – and in any case were beginning to suffer from a shortage of shells, common to the whole BEF, so that rationing was introduced and, in time, some guns were withdrawn for want of munitions.

A series of attacks was launched against the line, the Scots Guards in the salient once again being particularly vulnerable. Two companies of 1/South Staffs, between the Scots Guards and the Borders on their right, were overwhelmed at about 11 am. Those who survived fell back and formed a new line that held the Germans. The Borders, meanwhile, under attack from 9 am by Germans who assembled in woods to their front, were now attacked on their left flank and only about seventy men got away. A motley collection of these men, battalion HQ, battalion scouts and the machine gun section, however, succeeded in halting the Germans.

The worst affected were the Scots Guards; the line was rolled up from the left flank, though it took until 3 pm to complete the capture of their trenches, in particular those on the left, the least vulnerable. The Scots Guards' history, noting that in the early hours of the 26th that it became too light to continue to search for more Germans in the village, goes on:

But that difficulty was solved by the German artillery, which destroyed every house in it, and must have buried any Germans left behind there. Colonel Bolton was now, with Lieutenant Menzies, his adjutant, in the forward trenches, where he said he would remain. The German bombardment was terrific, Lord Dalrymple and his CSM counted over 120 shell bursts within a hundred yards round them every two minutes. About noon there were reports of giving way on the left, and about 1.30 pm some men of the company next to the Border Regiment on the right were seen to be retiring slowly across the rear. Here there was heavy firing along Kruiseecke village, and at the north end Lord

*Gerald Grosvenor, an officer of the battalion, was taken prisoner
in a house to which he had gone to have his wounds dressed.*

*About 2.30 pm the front trenches were heavily fired on from
the village in their rear, into which the Germans had penetrated
through the south face of the salient. The defenders might even
then have got away to their left; but their orders were definite –
to hold on to the last – and they held. At last the Germans were
on them on all sides in overwhelming numbers and surrender
could not be avoided. Bushes and houses in the rear screened the
assailants until they were actually on the trenches. Lord
Dalrymple never observed them till he saw them mixed up with
the British in the next trench. He had only five men at hand, whom
he ordered to smash their rifles before he surrendered.*

The Germans captured seven officers – of whom two were wounded –
and two others were killed. Not one man in the Scots Guards killed on
this day has a known grave.

Captain CV Fox, one of the two wounded
officers, had an eventful time as a prisoner
of war; in fact he had an eventful military
career altogether. Born in 1877 and
educated by the Jesuits and at Oxford, he
joined the Scots Guards in 1900. He was in
West Africa for several years and picked up
various campaign medals; then served in
Egypt and the Sudan until 1914. In this period, intriguingly enough,
he led the successful 'Elephant Poacher Hunt' in 1913 and at some
stage in his secondment was taken prisoner for a while. For his deeds
at Kruiseecke he was awarded the DSO. When captured he had
suffered three wounds; he was then imprisoned in a succession of
prisoner of war camps: Crefeld (Krefeld), Werl, Legarden,
Brandenburg and Schwarmstedt. He escaped from Crefeld and was
recaptured; he escaped from the Berlin Express and was recaptured;
and escaped successfully from Schwarmstedt in 1917. He arrived in
England on 6 July 1917 and was received by the King; and was
subsequently elected President of the Escapers. In spare moments in
his university and military career he managed to win the Diamond
Sculls in 1901 and the sculling championships of France and Ireland;
and was runner up in the Army Middle Weight Boxing Championship
of 1903. Quite a man! After the war he served for a time in Iraq and
died in his home town of Dublin at the early age of 51, in 1928.

This then left the Grenadiers in a most precarious position, all the more so since the orders from Brigade to move back to a new line south east of Gheluvelt never reached those in the firing line. The King's Company (Weld Forrester) did manage to escape; most others were taken.

Although the line had crumpled, the isolated pockets of determined resistance gave time for the new line to be established on the western (reverse) slope of the hill; this line connected with that of 2/Gordons, whose own position had held despite being under attack; indeed the Gordons had escaped with relatively minor casualties. 22 Brigade (Lawford), now fully relieved from its positions on the left of the division, was billeted around Veldhoek; at 2 pm it was instructed to go the assistance of 20 Brigade. Lawford moved his men forward, 1/Welsh Fusiliers right, 2/Warwicks left and 2/Queen's in support (the other battalion of the brigade, 1/South Staffs, was already committed). They were heavily shelled as they crossed the Gheluvelt-Zandvoorde road; when about a mile south east of Gheluvelt (at about 4 pm), they were halted and withdrew slightly to develop a new line south of Gheluvelt and westwards to the Zandvoorde road, i.e. facing south. This action was caused by what turned out to be erroneous reports that 20 Brigade had been forced back once more; but in fact this was a matter of the artillery being redeployed west of the Basseville Brook and the Grenadiers accompanying them to prepare a new position should it be needed.

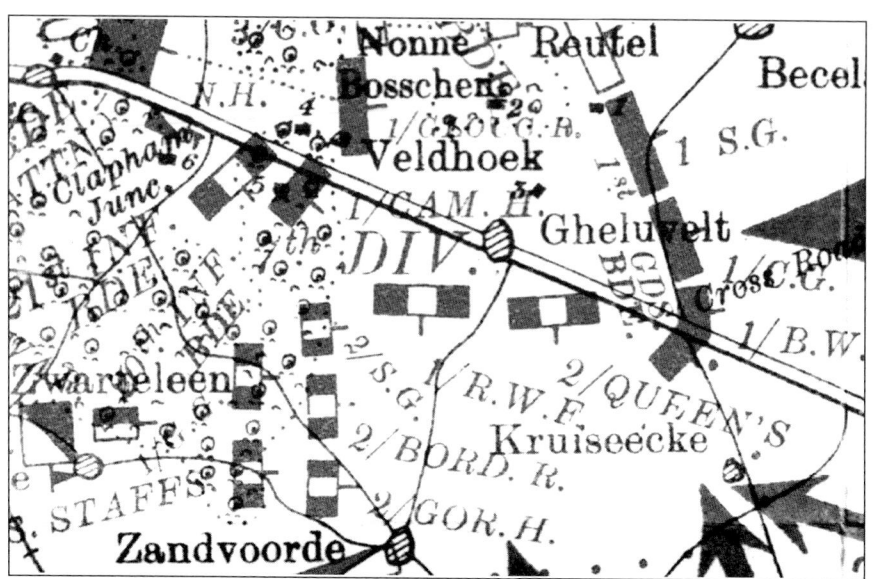

Situation evening of 26 October, Kruiseeke Salient.

51

A member of Leib-Dragoner Regiment 24 later reported:

At 10.00 am on 26 October, the British began to leave their front line trenches. When our troopers saw this, without waiting for orders, they rushed forward from their inadequate dugouts under the command of Hauptmann Riedesel Freiherr zu Eisenbach, determined to take revenge on an enemy who had inflicted such heavy losses upon them. Despite being swept at times by machine gunfire, they charged into the British trenches. Before the British knew what was happening and were able to defend themselves [we were amongst them]. *A few showed signs of attempting to resist so it was necessary to go in with lead and rifle butts to demonstrate that further resistance was useless. Encouraged, the dragoons pressed on into the narrow trenches and took one hundred prisoners.*

The Royal Scotch Guards [sic] *were astonished at the sight of our spurs and one officer, realising that their trenches had fallen to the cavalry, attempted suicide. The assault was continued on beyond these trenches towards Kruiseecke, where a great many of the enemy were taken prisoner. Orders were then given to halt any further advance. The edges of the village were all picketed and once initial duties were complete, the dragoons helped themselves to captured British tinned rations and cigarettes.*

The capture of the Kruiseecke salient was a feather in the cap of the German attackers, who moved swiftly to prepare it for defence in case the British army counter-attacked. Some dismounted cavalry remained in the area for the next three days to provide security, eventually being relieved by units of XV Corps. Reserve Infantry Regiment 242, which had suffered severely, formed three composite companies then, reinforced by Landwehr Regiments 77 and 78 of 1st Landwehr Division, later resumed the advance on 27 October and, having captured Oude Kruiseecke, continued to move as best it could towards Gheluvelt.

Simultaneously, off to the north of the Menin road, urgently needed French reinforcements went on the offensive in the Zonnebeke area, causing units of 53rd Reserve Division to go into hasty defence from totally inadequate, water and mud-filled shallow trenches so as to prevent the French from turning the flank of Criegern's brigade. Operating between Keiberg and Mispelaarhoek, Reserve Infantry Regiment 243, and especially its 3rd Battalion, commanded by Major Friedrich, was soon locked into a sharp close range battle. With its ammunition running low, it was reinforced in the nick of time by

A view down the Menin Road from a German barricade.

Reserve Infantry Regiment 244. This had the effect of hampering the French advance considerably, but it was unable to prevent British troops, which had been conforming to the French movements along the Broodseinde – Becelaere road, from occupying a group of houses and threatening the rear of 2nd Battalion Reserve Infantry Regiment 243. The overall position was becoming desperate and the divisional commander was obliged to deploy Reserve Infantry Regiment 241 to counter the threat. Unteroffizier Siegfried Brase, Reserve Infantry Regiment 241, later recalled what happened.

We came across some Schwabian Landwehr men who had been calmly occupying the trenches since the previous evening and were coolly firing at the clay coloured beings opposite whenever they spotted them up trees or attempting to fetch water. In order to help I removed my rifle stock and set about cleaning my rather ancient weapon. British Dum Dum rounds clattered harmlessly on the road to our rear, whilst our machine guns had soon discovered worthwhile targets in the shape of enemy columns. As we later discovered from the war diary of one of our opponents, they were reinforcements who had been called forward from France.

Suddenly very heavy artillery fire started coming down, initially around one of the buildings we had left back in Broodseinde, but then behind us and falling ever closer to our zig-zag trench, which actually offered almost no protection and we had barely begun to construct small fox holes ... shouting came from our right. To the left my comrade Körner, who had had a good laugh at my expense a little earlier, was hit by rifle bullets twice in the arm whilst out in the open. Our artillery fell silent, their guns in some cases destroyed, in others they had no ammunition left to fire. We could no longer hear our machine guns either; they had been wrecked by shellfire though, remarkably, their crews, sheltering in their holes, were completely unharmed.

As a result, the reinforced enemy could continue to work their way forward out on our right flank so, whenever we lifted our heads over the parapet to fire at the enemy, the howl of a shell made us duck our heads rapidly ... we then noted that the whole of the line to our right was pulling back. The commander of the Jägers, Major B., our former commanding officer when we were in the garrison ... having decided that to attempt to remain in our indefensible positions was tantamount to suicide, had given the orders for this. We tried also to conform. We had to leave the wounded behind, because to attempt to move them in the open would have put them at risk once more. We found some of them later, gruesomely beaten to death by the enemy ...

Back near Kruiseecke, with darkness falling on the 26th and their own men near to exhaustion, the Germans made little effort to push their advantage. Yet the position was very exposed and Ruggles-Brise, whose 20 Brigade had lost a third of its remaining manpower in the last twenty four hours, ordered a withdrawal at about 3.30 pm behind the Basseville Brook, the trenches facing east. Thus what had been a salient now became a re-entrant. Meanwhile, 21 Brigade, north of the Menin Road, had not moved and therefore had an open right flank; however, apart from persistent sniping, particularly against the Bedfords, no major effort was made against their line, apart from a half-hearted assault on 2/RSF.

Two battalions of 1(Guards) Brigade were also used to help resolve the situation; after reveille at 3.30 am on the 26th, 1/Camerons and 1/Black Watch were moved from their billeting area at Zillebeke to the south side of the Menin Road, in woods near Veldhoek. There they dug themselves in to protect against bombardment; and it was where a tragic incident took place.

During this halt a British aeroplane flew low over the trees and dropped bright lights just over the troops. As no warning had been given of this unexpected and, at that period, novel action, it was assumed that it was a German plane in disguise and the troops were ordered to fire on it. This order was carried out all too well; the plane caught fire and fell blazing to the ground, both occupants being killed – a deplorable and shocking event which will never fade from the memories of those who witnessed it.

The scene was witnessed by Major 'Ma' Jeffreys, 1/Grenadiers. He saw the plane dropping lights and 'heavily fired on by the Black Watch, who brought it down in flames, all the men cheering as it came down. A dreadful sight, as we were watching and realised it was British.' The Air Official History quotes the report on the incident by Major Raleigh of 4 Squadron:

'Ma' Jeffreys as a major general.

[Lieutenant LG] *Hoskins and* [Captain T] *Crean did a tactical reconnaissance early, but were unable to locate batteries owing to clouds. They went up later and did it. The clouds were low, so it was arranged that they should fly over one of our batteries to observe for ranging. The machine came down in flames and was completely demolished. Pilot and passenger had both been wounded by our own infantry fire when at a height of about a thousand feet with the large Union Jack plainly visible.*

Lieutenant LG Hosking.

The bodies of the airmen, buried locally, were not recovered and their names are to be found on the Air Forces Memorial at Arras. This mishap did have a considerable consequence, as it 'hastened the adoption of the suggestion (that the British should adopt the French circular marking) and thereafter the French target was painted on British aeroplanes, with the alteration only of blue for red and red for blue, to preserve national distinctions.'

Captain Crean.

At about 5 pm on the 26th 1/Black Watch was sent to the left of 20 Brigade, east of Gheluvelt; they were to clear any Germans near the crossroads north of Kruiseecke and to dig in south of the Menin Road, facing east and south east, including the road to Wervicq. B and D Companies of 1/Camerons were to dig in on the Zandvoorde road, half a mile south of Gheluvelt, whilst A and C were sent back to Battalion

HQ, got a meal and then dug themselves some shelters. However, their rest was not to last long; soon after 2 am they were roused and told to proceed down a side road to Kruiseecke, make contact with the right of 1/Black Watch and extend the line to the right, where they would be joined by men of 22 Brigade.

Off went the men of the two companies, accompanied by no less a personage than Capper and some of his staff, who wanted to be sure of the position of the Camerons' right.

It was dark, signs of heavy fighting were encountered ... and the road was strewn with debris of arms and equipment. When a

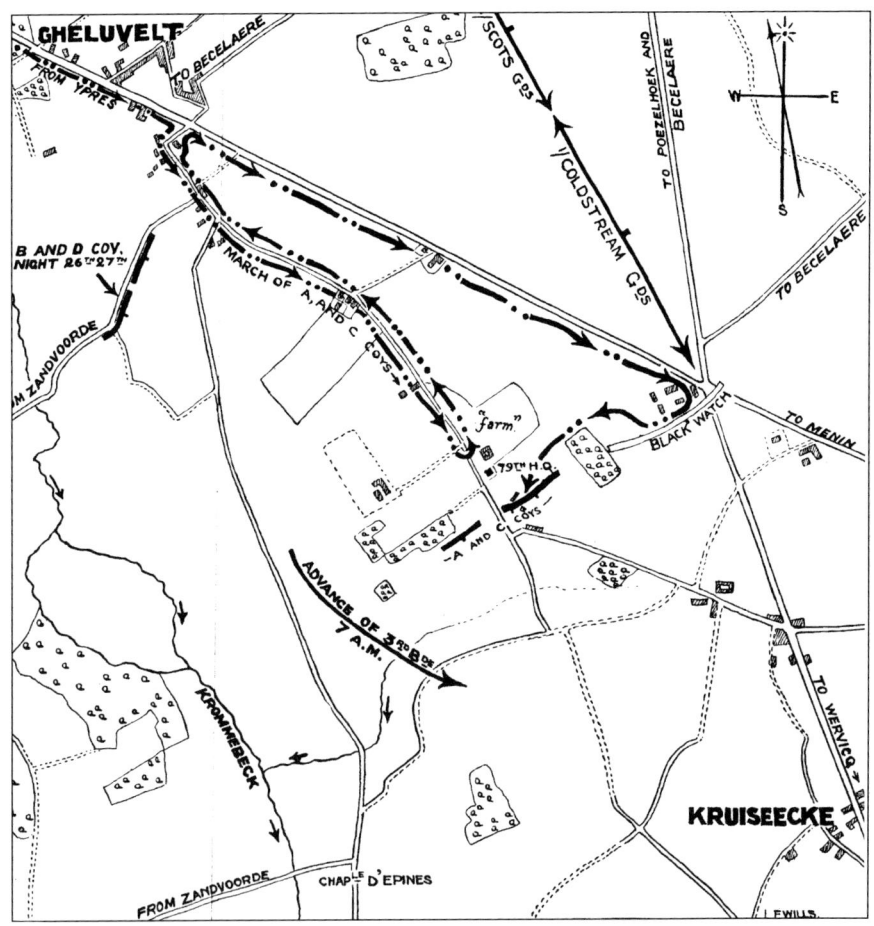

The wanderings of A and C Companies, 1/Camerons, during the night of 26-27 October.

point was reached estimated as the right spot, patrols were sent out to find the Black Watch, but without success. As the position of the enemy was quite unknown, [it was] decided to return to Gheluvelt and to march along the Menin Road until the Black Watch position was ascertained, and then to prolong the line to the right as directed. This plan met with General Capper's approval, and the weary return march commenced, the half battalion doubling sharply to its right at Gheluvelt and moving south east down the Menin Road. The Black Watch position was duly found and the Camerons stumbled in single file over the beetroot fields behind it until the right hand man of the [Black Watch] was reached.

Much valuable time and energy had been wasted by going along the side road in the first instance and there was only about an hour left in which to get out a covering party, lay down a trace and start digging before daybreak. A and C Companies had already dug themselves in at least twice since leaving Zillebeke, and they were also decidedly short of sleep. But luckily the soil was not hard, and in spite of weariness the men worked with a will and for their own safety. At dawn the enemy were still quiet and a patrol of the covering party ... secured some German wounded from a farm in front of the position.

In the account above one can almost hear the exasperated rage of the source of this account of confusion and wanderings! The battalion held the position until relieved by 2/Green Howards that evening and then moved back to Veldhoek (arriving about midnight) before assuming their new positions north of the Menin Road.

Capper considered a counter attack to restore the lost ground given up by 20 Brigade; hence the move with 1/Camerons to cover the left flank of any advance made by 22 Brigade. This advance, in turn, was made possible by the relief of 21 (Guards) Brigade after dark by the other two battalions of 1 (Guards) Brigade (Fitzclarence VC) of the 1st Division (Lomax).

An advance was ordered by 22 Brigade and, with hardly any opposition, it reached the original line of withdrawal. The move was delayed because it was made in the dark and for the need first to reorganise the much mixed up battalions of 22 Brigade. The intention that 22 Brigade would be replaced by the 3rd (Landon) was foiled by the time the advance had been completed, at about 7 am, as it would have to take place in the light of day; so that 22 Brigade had to wait for nightfall on the 27th before it could be relieved.

All this movement and the use of units from multiple brigades makes it very difficult to keep a clear sense of the comings and goings; how much more exhausting it must have been for tired, wet, hungry troops, in much weakened battalions, some of whom were new to the area and who had little idea of the ground. One can understand the irate tone of the historian of 1/Camerons as he recounted their meanderings of the night 26/27 October.

For once, the 7th Division had a quiet day on the **27th**; even 22 Brigade suffered little shelling, whilst 20 Brigade was in bivouac and 21 Brigade had an uneventful time in reserve at Veldhoek until in the evening, when they took over the line of 22 Brigade (Menin Road to Zandvoorde), the latter withdrawing to Klein Zillebeke.

The new position, though only inadequately entrenched, represented a real improvement on the Kruiseecke Salient, so tenaciously defended by 20 Brigade for five days of intense strain and shelling. A less satisfactory position it is hard to imagine ... Kruiseke [sic] *Hill, though only fifty feet above the general level, was terribly exposed, subjected to concentrated enfilade fire, and all units had fought most stubbornly.*

Meanwhile, optimism continued to shine at GHQ. French, on the evening of the 26th, informed Kitchener in London that II and III Corps, down in the south in the area of Armentières and La Bassée, could hold their positions, whilst 'reliable information' indicated that the Germans, 'were quite incapable of making any strong and sustained attack' because of their losses and were dependent upon their artillery to support their position. So, conforming with General d'Urbal, commander since 20 October of French forces in the north (Le Détachement d'Armée Belgique – DAB), the allied attack was to continue on the 27th, I Corps providing the British element, whilst the 7th Division and the Cavalry Corps were to assist as they could. Also on the 27th, IV Corps was temporarily disbanded. The 3rd (Cavalry) Division had already been transferred, on the 25th, to Allenby's Cavalry Corps and so it was a corps of only one division, a much weakened one at that. It now came under Haig and Rawlinson returned to England, to prepare the 8th Division for its move to France. When it landed on 6 November it joined the 7th Division to form the reconstituted IV Corps.

During the relative lull in the fighting, during the afternoon of the **27th**, Haig reorganised his forces in I Corps in an attempt to get some order restored in the command structure. He ordered the 7th Division to hold the line from Zandvoorde to the Menin Road; the 1st Division to cover up to a point west of Reutel and the 2nd to hold to the right of the French, near the Zonnebeke – Roulers road. The movements consequent on these orders were completed at about midnight – hard work for 7th Division, which had suffered considerably during the last week of operations. Indeed, I Corps had gone through exhausting marches from the time that the Battle of Mons had opened two months earlier and endured some very heavy fighting, most recently on the Aisne. For some the Aisne must have seemed like a distant memory.

Meanwhile the French had made little progress in their attack eastwards towards Passchendaele and Poelcappelle; 6 Brigade, on the left of the 2nd Division's front, did move forward a thousand yards, advancing into the bottom of the valley that lies between the Passchendaele-Broodseinde road and the Keiberg Spur, where they were halted. 2/South Staffs lost five officers and 115 men, whilst 1/KRRC suffered the loss of six officers (including Prince Maurice of Battenberg, Queen Victoria's youngest grandson, killed) and 167 men. On the evening of the 27th the left flank of the BEF, in the shape of 2/South Staffs, was on the Moorslede road. Field Marshal French remained confident; as the

Prince Maurice of Battenberg.

Official History puts it, 'he considered that it was only necessary to press the enemy hard in order to ensure complete success and victory'.

On the Yser line, a first attempt was made on the evening of the 27th to begin the inundation of the line east of Dixmude by opening the gates of the Furnes lock, a complex operation. The intention was to let in the sea between the railway embankment (to the west) and the Yser, but this failed. On the **28th**, another comparatively calm day in front of Ypres for the BEF (though 2nd Division did try to advance, making only insignificant progress in the afternoon), the locks were successfully opened under the skilled guidance of Belgian waterman Henry Geeraert and the slow process of the inundation began – so slow, indeed, that the Germans were initially oblivious to the fact that the seeping in of the sea was the cause of the ground becoming increasingly boggy.

All unaware, the allies had no notion that Falkenhayn, the German chief of staff, was preparing a major attack, using both his Fourth (in the north) and his Sixth Armies, but interposing between them a new formation, Army Group Fabeck. This was to take over the part of the line between St Yves to Gheluvelt currently occupied by four cavalry corps. Besides considerable infantry, the group also was to have its disposal 250 heavy guns with which to assist it in breaking through the British line.

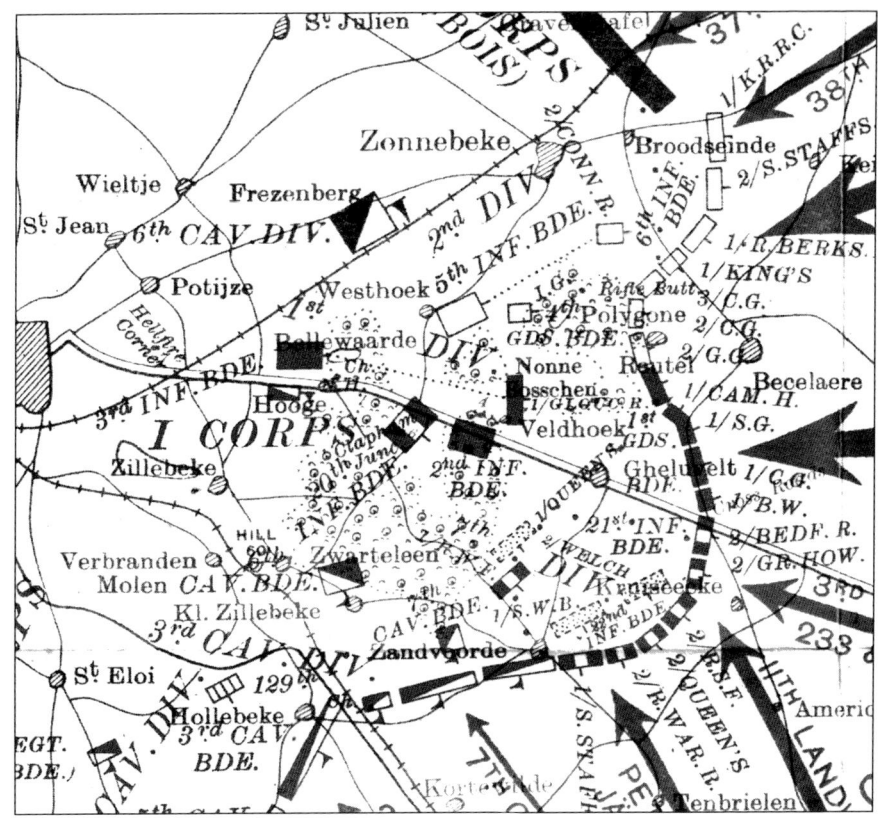

Situation on the evening of 28 October.

At 3 pm on 28 October, Haig received intelligence from an intercepted radio message that ordered an attack by XXVII Reserve Corps (which had been east of Ypres for over a week now) in the direction Kruiseecke-Gheluvelt, set for 5.30 am on the 29th. Since this did not indicate the use of new forces, Haig considered that he should continue to comply with orders to support the French attacks to the north by the 2nd Division, with the 1st Division in support. Air intelligence confirmed large movements of vehicles on the Roulers to Moorslede road – but a proportion of these were considered to be refugees' vehicles. Meanwhile, further to the north, there was a strong suspicion that the enemy were shifting troops south from the Yser front.

The Battle of Gheluvelt: The Preliminary Fighting

Fourth Army issued orders on **28 October** for a general resumption of the attacks on Gheluvelt. Leading elements of XV Corps, commanded by General Deimling, had moved into position to the left of XXVII Reserve

Corps and Reserve Infantry Regiment 247 quickly established contact. This was the first time Bavarian Reserve Infantry Regiment 16 – the so-called 'List Regiment' in which Adolf Hitler served – went into action but, although subsequently much was made of their participation, in fact the 29 October attack also involved Reserve Infantry Regiment 247 grouped to form 'Group Bendler', under the command of Oberst von Bendler of Reserve Infantry Regiment 247. Actually, every formation of XXVII Reserve Corps, with some elements of XV Corps operating to its left, was involved in an assault, the objective of which was to move the entire line forward from Poezelhoek to the crossroads a kilometre northwest of Vieux Chien.

As far as Group Bendler was concerned, the orders were to

work their way forward during the night 28/29 October, closing right up to the British positions; to direct the engineers to destroy any obstacles and to ensure that their light mortars opened fire immediately before the start of the attack, [which was scheduled for 6.30 am] *... The attack is to be pressed in the direction of Gheluvelt. Two battalions of Bavarian Reserve Infantry Regiment 16 will be subordinated to Group Bendler for the attack and are to be ready to move on the Gheluwe – Gheluvelt road, with leading elements located at the crossroads at Koelenberg by 5.00 am, ready to receive further orders brought by runner from Oberst von Bendler ... You are reminded once more that Bavarian Reserve Infantry Regiment 16 is equipped with Landsturm caps with a green covering.*

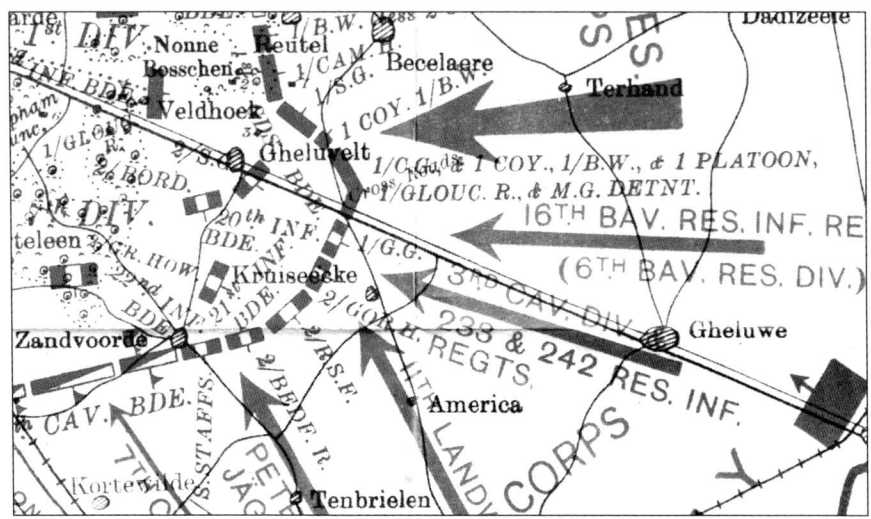

Extract from the Official History map for 28 October. Note the crossroads on the Menin Road, below the 'e' of Gheluvelt.

It was about midnight when the orders reached the forward troops. They were greeted with little enthusiasm. Nobody was under any illusion about what the day would bring and, despite general exhaustion, sleep proved elusive. The mood of apprehension was further intensified when the news arrived that the preliminary bombardment had been cancelled, apparently because of fog. The few stray shells fired by the guns furthest forward did little to inspire the attackers, who were all too well aware of the grave risks of attacking with inadequate fire support. However, in accordance with the orders, the early hours saw Bavarian Reserve Infantry Regiment 16 set out from its assembly areas. The 2nd Battalion was moved off to advance independently via Terhand to Becelaere to join Group Mühry (107 Reserve Infantry Brigade, 54th Reserve Division). Meanwhile, 1st and 3rd Battalions marched off to reinforce Group Bendler, which already comprised Reserve Infantry Regiments 242, 247 and 248 and the Saxon Infantry Regiment 105.

29 October

Taking advantage of his local knowledge, gained during an earlier reconnaissance, Hauptmann Obermann of Reserve Infantry Regiment 247 led his men via a concealed route towards the enemy trenches. This meant that his battalion suffered very few casualties initially when these forward British positions were overrun, but he himself was killed by machine gun fire from a well concealed position some three hundred metres further on. Obermann's death led to an urgent attempt to silence the offending machine gun. Eventually this proved to be possible, the machine gunner, described as an 'old soldier', died at his position, firing to the last. When the positions were finally consolidated, there were bodies strewn everywhere, many of them Scottish, but equally large numbers of German troops. 1st Company Reserve Infantry Regiment 247 alone suffering fifteen killed, including the company commander, Oberleutnant Meßbauer, whilst seventy-four men were wounded.

It was later claimed that Reserve Infantry Regiment 247 completely routed the enemy to its front but, whether or not that is true, the fact that those located opposite Reserve Infantry Regiment 248 held on ruled out any possibility of 3rd Company Reserve Infantry Regiment 247 pressing forward. Instead they concentrated on the enemy positions north of the main road. The situation on the ground was quickly becoming chaotic. Bavarian Reserve Infantry Regiment 16 was having great difficulty and suffering heavily in its attempts to advance, so shifted its point of main effort to the south, which meant that there was soon an appalling mixing of sub-units from different regiments. The problem was further compounded by the fact that despite explicit warnings about the wearing of forage caps by the Bavarians, they were mistaken for British troops at a distance and were fired on several times by their own side. Eventually the advance reached a line about 700 metres beyond the junction, but the cost had once again been high.

The 1st Battalion Bavarian Reserve Infantry Regiment 16 played a notable part in the attack. Setting off at about 6.45 am, it moved towards Gheluvelt on the northern side of the Menin – Ypres road, bypassing Vieux Chien. Shortly after the attack began the battalion came under unpleasantly accurate shrapnel fire, which caused it to spread out and to advance by dashes as quickly as possible, so as to pass through the danger area. Reserve Hauptmann Ottmar Rutz published, in 1917, a short memoir entitled *Bayernkämpfe* (Bavarian battles), in which he provided a graphic account of what happened.

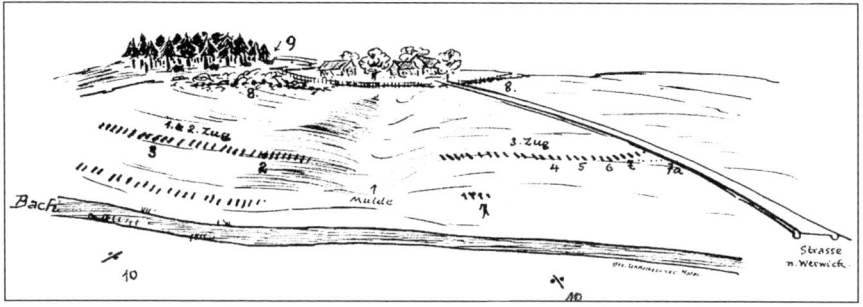

Represented on the panorama is the failed assault of 11th Company Bav RIR 16 on Geluveld on 29 October. That company's dead and missing reached an appalling seventy-five that day – worse than all other companies on a day when the regiment suffered 349 fatal casualties. On 30 October it suffered another 373 fatalities.
1. Place where the Company Commander, Res Oblt Johann Peuckert, was killed. 2. Place where Res Lt Karl Graf, who replaced Peuckert, was killed. 3. Place where Company Feldwebel Hans Mueller was killed. 4. Place where [Vize?]feldwebel Gies was wounded. 5. Place where [Vize?]feldwebel Spengler was killed. 6. Place where Gefreiter Hugo Schramm was killed. 7. Place where (the sketcher of the panorama) Einjaehrig Freiwilliger Gefreiter Ludwig Klein was wounded. 7a. Place where Klein crawled to and was rescued by stretcher bearers. 8. Camouflaged British positions. 9. Location of a British battery in a wood, on a hilltop about three kilometres distant. 10. German machine guns.

On 29 October, the reinforcements arrived. They were the Bavarian 16th, Reserve Regiment List, the flower of the youth of Munich, in many cases students, almost all volunteers and full of fresh enthusiasm. All-out attack! The fresh troops advanced as though on the drill square and the British fell back noticeably quickly. We had warned the new troops that the British were cunning, sly, opponents. This demanded the greatest care during the advance to contact. In the meantime we moved further to the left to link up with Prussian troops. The attack seemed to be progressing much better than expected. The British artillery fire caused us no casualties as we stood by, near some mean dwellings, ready to move.

The 16th stormed forward with youthful impetuousness. I was able to shout greetings to an old acquaintance, who was one of their company commanders, then they pressed on! Suddenly there was an appalling roaring and groaning noise mixed with whistles and cracks. The British, like us during the assault on Kruiseecke, were firing heavy artillery. To our front, about two hundred metres away, the first heavy shells crashed down, right in the centre of one of the advancing lines of the 16th. Simultaneously shrapnel balls rained down, shells exploded in grey-green clouds of sulphurous smoke and bullets from British small arms fire whistled through the air. In their careless forward thrust the men of the 16th found themselves trapped in the carefully planned cross fire of British riflemen and machine gunners, firing from the flanks. A Prussian officer came hurrying across from the left and shouted, 'Why aren't the Bavarians getting forward? Why are they lying down out there?'

Well there certainly was a line of riflemen from the 16th lying down, but they were not resting – they were either dead or wounded. We went into hasty defence and, silently, began to dig in. One heavy shell after another droned towards us. It was extraordinary how they groaned and droned through the air. Some of them came down not thirty metres to our front; the black fountains of earth flew into the air and cascaded down on us. These were moments of great tension. Would the next salvo hit us? Was it all over for us? But no, the next rounds crashed into a house to our rear, sending clouds of red tile dust, looking like a giant flower, into the heights. Off to our right shells and shrapnel bullets rained down on the twigs and branches of a copse. A shell splinter flew across, cutting off the calf of one of our runners. The poor man died as a result.

The dead and wounded were carried to the rear. My acquaintance, the company commander of the 16th, had been killed. Evening fell. Our doctors came right up to the front line to help. Taking advantage of the twilight we made our way forward

A German battlefield cemetery at Gheluwe, one of numerous such burial grounds. It was destroyed in post war years and its occupants were concentrated into one of the handful of large German cemeteries in the area today.

to a farmstead, which was already occupied by one of our patrols. A heavy shell had landed right in its dung heap, but the surrounding softness had completely contained it. The perimeter of the farm was immediately put into a state of defence and a trench was dug along the length of the farmhouse and extended to the left and right. It began to pour with rain.

Numerous patrols went out to bring the poor 16th in – those still alive that is. They had been dreadfully mauled. Some individuals had been wounded five, seven, or even more, times. We filled the barns with the most seriously wounded. The rain grew even heavier. The British, fearing a night attack, brought down idiotic, unaimed fire. This lasted for about an hour and greatly hindered the work of rescuing the 16th …

Of course, the remainder of 54th Reserve Division endured a day almost as bad as that of the Bavarians. In addition they had to put up with the indignity of being fired on repeatedly by their own artillery. That afternoon Hauptmann Theinert, of 1st Battalion Reserve Infantry Regiment 246, was forced to send this message:

2.00 pm. Report to Regiment. In the past five minutes our own artillery has fired eight rounds into our positions. In the name of all the men subordinated to me, I request your assistance. Enemy artillery fire is coming down heavily on our trenches either side of the lane leading westwards from Reutel. Where are our artillery observers? I am complaining officially about such incompetence. Update at 2.07 pm. Nine or ten shells fired by our own artillery have just landed immediately behind our trench.

This message was significant. Appalling training deficiencies meant that a great many German casualties were caused throughout the Fourth Army area by misdirected gun fire and numerous attacks withered away for precisely the same reason. Altogether Bavarian Reserve Infantry Regiment 16 suffered 349 all ranks killed in action that day, though there had been an advance towards Gheluvelt and some reasonably well-dug British trenches, complete with timber reinforcement, had been overrun, despite the striking lack of accurate artillery support. In addition, the British suffered many casualties, including the four hundred prisoners captured by XXVII Reserve Corps.

The British had not been simply recovering their breath in the relative interlude in the fighting. Warnings had been issued about the likely German attack at 5.30 am on the 29th; sunrise was shortly before 7 am. Its direction would hit the junction between the 7th and 1st Divisions at the Gheluvelt (Kruiseecke) cross roads, a kilometre south east of the village and just west of the 9 Km stone. The left battalion of the 7th Division was 1/Grenadiers, the right of the 1st Division 1/Coldstream, with only 350 men left, and covering a front of no less than 1,500 yards. Therefore a company of 1/Black Watch was posted on each flank. That on the left, however, did not have the numbers to make contact with 1/Scots Guards on its left, the Becelaere road at that point having thick woods on either side of it. This left a gap of a couple of hundred yards, so a platoon from 1/Glosters was used to cover it as far as possible. To make matters worse, the trenches were not good – originally these had been the 7th Division's support trenches. They not very deep and were narrow, lacking traverses and dug in short lengths with long intervals between them. There were no communication trenches and no dugouts – the manpower and materials needed for their construction was simply not available. They were defended by a single strand of wire, hung with tins containing pebbles, to act as a warning of German infiltration – certainly not meant as a meaningful obstacle.

Haig sought to improve the line south of the Menin Road; Capper and Haig's chief engineer, Brigadier General Rice, walked the line at

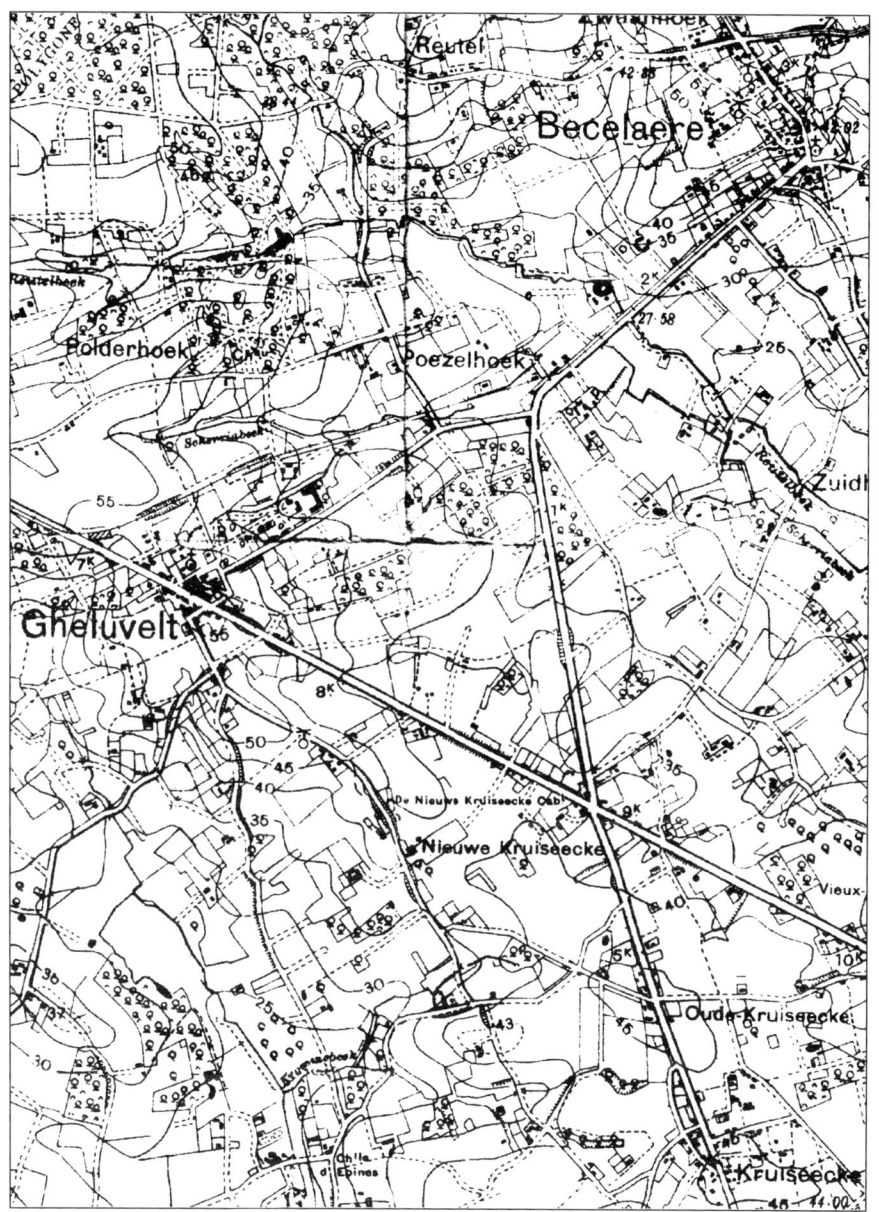

Contemporary map of the area. Note that the kilometre stones on the Menin Road are clearly marked.

daybreak on the 29th from left to right. The intention was to construct a new line to the rear, leaving the old to act as a dummy. But there were problems – even standing up there was a limited view, 'obstructed by cottages, trees, hedges and gardens'; from the trenches themselves there was practically no view. Not only was this a problem in dealing with an advancing enemy; it also meant that the defenders had very little idea of what was unfolding in their own area. As the Official History says, 'it accounts for the fact that when a mishap occurred, the troops on either side of those concerned remained for hours in ignorance of it'.

The German attack started at 5.30 am north of the Menin Road, not south, as rumour had had it. The advance was led by Bavarian Reserve Infantry Regiment 16, which broke into the Black Watch positions by the road and by 6.30 am had rolled up their position, from right and right rear, and that of the two right companies of 1/Coldstream. No British artillery support was forthcoming either; because of the extreme shell shortage, only nine rounds were available per gun and what ammunition was available, orders stated, was to be used against German artillery though, as has been mentioned, some artillery fire was indeed directed at the German infantry.

Further to the left, against the remainder of 1/Coldstream and the left company of the Black Watch, the Germans had no success in their attacks. The Coldstream endeavoured to create a defensive flank, to cover the German success to the south. When Fitzclarence at 1 (Guards) Brigade HQ heard what was going on – not until 7 am – he sent 1/Glosters (attached from 3 Brigade) to try and recover the situation. In this they partially succeeded, though the companies were sent in individually and piecemeal.

South of the Menin Road, 1/Grenadiers, with no view of the road due to obstructions such as houses and the like and which was in any case shrouded in fog, had no idea what was going on to the north; they neither heard the attack nor saw it. So great was this ignorance that, by 6.45 am, Ruggles-Brise (20 Brigade) decided to withdraw two battalions into reserve. These were 2/Scots Guards and 2/Borders: left where they were they would have been vulnerable to artillery fire in daylight hours. The German attack was preceded by a heavy bombardment from about 7.30 am and then the Germans came forward on the battalion's front and left flank. Soon the Grenadiers were fighting against attacks from their rear as well as the front, which soon developed into hand to hand fighting. Counter attacks were attempted, with the assistance of 2/Gordons on the right (who held their position throughout the day), to no lasting avail. Eventually, by about 9.30 am, the battalion withdrew as best it could to a ditch south of the Menin Road and to the east of Gheluvelt, where they were joined in their new position by a company of 1/Glosters and 2/Borders, brought back up from the reserve. This line held, despite being under considerable attack for much of the rest of the day. By the time that night came 1/Grenadiers had lost 470 men. Having had eleven officers killed, eight wounded and the CO, Lieutenant Colonel Earle, wounded and captured; they were left with five officers and under 200 men. Lieutenant J Brooke of 2/Gordons won a posthumous VC for his part in the fighting, particularly for leading two counter attacks early on in the day.

With reports sketchy, higher command was working in a literal as well as metaphorical 'fog of war', with contradictory, but broadly reassuring, reports coming back to the 1st Division's HQ. It only became clear at 10.15 am that 1/Grenadiers' line had given way and so Lomax and Ruggles-Brise decided to restore the Gheluvelt cross roads line by means of a

Lieutenant James Brooke, 2/Gordons.

counter attack by 3 Brigade. 2/Welsh had already been sent forward in support behind Gheluvelt at 7 am, replacing 1/Glosters; to these were added 1/Queen's, approaching from the south of the Menin Road and 1/South Wales Borderers (SWB) north of it. On the right of this movement, 2/Scots Guards and 2/Queen's were instructed to take the lost position of 1/Grenadiers.

The Germans, it would seem, were not fully aware until after 10 am of what their early morning attacks had achieved. At that stage they made the decision to make the attack general along the fronts of the 7th and 1st Divisions and on the right of the 2nd. However, they did not devote sufficient resources to the attack (if, indeed, these were immediately available) and, with the arrival of the British battalions coming forward to retake lost positions, a full scale encounter battle took place.

Before the new battalions could implement their attacks, however, the left half battalion of 1/Coldstream and its accompanying company of 1/Black Watch were attacked in front and rear by the Germans, who had been able to move up behind the position as a result of their success at the cross roads on the Menin Road. The Germans simply overran the position by about 10 am, so that by nightfall it was thought that 1/Coldstream were reduced to eighty men and the quartermaster; however sixty, who had become attached to 1/Scots Guards, returned the next day. This battalion was generally able to hold its own after ferocious fighting – losing eight officers and 336 other ranks – though positions on the right were lost, largely as a consequence of the defenders running out of ammunition.

Before midday 1 (Guards) Brigade had suffered massive losses of

over half of its strength and much of its front –
except on the left, to the west and south of Reutel,
defended by half 1/Black Watch and 1/Camerons
– had been lost.

Somewhat belatedly – for had it been
launched simultaneously with the more southerly
attack the effect might have been truly disastrous
for 1 (Guards) Brigade – at about 11.30 am
German troops on the right threatened an attack
on Polderhoek Chateau and the front of 1/Scots
Guards and 1/Camerons. Two companies were
sent up to support the Camerons and, at noon,
Monro sent his available troops from the 2nd
Division to assist in dealing with this new danger.
He did this by thinning out the fronts of 5 and 6

The Earl of Cavan.

Brigade, who had anticipated assisting in the continuing French attack,
and thus creating a reserve for his division of four battalions positioned
behind Polygon Wood under the command of Lord Cavan.

The counter attacks to the south
managed to make some limited progress and
a line was restored just forward of Gheluvelt
– a long way short of the original intention
of recapturing lost ground around the cross
roads. By 4 pm it had become clear that
attempts at enveloping the German thrusts
were going to get nowhere and, at a
conference of Landon and five battalion
commanders at Gheluvelt Chateau, it was
decided that the counter attack would cease
and, with the arrival of Fitzclarence and
Bulfin at the chateau, it was determined that
a new line was to be dug. Apart from a very
high casualty rate, the main loss was a
stretch of five hundred yards or so at the
cross roads. To add to the misery of the day,

Edward Bulfin in later life.

2/Scots Guards, which had outrun the advance in the counter attack,
suffered considerable casualties from accidental fire as it withdrew; then,
to cap it all, it proceeded to pour with rain that evening.

The new line ran approximately north south through the 8 km stone,
that is about a kilometre further back from where it had been in the
morning. Lomax and Monro, meeting at Hooge Chateau that evening,
agreed a strategy for dealing with any breakthrough by the Germans

before Gheluvelt. The 2nd Division's reserve, west of Polygon Wood, would be prepared to launch a counter attack southwards, with the intention of catching the Germans in enfilade. Most seriously, Haig now had hardly any reserve to speak of – from four brigades (admittedly at considerably reduced strength) he was reduced to the battered 20th and a couple of battalions. Even the continuing French attacks by IX Corps on the left made no progress, though de Mitry's 3rd Dragoon Brigade did succeed in capturing Bixschoote and Kortekeer Cabaret. French determined that British co-operation with Dubois' IX Corps attack on the left should continue, though with what immediate resources it is far from clear. To be fair, French had no knowledge until 31 October of the new German forces – five new divisions in Army Group Fabeck – before the BEF. He cheerily informed Kitchener that, 'although the enemy's resistance is very stubborn, slow but decided success is being made everywhere'. II Corps, around La Bassée, was being relieved and would be made available in the north; but the London Scottish were the only fresh troops that came up to Ypres that day, arriving there about midnight.

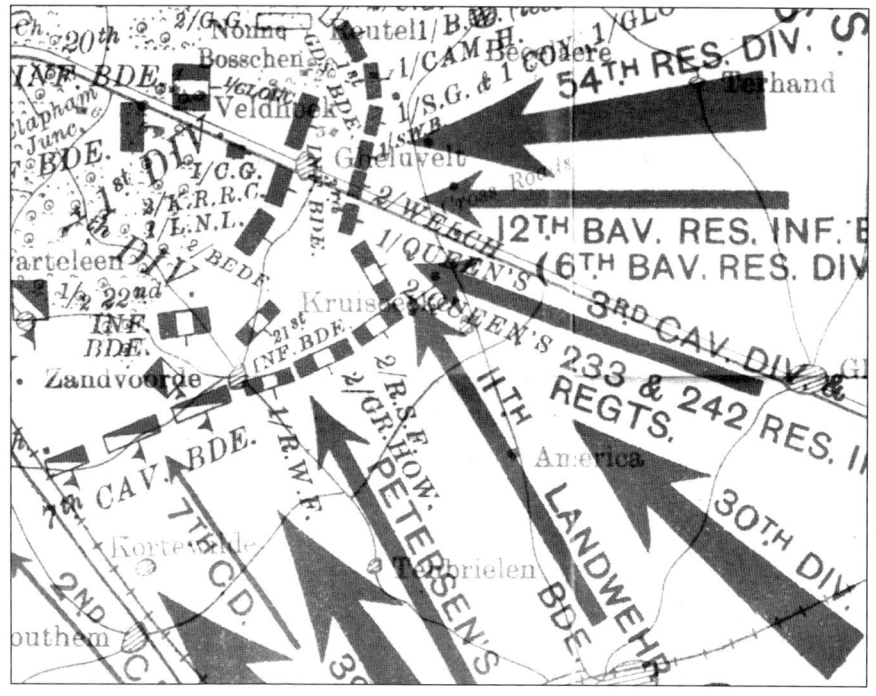

Extract from the Official History map for the situation in the evening of 29 October.

Chapter Two

30 October 1914

Despite all the difficulties and high losses suffered by the German army on 29 October, the decision was taken that the reinforced 54th Reserve Division was to renew the attack the following day. The order when it arrived at unit level stated,

> *Today the Division, including attached troops, namely Bavarian Reserve Infantry Regiment 16, Reserve Infantry Regiment 242, 2nd Battalion Reserve Field Artillery Regiment 53 and Landwehr Detachment Waxmann, is to attack the enemy opposite it and is to carry the attack on to Gheluvelt once the assault has been prepared by the artillery.*
>
> *Group Mühry, linking up on the right with 53rd Reserve Division and on the left with Group Bendler, is to advance on the sector southern edge Polygon Wood – Polderhoek – Poezelhoek.*
>
> *Group von Bendler, continuing the line, is to advance on the chapel just to the south of Gheluvelt and Group Waxmann is to conform to this from the positions taken up tonight, maintaining close contact with Group von Bendler.*
>
> *For the purpose of preparing the attack, the artillery is to open fire as soon as observation is possible.*
>
> *The Divisional staff and reserve will remain initially in Terhand.*

For his part, Haig's orders for the night of the 29th were for entrenching in favourable positions, reorganising and engaging in active reconnaissance. The events of the following day were broadly similar in nature to those of the 29th – a German penetration of a small part of the line before Gheluvelt and then the consequent scramble to 'putty up' with what forces were available. The German intentions were to break through south east of Ypres and take the Kemmel Heights, cutting off allied forces in the north. An order of the day for 29 October, recovered from a dead German officer of XV Corps on the 30th, included the following ringing call to action:

The break-through will be of decisive importance, settle for ever with the centuries-long struggle, end the war, and strike the decisive blow against our most detested enemy. We will finish with the British, Indians, Canadians [sic.], Moroccans, and other trash; feeble adversaries, who surrender in great numbers if they are attacked with vigour.

Much of the fighting on this day, which included most of the ground defended by the Cavalry Corps, is covered in *Messines* in this trilogy of books on First Ypres. To the Cavalry Corps' left lay the battered 7th Division – reduced to less than half its establishment strength and which had received only 400 men in drafts since it had landed on the continent. A whole variety of reasons made a German attack early on 30 October impractical, so instead 3rd Battalion Bavarian Reserve Infantry Regiment 16 and Infantry Regiment 105 were directed to begin a fresh advance along the Ypres – Menin road at 3.00 pm. Initial progress of a few hundred metres provoked decisive counter action by the British defenders, who cut down swathes of men from the already reduced ranks, not only of Bavarian Reserve Infantry Regiment 16 but also amongst the units which spearheaded the advance on the windmill east of Gheluvelt and which were subject to rapid small arms fire once they hove into view of the defence. Some field guns of Reserve Field Artillery Regiment 54 were rushed forward to provide direct fire support over open sights and 1st Battalion Bavarian Reserve Infantry Regiment 16 was also deployed – but all to no avail. The entire attack was called off at 5.00 pm and the participants were ordered to withdraw to their start lines. All the sacrifice had been for absolutely nothing and there was worse to come the following day.

From the British perspective and starting from the north of the BEF line, the 2nd Division's front emerged unscathed as a result of the day's fighting. It had the advantage of a line that had not been shaken much by enemy action and was thus able to make good its defences, even so far as being able to place some reasonable barbed wired defences. In addition, it is almost certain that these attacks were designed to fix the British defenders in place. If this was the intention, it succeeded but, on the other hand, the line was already held with dangerously small manpower, which could not prudently be diminished whatever the circumstances elsewhere. Thus, after a bombardment which commenced at about 6.00 am on the 30th, an attack against the junction of the allied line before Zonnebeke was launched in the pre-dawn light, only moderately assisted by a slight mist. 6 Brigade and its French neighbours saw off the attacks, which continued until about 9.00 am, with a further,

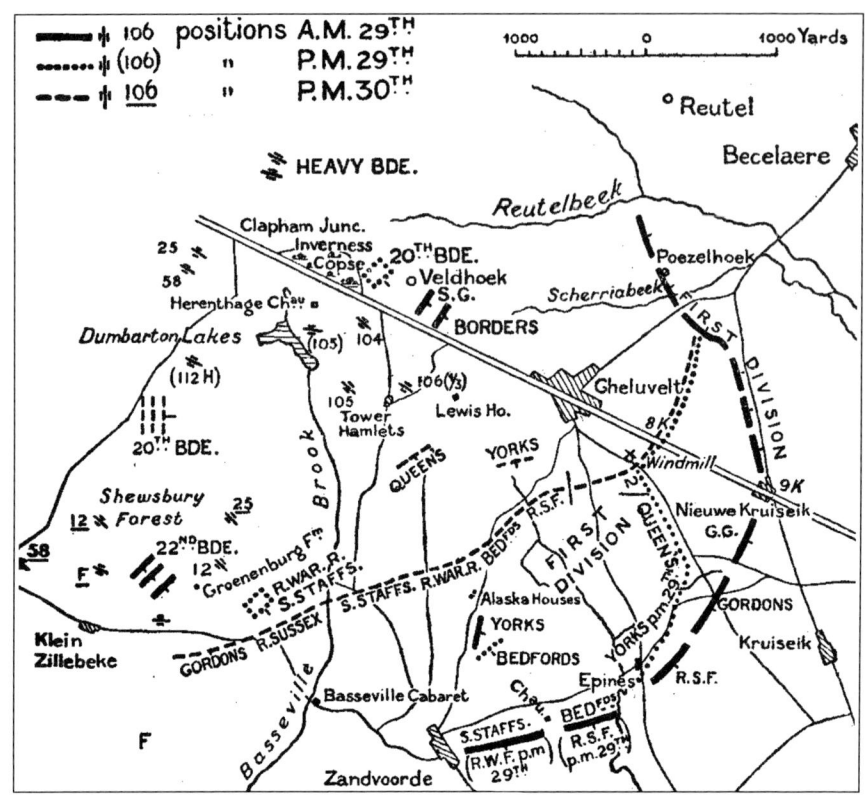

A map from the 7th Division's history indicating operations for 29-30 October. The key relates to the changing locations of gun batteries.

more feeble effort, launched at about 11.20 am and one against 5 Brigade some forty minutes later.

The 7th Division's story in this area, as explained above, is in the main covered in *Messines*. This account deals only with the severe fighting around Zandvoorde, which entailed the loss of that village, sucked in the three battalions of 22 Brigade's reserve and the two battalions of 2 Brigade in reserve, the latter being accompanied by Major General Bulfin. 1/Royal Welsh Fusiliers (RWF), holding positions to the north of Zandvoorde, were overrun and by evening roll call was reduced to eighty-six men out of the 420 odd who had started the day. All attempts during the day to recover the Zandvoorde position failed; the reinforcements were able to establish a new line, which became known as the Klein Zillebeke line, about a kilometre west of Zandvoorde; whilst the Germans made no attempt to take advantage of their gains to envelope the British line to the north.

To the left of 1/RWF lay 2/Royal Scots Fusiliers (2/RSF) and, beyond them, 2/Green Howards (2/Yorks), with two battalions of the Queen's extending the line almost to the Menin Road. 2/Bedfords provided the only support; whilst the whole was a mixture of units from 21, 20 and 3 Brigades.

In the light of the developing situation to the south, the position of 2/RSF and 2/Yorks was now dangerous, especially that of the latter, which was the unit furthest east of Gheluvelt. At 12.45 pm these two battalions were instructed to withdraw in conformity with the new line – a distance of a thousand metres on the right – and to link up with 3 Brigade's position before Gheluvelt. 2/RSF in part managed to follow these orders, although there was considerable confusion, not least because the orders did not reach all parts of the battalion. Some, including the CO, Major Burgoyne, walked into German troops, unaware of their presence, and were taken prisoner. It was a pale reflection of a battalion that took up its new position that evening.

The orders to withdraw did not get through to 2/Yorks until 3.30 pm. However, they had been able to hold their ground and to inflict significant losses on the Germans; so much so, that the battalion was able to withdraw almost intact, losing only eleven men in the course of the manoeuvre.

2/Yorks, about 300 strong, had been under moderate shellfire all morning; the main danger came from snipers, whose victims included the CO, Lieutenant Colonel King.

At 3.30 pm we got a message from the Brigade telling us to retire. The message had been delayed three hours as the orderly had been cut off and had had to work his way through a wood which was full of snipers. When Moss-Blundell (the new CO) got this message he had to make up his mind what to do; it was one of two things – hang on till dark, or go at once and risk a larger loss of life. His mind was made up by hearing heavy firing on his left, and he took the Battalion back by companies, working from the left and starting with D Company. Owing to some very bad shooting by the enemy, and our men keeping their heads, we were able to get back with only eleven casualties; this did not include our losses in the trenches before we retired. We got back to our new position in the dark and were ordered to dig bomb proof shelters behind the second line of trenches.

At about 11 am Haig warned Dubois' IX Corps of the serious situation around Klein Zillebeke and Hollebeke and that he might need assistance.

Dubois, in response, sent a brigade of cavalry towards Hooge. Haig sent another message, at about 3 pm, indicating the seriousness of a German breakthrough south of Ypres; Dubois responded by halting all his operations and despatching first three battalions from his reserve and, at night, two more, with a group of field artillery, to Zillebeke. These all reached the village by 6 pm (though none were involved in the fighting on the 30th) and were put under the command of General Moussy.

General Pierre Dubois, Commanding the French IX Corps.

Whatever other outcome there might have been to the day's fighting on 30 October, there was no more talk of offensive action by the BEF. The three divisions which had responsibility for the Menin Road position were spread out as follows: the 7th Division's 22 Brigade (now just three battalions, 1/RWF reorganising) and 21 Brigade (three battalions, 2/Wilts reorganising) were spread between Zandvoorde to just over a kilometre south of Gheluvelt, with two battalions of 20 Brigade in reserve, 2/Gordons with General Bulfin and 1/Grenadiers reorganising. 'Reorganising' in this context means that the battalions had ceased to be functioning units. To their left were 3 Brigade, covering Gheluvelt, with a battalion in reserve; 1

General Jean Baptiste Moussy, who was killed by a shell near Grenay on 21 May 1915.

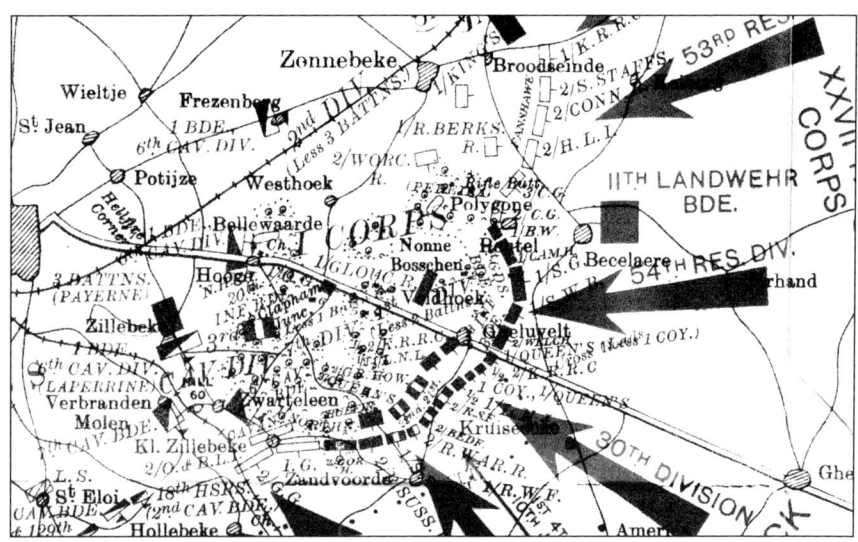

Situation on the evening of 30 October. The intensity of the fighting along the Menin Road is clearly illustrated by the number of units jammed into an ever decreasing area.

(Guards) Brigade, covering from Poezelhoek to Reutel with three battalions, 1/Coldstream reorganising; and the two remaining battalions of 2 Brigade (the others with General Bulfin) were in support of 3 Brigade. Finally, the 2nd Division held the line Reutel to the Zonnebeke-Roulers road – 4 Brigade with two battalions (two with Bulfin), 5 Brigade with three battalions (one battalion with Bulfin) and 6 Brigade complete. Twenty-one battalions were in the front line, eight were in brigade or divisional reserve and the Corps reserve, stationed near Veldhoek, comprised two battalions, a brigade of French cavalry and the Northumberland Hussars. The situation was indeed serious.

There were, nevertheless, a couple of bright spots. The first, generally, it seems to us, rather under-rated by most writers of whatever nation, was the full-hearted cooperation of the French commanders in coming to the assistance of I Corps and the Cavalry Corps. Relations had not always been good between the BEF and the French, but there is no doubt about those between the commanders at Ypres. Without timely French assistance it is virtually certain that the Germans would have broken through the BEF and doubtless caused huge damage to Britain's ability to fight the war on the continent – indeed, if it could do so without first withdrawing into a port enclave or from the mainland altogether. The second was that the inundation north of Dixmude had, by the evening, effectively secured the northern flank; though, of course, at the same time it also secured it for the Germans.

On the German side there seemed to be a lack of appreciation of the dire straits into which the BEF had been thrown by the events of 30 October; this has often been put down to the fear that the British had brought fresh reserves to France, notably some or all of the (theoretical) fourteen Territorial Divisions and their mounted brigades; and that therefore some caution had to be observed. Nevertheless there was some optimism that the decisive moment was at hand; so much so that the All Highest himself was present at Rupprecht's Sixth Army HQ on 31 October.

Emperor William II, the 'All Highest'.

Chapter Three

31 October 1914:
The decisive day for the BEF before Ypres?

 The day and the following night is well known for the attacks on Messines Ridge and the Gheluvelt spur. The defence mounted by the Cavalry Corps is covered in *Messines* in this trilogy.

Called to a 54th Reserve Division orders group in Kruiseecke during the evening of 30 October for a dawn attack on Gheluvelt on 31 October, Hauptmann Rubenbauer, the commanding officer of 1st Battalion Bavarian Reserve Infantry Regiment 16, objected to the entire premise, stating, allegedly,

> *We in the centre no longer have a battalion; scarcely a recognisable company. The men have been in battle now for forty-eight hours and they have had no sleep for three nights. The troops are exhausted. We have no infantry reserves behind the front. I regard it as impossible to conduct a purely infantry assault against the strongly dug in British positions successfully, unless it has been preceded by really heavy artillery preparation.*

This objection was ridden over roughshod by Oberst von Oldershausen, the deputy sector commander, but Oberst List, himself, also joined in, saying,

Oberst Julius List, commander Bavarian RIR 16. Killed in action at Gheluvelt on 16 October and now buried in the Kamaradengrab at Langemark.

> *If I may add a word – I too am of the opinion that a simple infantry attack conducted against such a cunning, intelligent and strongly dug in enemy will either fail or simply lead to a bloody sacrifice of immense proportions. I would urge that heavy artillery be brought to bear during the course of the night and to continue [its work] until the positions are thoroughly softened up for an assault. Only then should we advance with infantry – otherwise what remains of my regiment will be lost as well!*

In the event, he was not very wide of the mark.

The main attack was entrusted to Rubenbauer's 1st Battalion Bavarian Reserve Infantry Regiment 16 and was a thrust towards the grounds of Gheluvelt Chateau. Reserve Infantry Regiment 248 was deployed, whilst out to the left was the 3rd Battalion. Reserve Infantry Regiment 247 and Infantry Regiment 105, in extension of this line, attacked south of the main road. Later in the day elements of Infantry Regiment 143 were also introduced into the firing line. The battalions were ordered to move forward during the hours of darkness with unloaded weapons and bayonets fixed. The artillery was directed 'as far as possible' to support the attack with fire; but this was only expected to last from 5.30 to 5.40 am, so as to ensure that some ammunition would be available to respond to fire missions later in the day.

Hauptmann Rubenbauer, who had expressed his reservations about the attack the previous evening, survived the day and was able to record his impressions of it.

Midnight had come and gone by the time orders for the forthcoming major attack on 31 October reached the forward positions. It was a cold, rainy night, lit only by the flames of the burning Becelaere and the countless great stacks of straw which dotted the landscape and which had been set alight by the fire of the enemy. Rifle fire cracked overhead constantly, but we did not reply, concentrating instead on silently preparing for the start of the operation under cover of darkness. At 5.30 am precisely, just as ordered, there was the crash of a surprise concentration of fire to the front of 1st Battalion where the British were occupying positions on the southeast edge of the village. As dawn gradually broke there was activity all along our lines. Surging forward from the dense hedgerows and up the slope, the lines of infantrymen, mostly from our 3rd Battalion, worked their way in bounds, wave after wave, up the rising ground.

British shrapnel fire fell on them like iron rain. A densely held British trench was overrun and about two hundred prisoners were taken. Hardly had they been assembled on the Ypres road, ready to be moved back, than enemy shells came down amongst the column of prisoners. Shouting fearfully, they scattered. Dozens of them lay where they had fallen on the road, the remainder rushed wildly down the hill where they were reassembled by our reserves. The attack continued, but more slowly, making forward progress step by step. On the southern slope below the village around the windmill, the British had dug themselves in strongly.

The defenders' fire beat off every attempt to close up to it. Salvoes of artillery fire thundered from the direction of the village and machine guns hammered away… Each assault was pushed back disdainfully and the battlefield became littered with dead and wounded soldiers as the intense fighting went on hour after hour.

Finally, at 2.12 pm, our heavy artillery, which had been moved forward during the previous hour, brought fire down on the windmill. One round, followed by a second, then a third sent it spinning into the air. How it cracked and splintered! That was the turning point. The garrison fled and the way was open. In no time flat our lines rushed it, tumbling forward one after the other. Everyone charged forward against Gheluvelt. For a moment there was a pause in the enemy fire, rather as if they were taking a deep breath, then down it came again, with renewed strength, like a violent storm. It was clear that the enemy could tell what was at stake! Suddenly the leading troops wavered then fell back into the hurricane of fire which was being directed at them. It was a truly critical moment. The trumpeters from the left to the right flank blew the call for the charge and, their blood up, everyone responded, Emerging from behind hedges and out of cover, the assault was carried forward: line after line pressed on, closing gaps – Bavarians, Saxons and Württembergers. A thousand shouts of Hurra! echoed over the battlefield in one great cry of victory, which could be heard above the rattle of machine guns and the thunder of the guns.

Rolling forward violently in waves like giant breakers crashing ashore the storm formations forced their way into the village. Gheluvelt was ours! After a short period of fighting from house to house, the enemy pulled back, abandoning their positions. The firing died away, evening fell with early mist gradually clearing to a clear starry night enfolding the bloody Flanders battlefield. Listening posts were sent forward whilst the remainder, nerves trembling and totally worn out dug in.

Suddenly a runner came rushing up and tumbled breathlessly into the trench, throwing himself exhausted at our feet. 'The regimental commander has been killed!' 'What are you saying – the Oberst?' 'Dead – over there by the hedge in the grounds of the chateau – during tonight's assault – right in the front line!' Good Heavens! We had not even been spared that! We looked at each other and there were tears in every eye. A need for revenge grew silently and bloodily in our hearts. He lay there in the grounds of the chateau, his white face set and determined; in amongst his

A German casualty clearing post east of Ypres, photographed in October 1914.

faithful soldiers. Covered in a blood-soaked coat, he was laid to rest there for all eternity at the foot of a severed tree stump, upon which hung his field cap. God grant him peace!

It was not only List who fell on that day of dreadful casualties. 3rd Battalion Bavarian Reserve Infantry Regiment 16 was hit particularly hard, whilst Reserve Infantry Regiment 247 lost almost every one of its officers, with virtually all the platoon commanders dead, wounded or missing. All in all it was day when the British defence came close to breaking, but it came at a completely unsustainable rate of loss for the German army. The assault began promptly at 5.30 am precisely and because in the centre the German units were able to move forward very close to the British defensive lines near the chateau, troops from Bavarian Reserve Infantry Regiment 16 were able easily and very quickly to overcome the defences in that sector. Down to the south, however, the situation was quite different. The attack of Reserve Infantry Regiment 247 and 3rd Battalion Bavarian Reserve Infantry Regiment 16 soon stalled in front of the windmill, which meant that there was no alternative but to order the sub-units to halt where they were and maintain their newly gained positions.

Additional German reinforcements were launched forward and for several hours men of three regiments fought their way forward slowly and painfully as great gaps were hacked in the ranks by the British artillery and infantry. There was little supporting fire but despite what was described as an 'extraordinary hurricane' of small arms fire, inexorable progress was made and, by 2.00 pm, the area around the windmill to the south of Gheluvelt was in German hands. Within the village itself, from about 11.30 am, when the survivors of the King's Royal Rifle Corps (less those captured), the Queen's and the Loyal North Lancashires had been pushed out of the village, some 60 pounder guns had been captured and an attempted British counter-attack had been beaten off, the Germans had a precarious hold on Gheluvelt, but it was not until rather later when the numbers built up that this improved. It was at about this time that the famous counter attack by about 350 men of 2nd Battalion Worcestershire Regiment, commanded by Major EB Hankey, stepped off across the open ground between the village and Polygon Wood. The British Official Historian later claimed that this put an end to all German attempts to secure Gheluvelt, but this is completely incompatible with what actually happened.

The one part of I Corps' line that was not attacked in any significant way on 31 October was at the northern end, held by the 2nd Division. The day was remarkable for two things, however. At about 11.30 am 2/Connaught Rangers (2/Connaughts) complained that they were being shelled by 'a sort of howitzer' from trenches three hundred yards away. It was the first time a minenwerfer had been seen against the British (though they had been used against them before); it was then knocked out by the first shell of a gun manhandled up near the line for the first time for such a purpose; which in turn was the first time an HE (high explosive) shell, as opposed to shrapnel, had been fired by an 18 pdr field gun at Ypres. Apart from that, and warning orders to thin out the line as the situation developed to the south, the division had a remarkably quiet day – with the exception of its commander becoming a casualty. That evening French cavalry took over 1/KRRC's line – the left of the division – and, because of developments to the south described below, the line was brought back from the south eastern edge of Polygon Wood to its south western edge.

For the British, Gheluvelt was important because of its value for observation to the east. Becelaere to the north and Zandvoorde to the south had already been lost, leaving Gheluvelt alone for this function. From the German perspective it happened to be a defended part of the enemy line on the best road at the head of a gentle rise to the highest point of the Ridge in the area near Clapham Junction. Landon's 3 Brigade had the responsibility for its defence, assisted by two battalions of 2 Brigade. The British line was on the eastern outskirts of the village,

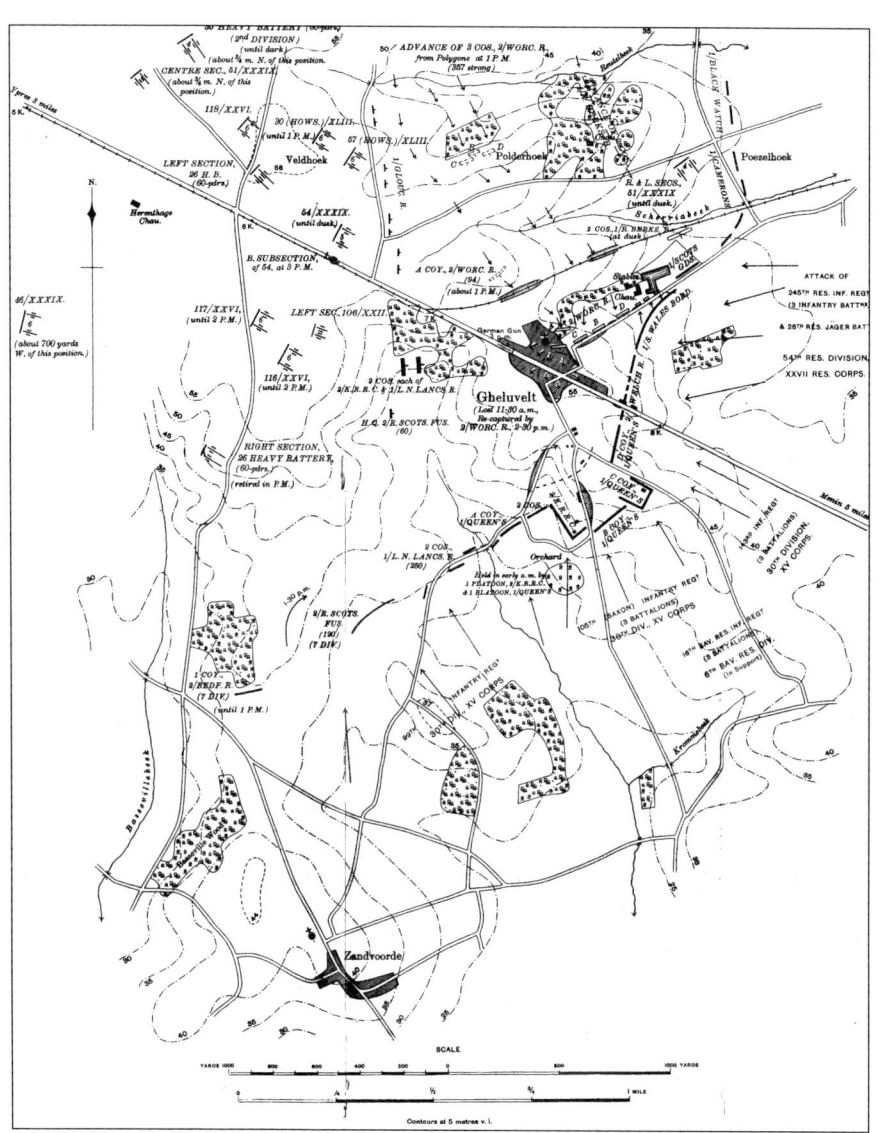

Extract from the Official History map, The Defence of Gheluvelt, 31 October.

about four hundred yards from the village church. This was held by 2/Welsh, with 1/Queen's on the right assisted, in a small salient in an orchard, by two companies of 2/KRRC. Then came men of 1/Loyal North Lancashire (1/Loyals) and 2/RSF. To the left of 1/Welsh were 1/South Wales Borderers (1/SWB), up to the east of the chateau, followed in order by 1/Scots Guards, 1/Camerons and 1/Black Watch.

Gheluvelt Church before its destruction.

The shell damaged remnants of Gheluvelt Church.

1/Glosters were in front of Veldhoek. Many of these battalions were very weak – for example 1/RSF had a total fighting strength of only about 180 men.

The German attack commenced at 6 am – about the same time as that on Messines and an hour or so after heavy shelling on Wytschaete started. The initial attack was beaten off, except for a part of the orchard. This loss was important, as it exposed the Queen's to enfilade fire and, because there were only restricted fields of fire, attempts to recapture it failed. Making full use of cover, by 9.30 am 2/Welsh were being blown out of their trenches and the CO decided to withdraw the left half of his battalion to the support line, leaving the rest to cover 1/SWB's flank. Of this the Queen's were unaware, because they could not see what was happening north of the road. The support line of the Welsh was in reality merely a sunken road and provided little protection against German shells, so Colonel Morland withdrew his men, about a hundred in total, out of the village and then placed them in support of the remaining right half of his battalion still in the line. In the confusion some of the men did not follow when the rest of the battalion moved to the right (north) and eventually were absorbed into the Glosters at Veldhoek.

The Queen's were soon in trouble – their CO was mortally wounded – although one company could cheerily report that 'it was quite all right'. There was only minimal artillery support, because it was impossible to communicate with the rear and make contact with the gun lines. All the runners that were sent were brought down. At 10 am the Germans began an advance north and south of the road on Gheluvelt, at the same time also attacking from the south east. The attack was made with gusto, with 'singing and cheering'.

For about an hour the onslaught was held off. South of the road the Germans brought up guns to fire a mixture of shrapnel and high explosive at close range and machine guns in the orchard and the bank of the Menin Road enfiladed the trenches. At 11.15 am the southern part of the bulge in the Queen's/KRRC's line was broken and the KRRC fell back to the other half of their battalion; but the Queen's to the south still held on. Their CO, Major Watson, determined that the cause could best be served by staying put in the hope of reinforcements or a counter attack. When a withdrawal to join the remainder of the battalion became inevitable it was too late, as the Germans had already forced their way into Gheluvelt. When they got to these rear positions the battalion was gone and Watson's force was practically surrounded; ultimately only two officers and twelve other ranks managed to escape.

The troops in Gheluvelt and to its immediate west were largely swept away by artillery fire and then mopped up by the advancing infantry; the survivors of 2/KKRC and 1/Loyals and some men of the Queen's fell back to the road running south of Veldhoek. 2/KRRC lost 408 men, being reduced to a rump of a battalion of 150 by the end of the day. The *BOH* notes:

> *To the everlasting disgrace of the German 143rd Regiment, it must be recorded that not only were many of the wounded and unwounded prisoners of the Queen's stripped of their uniforms and robbed of their possessions, but some were clubbed and bayoneted to death.*

Though it adds, in a footnote, that the Saxon Infantry Regiment 105, which attacked south of the Menin Road, 'behaved well to the prisoners'. By this stage, with men drifting back (and it is very difficult to establish confirmed timings), Haig was informed by a liaison officer with the 1st Division that Gheluvelt had fallen, that its defending artillery batteries had been withdrawn – including one of 60 pdrs – and half a dozen guns lost (though disabled and recaptured later), but that the withdrawal was not a complete disaster and that there was order in the midst of confusion. An attempt by Landon to counter attack was aborted about noon when it became clear that the German heavy artillery fire was dominant and that the Queen's position had already crumbled. This force returned to positions before Veldhoek. The Germans reported in *Ypres 1914*, their earliest semi official account of the battle, written during the war and consequently somewhat suspect, that they had taken the whole of Gheluvelt, including the chateau and its grounds by 2 pm; the BOH challenges this by saying that the chateau area was never taken and only fell when the British withdrew at around 6 pm – the issue is discussed elsewhere in this chapter. In fact the village was probably captured about 11.30 am, the northern part earlier – but it could have been about 1 pm when the whole, minus parts of the chateau area, were actually taken: and how firmly is not clear.

To the south of the Queen's position 1/Loyals held on until about 1.30 pm, when the position was surrounded: forty of the eighty Loyals who remained to be captured were wounded. On the morning of 1 November the battalion was reduced to one officer and thirty five men. 2/RSF suffered a similar fate, with many men captured – including the CO, second in command and adjutant; it was reduced to a total of 151 men. Thus the whole of the defensive position south of the village was overrun somewhere between noon and 1 pm.

Some two hundred yards north of the Menin Road, a company of 2/Welsh, men of 1/SWB and the remnants of 1/Scots Guards held the

Gheluvelt Church and village after the battle.

line to the northeast corner of the walls of the chateau grounds. About 10 am a full scale infantry assault commenced, about the same time as that on the Queen's. This soon threatened to degenerate into hand to hand fighting. The main contrast with what was going on south of the road was that telephone communications remained open, more often than not, from the chateau stables to Brigade HQ up near Glencorse Wood.

By 11.45 am the remnants of 2/Welsh had succumbed – at 10 am there were only forty five alive of the original 130, with only sixteen rifles firing; thirty seven men were captured. Shortly before 1 pm the two right companies of the 1/SWB gave way and fell back to the northwest side of the chateau grounds, the rest of the battalion mixing in with 1/Scots Guards. This line – and that to the north of it – continued to hold. The CO of 1/SWB, Lieutenant Colonel Leach, decided on an immediate counter attack and launched a charge with his two right companies (the ones that had withdrawn), some Scots Guards and his battalion headquarters. This succeeded in retaking the chateau grounds to its south eastern corner and Leach then brought his line back to the enclosing walls, making no attempt to restore his old position.

Leach then sought reinforcements from 3 Brigade, which then ordered 1/SWB and the Scots Guards (1 (Guards) Brigade) to fall back to Polderhoek Wood; but the remainder of 1 (Guards) Brigade was ordered by telephone to stand fast and so Leach ignored his own brigade commander's orders. FitzClarence sent up what reinforcements he could – elements of 1/Black Watch and a company of 2/Worcesters (5

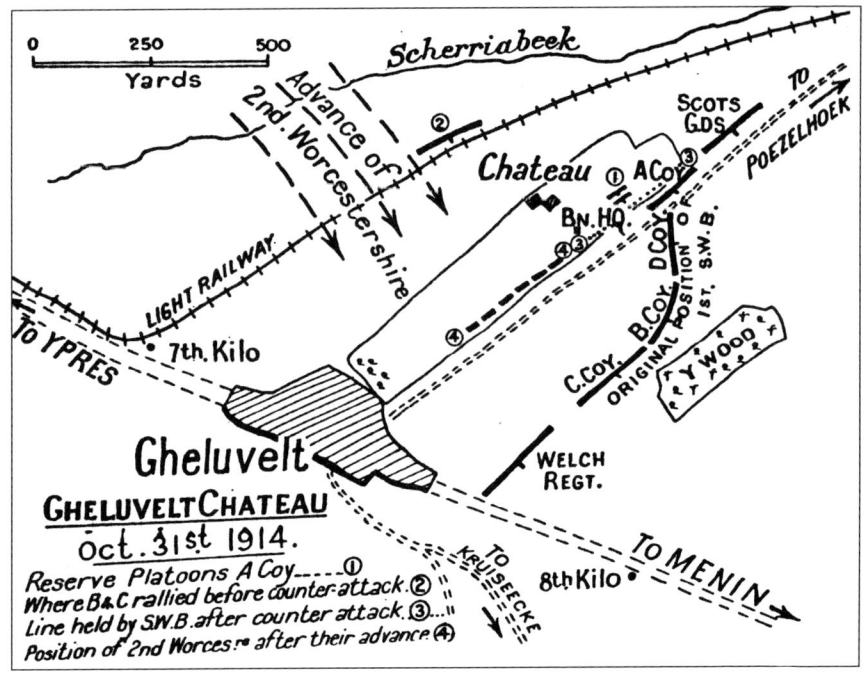

The South Wales Borderers at Gheluvelt, 31 October.

Brigade), currently under his command, and these were positioned on the right flank. FitzClarence then appeared in person and quickly saw that the whole line threatened to be split asunder if the Germans were able to build on their success of taking Gheluvelt. Galloping back to his HQ near Glencorse Wood, he briefed Lomax, who was posted near Clapham Junction. (It is important to note here that the fact that telephone communications, from the firing line to 1 (Guards) Brigade and from brigade to division, remained open during this crisis was essential to the success of what subsequently happened.) FitzClarence was instructed to use 2nd Division's reserve – 1/King's, the bulk of 2/Worcesters and half of 1/Berks, which had been pre-positioned for just such an eventuality at the south west of Polygon Wood. Lomax cantered off to Hooge Chateau, where Monro was established, arriving at about 12.45, and informed him 'laconically', 'My line is broken'.

It was not only his line that was broken; soon after, so was the roof over his head. On the evening of the 30th the HQs of both the the 1st and 2nd Divisions were at Hooge. The 2nd Division's HQ was on the verge of moving to Westhoek (which often appears as Eksternest in many accounts of the battle), about a kilometre to the north and closer to the bulk of the 2nd Division's troops. The two staffs were assembled in an

Hooge Chateau. The photographer is standing close to the Menin Road. (Baron de Vinck)

annexe on the western side of the chateau, which was built in 1896 by Baron Gaston de Vinck. It was designed as a mini artists' colony – he was a patron of the arts, particularly painting and music. It comprised a coach house, a studio and conservatory and a small room with a glazed veranda. Monro was using the last as an office and there he and Lomax, along with their chief operations staff officers, met on his arrival. They discussed the situation and agreed that a retirement would be disastrous in the circumstances, with so many units heavily engaged in direct contact with the enemy and given the ferocity of the German shelling. At about 1.15 pm several shells landed in the immediate area of the annexe,

Hooge Chateau's Annexe. Baron Gaston de Vinck is standing on the lawn, bottom centre. (Baron de Vinck)

including one which hit the studio and one which impacted just outside Monro's office, where those mentioned above were still gathered. Lomax was severely wounded, never recovered and died in April 1915 in a nursing home in the UK. Colonel Kerr and Major Paley of the 1st Division general staff and Lieutenant Percival and Captain Ommanney of the 2nd Division's general staff and two others were killed, whilst Lomax's ADC, Captain Giffard, was mortally wounded by another shell. Monro, standing at the doorway, got away with being badly stunned and was able to stay in command; Major General Bulfin was named as Lomax's replacement, but because he had his hands

Lieutenant General Samuel Lomax died of his wounds in April 1915.

full at Hollebeke, Major General Landon acted for him – once they could locate him. [In case of confusion over these major generals commanding brigades, on 26 October a number of senior officers had been promoted – including Lomax to lieutenant general and Bulfin and Landon to major general.] Lovett of the Glosters became 3 Brigade's commander.

I Corps HQ was situated at the White Chateau (one of many 'white chateaux' in France and Belgium), on the Ypres side of Hell Fire Corner – or Halte, as it was still known – and had been getting bad, if contradictory, news, throughout the morning. Haig decided to go out himself to see something of the situation – a ride that has probably produced more learned discussion than any other in the war. Some argue that this was micro-managing and a Corps commander should be where he can most influence events; on the other hand, a calm appearance on the Menin Road could do no harm, could do some good in helping to soothe nerves and also enabled him to get a feel for the mood of the men. The latter argument is reinforced by the reality that at this stage it was the lower level commanders who were the only ones really capable of dealing with the rapidly unfolding situation on the ground, especially when consideration is taken of the generally poor quality of communications.

Haig returned and issued orders at 1.30 pm for a new line, Klein Zillebeke – Frezenberg via Westhoek to be prepared to be be held at all costs. Meanwhile, he was still pretty much in the dark as to what exactly was going on and so sent Brigadier General Rice, his chief engineer, to attempt to contact a commander at the front who could clarify things.

FitzClarence, meanwhile, briefed the adjutant of 2/Worcesters. After some time spent looking at the map and ground, preliminary instructions were issued.

Scouts were sent out to cut any wire that might delay progress – most of them killed by artillery fire before that work could be accomplished – packs were discarded, extra ammunition issued, and every preparation made for a rapid advance.

The initial intention to use 1/King's as well in the attack was countermanded by Monro; instead they were despatched to fill a very weakly held part of the line between the 2nd Division and 1 (Guards) Brigade. At 1 pm FitzClarence gave 2/Worcesters the order, 'to advance with the utmost vigour against the enemy who are in possession of Gheluvelt and to re-establish our line there'. The attack was to be conducted by three companies (one had been earlier detached to 1 (Guards) Brigade), with a total strength of seven officers and 350 other ranks, supported by XLI Brigade RFA, whose CO had a grandstand view over the advance.

Major General (then Brigadier General) SR Rice, who went on to become the Engineer in Chief at GHQ and was instrumental in forming Tunnelling Companies as a distinctive branch of the Royal Engineers.

The woods provided cover from view for the first 600 yards, and so the men were able to move in columns of four, which were easier to control. West of Polderhoek Chateau, with some cover provided by trees, the CO, Major Hankey, deployed the men into two lines, fifty yards apart. There were two companies in the first wave with a small group under an officer to guard the vulnerable right flank. They had to cross a thousand yards of open ground that offered no cover at all. All that could be seen were burning buildings in Gheluvelt and scattered individuals making their way back from the line. The first couple of hundred yards were covered in a rush, all the time under considerable artillery fire, which opened up as soon as they came into sight. In all, one hundred men fell during the advance. When they hit the Chateau grounds it was to find the Germans disorganised, taking advantage of their victory in search of water and loot and certainly not

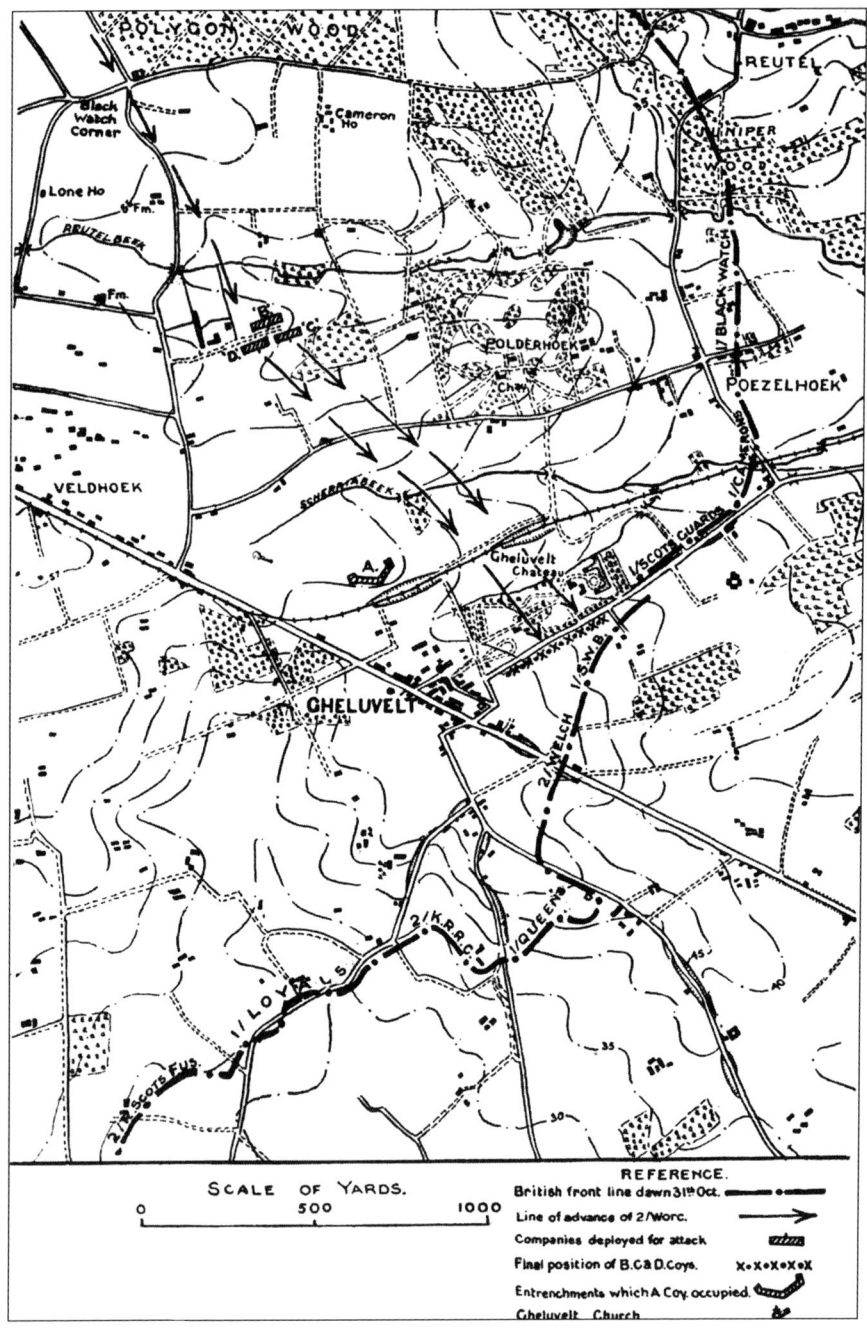

REFERENCE.

British front line dawn 31st Oct.	━━━◆━━━
Line of advance of 2/Worc.	➛
Companies deployed for attack	▨▨▨
Final position of B.C & D.Coys.	X•X•X•X•X
Entrenchments which A Coy. occupied.	〰〰
Gheluvelt Church	♁

SCALE OF YARDS.

0   500   1000

The counter-attack of the Worcesters at Gheluvelt, 31 October.

92

anticipating a counter attack. The Worcesters found the SWB and Scots Guards in the south west of the chateau grounds, still fighting but almost surrounded. The three companies then spread out along the sunken road leading into the village and patrols set about clearing that part nearest to the British line. The Worcesters' fourth company was brought forward at 3.45 pm and extended the line to the village church and churchyard, there forming a defensive flank. Patrols went further into Gheluvelt and down the Menin Road, to its outskirts at the south eastern end. Having started the day with eleven officers and 450 other ranks, the battalion lost three officers and 189 men on 31 October. Thus, although the Germans seem to have had control of the whole village before the attack, it was – so it appears – not robustly held.

The Worcesters' attack was, of course, critical; it prevented the Germans from breaking the British line, although it can be argued that the time delay imposed by the defenders around the windmill was of equal importance. However, it is impossible to sustain the view that it ended all efforts to take and hold Gheluvelt. There are numerous German accounts concerning the events of that day, only one of which even alludes to the Worcesters. It is to be found in the regimental history of Reserve Infantry Regiment 247 from Württemberg.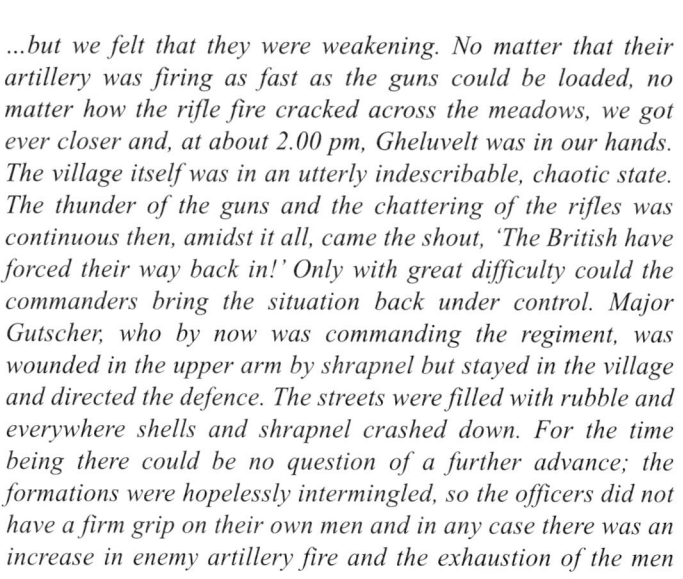

> *...but we felt that they were weakening. No matter that their artillery was firing as fast as the guns could be loaded, no matter how the rifle fire cracked across the meadows, we got ever closer and, at about 2.00 pm, Gheluvelt was in our hands. The village itself was in an utterly indescribable, chaotic state. The thunder of the guns and the chattering of the rifles was continuous then, amidst it all, came the shout, 'The British have forced their way back in!' Only with great difficulty could the commanders bring the situation back under control. Major Gutscher, who by now was commanding the regiment, was wounded in the upper arm by shrapnel but stayed in the village and directed the defence. The streets were filled with rubble and everywhere shells and shrapnel crashed down. For the time being there could be no question of a further advance; the formations were hopelessly intermingled, so the officers did not have a firm grip on their own men and in any case there was an increase in enemy artillery fire and the exhaustion of the men was too great.*

In fact, according to all other regiments present, although there were major problems to be resolved, by nightfall, the entire village was firmly in

German hands. Nearly 1,000 prisoners, three guns and a machine gun had been captured and the British were gone, either of their own volition or because of German pressure. The possession of Gheluvelt, however, meant nothing. It represented not the summit of German ambitions but a necessary stop along the way to Ypres and beyond. Furthermore the price paid had been very high. Apart from its commander, Oberst Julius List, Bavarian Reserve Infantry Regiment 16 had suffered many hundreds of other casualties and the situation was much the same for Reserve Infantry Regiment 247.

Meanwhile, the two companies of 1/Berks in reserve were brought over from Polygon Wood and reinforced the line on the left of 1/Scots Guards then, at 1.50 pm, the news arrived at I Corps HQ of the result of the shelling of Hooge Chateau. New orders were prepared, sent out at 2.40 pm, that another, last ditch, position, a mile behind the one described above, should be marked out: Verbrandenmolen-Zillebeke-Hellfire Corner (Halte)-Potijze, connecting up with the French on either flank. French himself arrived at 2 pm, on foot, his car a short distance away, to find Haig and his GSO 1 and chief staff officer (Johnnie Gough VC) at a table on which lay the shattered remnants of a chandelier, the victim of shell blast. He was given the depressing news and set off in search of General Foch, commanding French troops in the north. Haig then prepared to set off to head back up the Menin Road to the 1st Division's HQ when Rice returned, hot and bothered by his exertions, with the news that Gheluvelt was retaken and that the immediate crisis was over;

Brigadier General 'Johnnie' Gough VC. He died of an abdominal wound received at Fauquissart and died in Estaires two days later, on 22 February 1915.

which news was hurriedly passed on to French before he set off towards Poperinghe.

Although there might well have been a reprieve from a very serious situation at Gheluvelt, the Germans immediately south of the Menin Road had not been inactive. A large detachment moved forward and came into contact with the mixed force of Glosters, Queen's, KRRC and Loyals before Veldhoek, with part of 6 Cavalry Brigade (Royals and 10th Hussars), a reserve which had come forward dismounted from Hooge, on its right. The force available was sufficient to drive the Germans off and a counter attack sent them back towards Gheluvelt, probably at about the same time as the Worcesters were making their charge. In *Ypres 1914*, it states that, 'further advance beyond Gheluvelt was prevented by heavy fire from a new and strong position along the edge of the woods west of Gheluvelt. Here a new fortress had been made, which would have to be broken down by our artillery before it could be attacked.' As is evident, there was no such 'strong position', let alone 'a new fortress'.

At 4 pm Haig came forward to confer with Landon and FitzClarence at the cross roads east of Hooge, later to be known as Clapham Junction; with the situation to the south still very much in the balance and ground almost certainly to be given up there, it was decided to withdraw from Gheluvelt that evening and to take up positions on the reverse slope to the west of it. French troops, in the shape of a cavalry brigade that arrived at about 5 pm at Hooge, were used to assist in clearing the woods west of Gheluvelt. 1 (Guards) Brigade and its attached battalions took up a position north of the Menin Road and to the right of the Glosters group, which was under Lovett's command. Beyond on the right, FitzClarence's 1 (Guards) Brigade's left flank met the 2nd Division's adjusted right flank at the south western edge of Polygon Wood, later to be known as Black Watch Corner.

The very serious situation facing the 7th Division around and to the north east of Klein Zillebeke, was finally resolved – at least for the

Looking down the Menin Road towards Ypres and the Halte, a location that later became known as Hell Fire Corner. October 1914.

moment – by a desperate counter attack, which included men of the Royal Engineers acting as infantry, at about 4 pm. Much of the ground lost during the day was recaptured, and a new line, running through Herenthage Wood and adjusted to take account of developments to the north, was established during the night.

The French were still hopeful of making new attacks the following day – ever the method of Foch. In this case, they were to be on either flank of I Corps, which would help ease the pressure upon it; Haig issued orders that the units and formations of his Corps were to hold their positions but to be prepared to join in any French advance. At least now he had some sort of reserve, because the 3rd Cavalry Division was withdrawn from the line. To the south, more and more French troops were arriving along Messines Ridge and to the north, near Klein Zillebeke – the situation there being just as critical as the events along the Menin Road. After days of continuous fighting, the 7th Division's brigades were reduced to shadows of their embarkation selves – 20 Brigade had a total of 940 men (this means everyone in the Brigade, including transport, signallers etc.); the 21st a total of 750 and the 22nd (though no precise figure is available) had barely 800. In short, and given that it was not fully up to strength when it left for the continent, the Division's manpower total was about 80% below what it should have been.

General Foch, who from mid October commanded French forces in the north.

Chapter Four

1–10 November 1914

1st to 5th November

As the German army tried to reorganise after the long drawn out battle for Gheluvelt, it had to deal not only with the psychological trauma of all the losses and the need to provide succour for the wounded, but also with the general utter exhaustion of seventy-two hours of continuous action. It took a major effort of leadership from the surviving officers and NCOs to restore order, arrange for the defence of the latest gains and try to resupply the survivors. For once, some rations were got forward, thanks to the company feldwebels located back with the quartermasters, who mustered every spare man to carry basic rations and drinks forward. Despite all the losses, there was little enough to issue, but the arrival of these teams in the middle of the night boosted morale at a critical moment. Meanwhile, steps were being taken to restore a clear chain of command and to attempt to maintain the momentum of the advance. Oberst von Hügel, commander of Reserve Infantry Regiment 248, sent this written order to Bavarian Reserve Infantry Regiment 16 during the early hours of 1 November:

> *I am assuming command of all the detachments located to the right of the main road running through Gheluvelt. The attack will be continued today. Bavarian* [Reserve Infantry] *Regiment 16, with its left flank anchored on the road and maintaining contact with Reserve Infantry Regiment 248 on its right, is to advance via Gheluvelt Chateau towards the Gheluvelt – Poezelhoek railway line. The intervening wooded areas are to be cleared of the enemy. Reports are to be sent to Gheluvelt Chateau. Today, after a battle of several days, a decision is to be sought.*

With a supreme effort, all that was left of Bavarian Reserve Infantry Regiment 16 advanced west at dawn with 3rd Battalion, commanded by Hauptmann Butterfaß on the left and 1st Battalion under Leutnant Schmidt on the right. Shortly afterwards the Bavarians were moving forward past the chateau, where they discovered a well dug system of trenches. Crate after crate of small arms ammunition were found, together with maps, rangefinders, waterproof coats and telephones, as well as large quantities of rations and comforts for the troops. A considerable quantity of corned beef was recovered, as were with crates of biscuits, tobacco, cigarettes and spirits, all of which were immediately distributed. This was good for morale, not only because of their value, but because it showed that the British army had originally intended to fight far harder to retain Gheluvelt.

This final minor action was the temporary end of operations for Bavarian Reserve Infantry Regiment 16. Fought out, it was to be withdrawn to Wervicq, its battle over for the time being. It was directed to advance no further and to prepare to be withdrawn that evening. Buoyed up by the thought that Gheluvelt now lay to the rear and was securely in German hands, the 1st and 3rd Battalions, together with 2nd Battalion, which had been operating independently for the past few days, duly withdrew into rest at Wervicq that night. Reserve Infantry Regiment 245, deployed to the north, took part in a minor attack designed to straighten the line. This forced the British to withdraw from Polderhoek Chateau to the edge of Polygon Wood. It was the final significant action for several days in this area; the following week was devoted by both sides to digging in and improving their positions.

There was in fact a resumption of the attack on 2 November, but there was very little progress. However, the lines were advanced near Polderhoek Chateau and a link up was established between Group Mühry and Infantry Regiment 99 of 30th Infantry Division, on the right flank of XV Corps near Veldhoek. The British account provided in the Official History claims that even this limited success was due to the fortunate fact that the British guns had been directed to cease firing at midday (German time). This allegedly enabled Infantry Regiments 99 and 143 to advance along the line of the road in groups of thirty to forty men, overpower what was left of the Coldstream Guards and then attack the King's Royal Rifle Corps and capture more than four hundred men. Generalleutnant von Altrock, Commander 60 Infantry Brigade, later described the day's actions.

During the afternoon of 2 November, Infantry Regiment 99 captured British trenches in front of Veldhoek, taking 400 prisoners, including ten officers of the 'Rifles, Buffs, Coldstreams and Guards Regiments' [sic.]. A French attack threatened from the right, but General von Altrock directed artillery fire against it. Reinforcement was requested from Headquarters XV Corps. Infantry Regiment 143, Reserve Hussar Regiment 8 and two

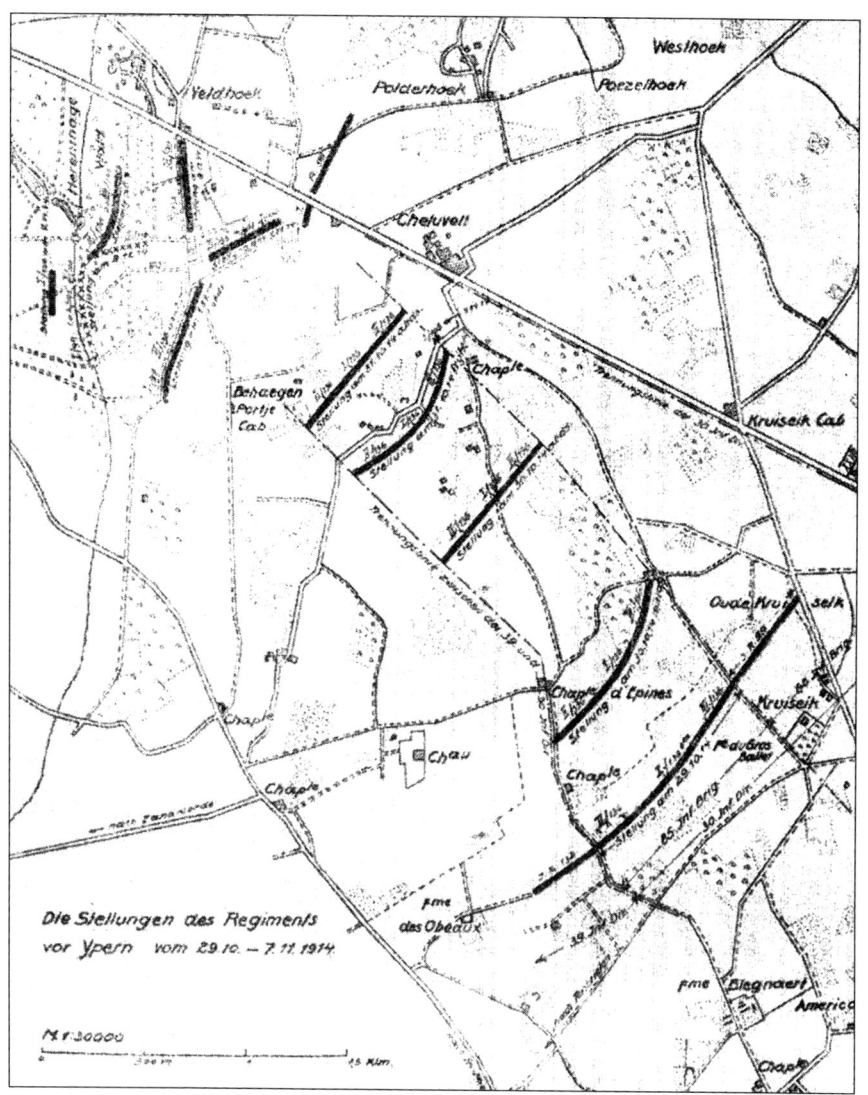

The advance of Infantry Regiment 136 towards Veldhoek, 29 October – 7 November.

companies of engineers were despatched and were sent into action. *Infantry Regiment 143 advanced south of the Gheluvelt – Veldhoek road and succeeded in capturing two British guns, together with their crews. These were the only ones taken by XV Corps on the Ypres front.*

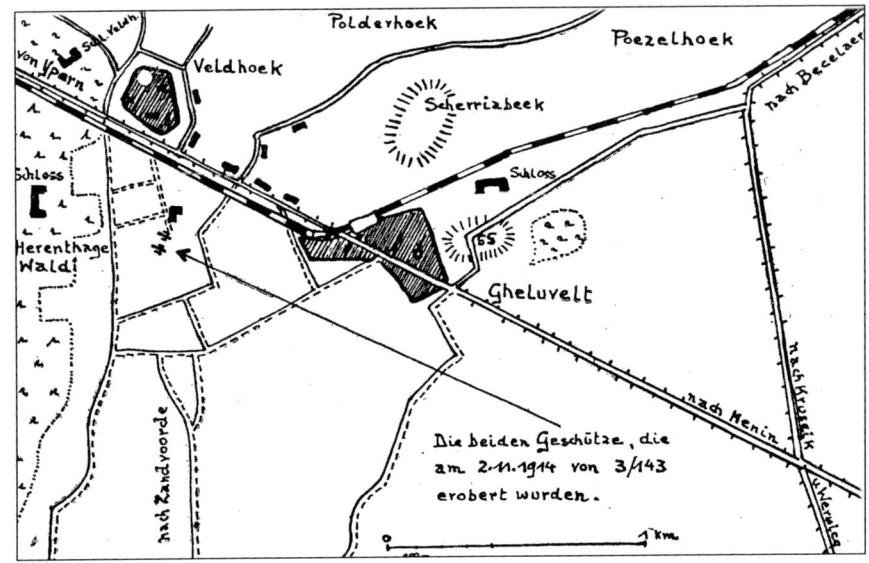

Location of the guns captured by 3rd Company Infantry Regiment 43 on 2 November.

The guns, the first the BEF had lost since Le Cateau the previous August, were later taken back to Strasbourg, where they were displayed for some weeks on Kaiserplatz, then claimed by Infantry Regiment 143 and given an honoured place in their barracks.

On 3 November the attack along the Menin road was renewed, but there had by then been French reinforcement of the depleted British ranks, which resulted in a stalemated day of minor attacks launched by both sides. Despite the fact that the severely reduced regiments of 54th Reserve Division, which were effectively fought out, were finding it increasingly difficult to contribute to the momentum of the advance, they were nevertheless ordered, together with 30th Infantry Division, to maintain pressure on the defence and to attack again on 4 November. Specifically, Reserve Infantry Regiment 248 of 54th Reserve Division was directed to capture Pottyn Farm, whilst Infantry Regiment 143 was tasked with the capture of the forward edge of Herenthage Wood, south of the main Menin – Ypres road. Herenthage Wood was a particularly difficult objective, so 60 Infantry Brigade spent the day sapping forward. In all Infantry Regiment 143 advanced its lines about fifty metres that day, but the British cavalrymen who opposed them also took the opportunity to improve their positions, rendering its capture even more awkward.

Reserve Infantry Regiment 248, responsible for the capture of Pottyn Farm, managed to arrange a suitable artillery bombardment then,

The situation along the Menin Road after the events of 2 November.

attacking at 3.15 pm on 4 November, a composite battalion took the objective and dug in. It was the final offensive action of 54th Reserve Division. The German High Command had by now decided to introduce an *ad hoc* Guards infantry division astride the Menin Road in a final attempt to force a decision so, whilst there were no more attacks for the time being, work went on day and night to sap forward and to attempt to dominate the British lines with sniper fire. Reserve Infantry Regiment 247 later commented of this work, 'that the casualties were disproportionate to what was achieved'.

These days were, in the great scheme of things, rather quiet for the British I Corps, except on the right, where all of the 7th Division and extra battalions drafted in from the other divisions in the Corps had a torrid time. The main weight of the German thrusts was along the Messines Ridge, but pressure also continued to the northeast of Klein Zillebeke. Indeed, by the evening of 1 November, French troops held the line from south of Klein Zillebeke to several hundred metres south west of Wytschaete and by the end of 5 November the French XVIth Corps now held this line, its southern flank extending west of Spanbroekmoelen. By that same evening 7th Division finally came out of the firing line – two brigades (20 and 21) concentrating around Locre, on the French border, and one (22) north east of Ypres.

Various fairly small scale attempts by the French to advance, as urged by Foch, failed to change anything at all but, on the contrary, in general they had to give ground, especially in the south, where the Germans completed the capture of Messines Ridge and moved on to the lower ridge to the west. On the 2nd Division's front on 1 November, 2/HLI, on the left, was relieved, their position taken over by the French, and went to reinforce the Division's rather pathetic reserve of a solitary company of 1/Berks. On 2 November there was some pressure on the

101

right of the line and some difficulties faced by 2/Connaught Rangers, but nothing significant.

On the 2nd, it was planned that the French IX Corps (Vidal) was to attack the German line at about 10 am, on the north side of Gheluvelt, for which purpose the troops had to move through British positions between Polygon Wood and the Menin Road. In fact the start had to be delayed until noon; and in that time gap the Germans were given an excellent opportunity. The British artillery had been instructed not to fire along the Menin Road from 10.30 am onwards; lacking observation, they could do nothing about a movement against the British defenders – a company of 1/Berks, three companies of 1/KRRC and 1/Coldstream, the latter, with the arrival of drafts, now about 200 strong, including only two officers. For these defenders, who had arrived only twelve hours earlier and did not know the ground, there had been no time to make any sort of realistic defensive line and their field of fire was extremely limited, ranging from fifty to a hundred and fifty yards.

Attacks had begun with an artillery bombardment, which destroyed a barricade erected across the road and a German machine gun was moved into a position from which it could fire into the backs of the KRRC, just south of the road. The Germans, instead of attacking en masse, came forward in medium sized groups and small bodies; 1/Coldstream was overpowered and lost about 50% of its men; then, almost surrounded, the two left companies of 1/KRRC were overrun, soon followed by the right company, for a casualty list of nine officers and 437 men. In addition, as has been mentioned, two guns of 116 Battery were taken by the German Infantry Regiment 143. The thrust was halted, but men both to the immediate north and south of the road were in danger of being hit by German attacks in enfilade. All of this had taken place by 11.35 am.

The situation, which had threatened to get out of hand, with Germans reaching Veldhoek and infiltrating Herenthage Wood, was resolved by a counter attack by the 3 Brigade group and by French troops (including a Zouave battalion); whilst the stalled French attack from the direction of Polygon Wood took place, albeit on a smaller scale. The end result was that most of the lost ground was retaken, though again, once night fell, there was a withdrawal, this time to a line along the north eastern edge of Herenthage Wood, to the 6 km stone on the Menin Road, behind (instead of in front of) Veldhoek and so on to Polygon Wood. One cheering bit of news for the British was the arrival of thirteen officers and 540 men, reinforcements for a variety of units; these were held back at Hooge to act as a Corps reserve. Corps HQ – both advanced (at the White Chateau) and in Ypres itself – were shelled by the Germans during

Haig's Forward HQ for the First Battle of Ypres until 2 November: the White Chateau, near Hell Fire Corner (or Halte, as it was then known).

the day, so these were moved to the right angle bend in the Menin Road, a short distance to the east of the Menin Gate, and Poperinghe respectively. Forward HQ was no safer there, however, and on 4 November it was shifted to the Chateau Les Trois Tours at Brielen.

By the evening of the 3rd, after a quiet day, the allies were becoming quietly confident that the worst at Ypres might be over; indeed both French and Foch thought that the Germans might be withdrawing troops to the Eastern Front. Meanwhile, Haig had been told that more French troops were coming up to the front and that these would not be used to plug gaps but were for a counter stroke. Haig was increasingly concerned by the lack of shells for his artillery; he withdrew three field batteries and a howitzer battery from each of his three divisions – a third of his field artillery – and sent them southwest of Ypres. There was no point having them under enemy shelling if they themselves had no shells with which to reply. Not totally convinced that the Germans had given up their designs on Ypres, Haig tried to make up for the weak defensive line by ordering Brigadier General Rice to ensure that small strong points, with all round defence, were carefully positioned and constructed behind the line. Rice, interestingly enough, had made a name for himself by the design for a simple blockhouse in the South African war, subsequently much used in that campaign: an ideal man, therefore, for supervising this task.

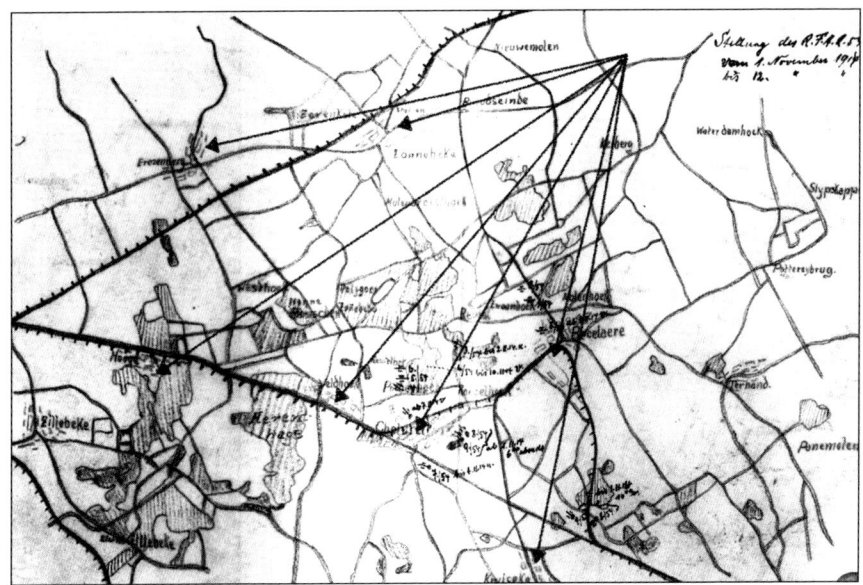

The gun lines of Reserve Field Artillery Regiment 54, 1 - 12 November. The arrows indicate built up areas which have been added to the original map.

So things continued though to the evening of the 5th. German shell fire continued to exact a heavy toll, especially on the centre and south of 1 Corps' line, covered by the 1st and 2nd Divisions and Lord Cavan's force. For 3 Brigade and its two attached battalions from the 2nd Division there was good news: that evening it was relieved of its positions on and south of the Menin Road by 6 (Cavalry) Brigade. The 7th Division, at long last, was also relieved (though 22 Brigade remained as a I Corps reserve, in Ypres; and its artillery was retained) – by men from II Corps (hitherto, until early on 31 October, around La Bassée), who were organised into two groups: Brigadier General McCracken's and Gleichen's.

Brigadier General Frederick McCracken.

Brigadier General (later major general) Count Gleichen, pictured after the war; he went on to command the 37th Division. His sister, Lady Feodora, was responsible for the magnificent bronze figures of the 37th Division's memorial at Monchy le Preux.

104

To the north the Germans had taken to sapping their way forward against 2nd Division's lines; but an evening attack on 2/HLI and 2/Connaughts, though dangerous at one point, came to nothing.

6th to 10th November

As for much of the time in November thus far, the main threat from the Germans lay to the south. On **6 November** they captured Zwarteleen and came close to St Eloi, creeping ever closer to Ypres; an attack on the Menin Road itself against Zouaves, which initially pushed them back, was seen off by a counter attack by 1/Berks. What was most significant was the arrival of further reinforcements from the line south of the border, where major operations had effectively ceased by the end of the month. Major General F. Wing (3rd Division) now took command of units from, chiefly, his and the 5th Division: Brigadier General Shaw's group (mainly of 9 Brigade), relieved 6 Cavalry Brigade late that night, south of the Menin Road; it thus joined Brigadier General McCracken's (mainly 7 Brigade) and Brigadier General Gleichen's (mainly 15 Brigade), which were already in the line. In addition, Wing had his own 3rd Division's staff,

Major General Edward Wing. He was killed in Mazingarbe outside his Report Centre on 2 October 1915, towards the end of the Battle of Loos

part of the 1st Division's artillery and the engineers of both the 3rd and 5th Divisions.

The 6th had been a very foggy day; the **7th** brought winter – mud made movement difficult and it was now so cold at night that sleeping in the open was nigh on impossible. Fighting was heaviest from the Lys to Zandvoorde, but Ypres was set on fire in many places and those further north would hardly have called it a quiet day. Counter attacks to try and restore the line to the south by Cavan's force eventually came to nothing. The Germans continued to press along the Menin Road, with little territorial effect, though the heavy shelling and the need to stay constantly on the alert was wearing. The greatest success involved the loss of a section of line south of Herenthage Chateau, about a hundred

The eastern entrance to the park of Herenthage Chateau.

yards deep, between 1/Beds and 1/Northumberland Fusiliers (1/NF). On the 2nd Division's front, the Germans took advantage of their sapping, with the trenches as close as fifteen yards apart, to try and rush a company of 2/HLI at about 4.40 am. After confused fighting and hand to hand combat, the Germans were ejected at a cost to them of fifty four prisoners and eighty killed or wounded; the HLI had forty five casualties and for his actions in the fight Second Lieutenant Brodie, the battalion machine gun officer, was awarded the VC. (The London Gazette says this happened on 11 November; the regimental record says the 7th.) At about 5 pm a similar attempt to rush the line was made against 2/Connaughts. This forced them out of their trenches, but 1/Berks counter attacked and restored the line. 5 Field Company RE was brought up to

Lieutenant Walter Brodie VC. He was killed in August 1918, during the advance to Victory, when he was commanding 2/HLI.

support the Connaughts' line and the strong points behind were manned by the Divisional Cyclists.

On **8 November**, two serious attempts were made by the Germans on the Menin Road. That day Infantry Regiment 143 attacked Herenthage Wood once more. A well directed bombardment and aggressive action led to initial success, but the attack soon stalled with severe losses, including many amongst reservists who had only just joined the regiment. By nightfall hardly one single officer of Infantry Regiment 143 was still on his feet. 1st Company was commanded by Vizefeldwebel Bormann, the Machine Gun Company by Offizierstellvertreter Aurisch. All that the enormous casualty list had achieved was a precarious hold on the forward edge of Herenthage Wood. It was a dismal return for such sacrifice and it brought to an end the efforts of Infantry Regiment 143, which was relieved on 9 November by Grenadier Guard Regiment 4. Reserve Infantry Regiment 247 was also pulled out of the line the same night when Grenadier Guard Regiment 2 (Kaiser Franz) arrived to relieve them.

Another attack was launched after noon on 8 November north of the Menin Road against the line on the edge of the woods to the immediate east of Veldhoek Chateau. Some Zouaves and men of 1/Loyals fell back on the Loyals' reserve companies on the far side of the chateau, though the neighbouring 1/Scots Guards held on. The loss of the trenches meant that 4/Royal Fusiliers (4/RF) were vulnerable to enfilade fire from the other side of the road; a forceful counter attack restored the line. However, a stronger attack launched at 2.30 pm pushed the line well

Pre-war visit by the Grand Duchess of Baden to Grenadier Guard Regiment 4 (Queen Augusta).

back into the woods. Again the Germans were forced back, but it took the assistance of Landon's last reserve battalion (1/Northants) and his cyclist company to do it. When that was not enough to restore the Loyals' trenches, FitzClarence – for some time now known as 'GOC Menin Road' – launched an attack at 4.15 pm along the front of the Scots Guards with his brigade reserve: all of eighty men of 1/Black Watch. This restored the line. The Germans remained close, however, and at 6 pm attacked the south of the road, sometimes reaching the parapets but getting no further. Although relatively small affairs, the attacks cost the British some 370 casualties, including at least fifteen officers. On the same day, Kitchener informed French that the total reinforcements available to him in the UK amounted to no more than 150 officers and 9,500 men (this has to be understood as meaning regular and reservist troops, of whatever category; and thus excludes the Territorial Army).

9 November continued with autumnal conditions, notably mist, which had precluded effective aerial reconnaissance for the past few days. Both it and the 10th were 'quiet' days for the British; reliefs took place and, by the 10th, all lost or broken machine guns had been replaced, bar two. For the French to the north, however, between Langemarck and Dixmude, **10 November** was far from quiet.

This was the day when the Germans were supposed to be making an all out effort to break the impasse – both along the Yser line, south of the main inundation, against the French and the Belgians and against the British, along – more or less – the axis of the Menin Road. After a

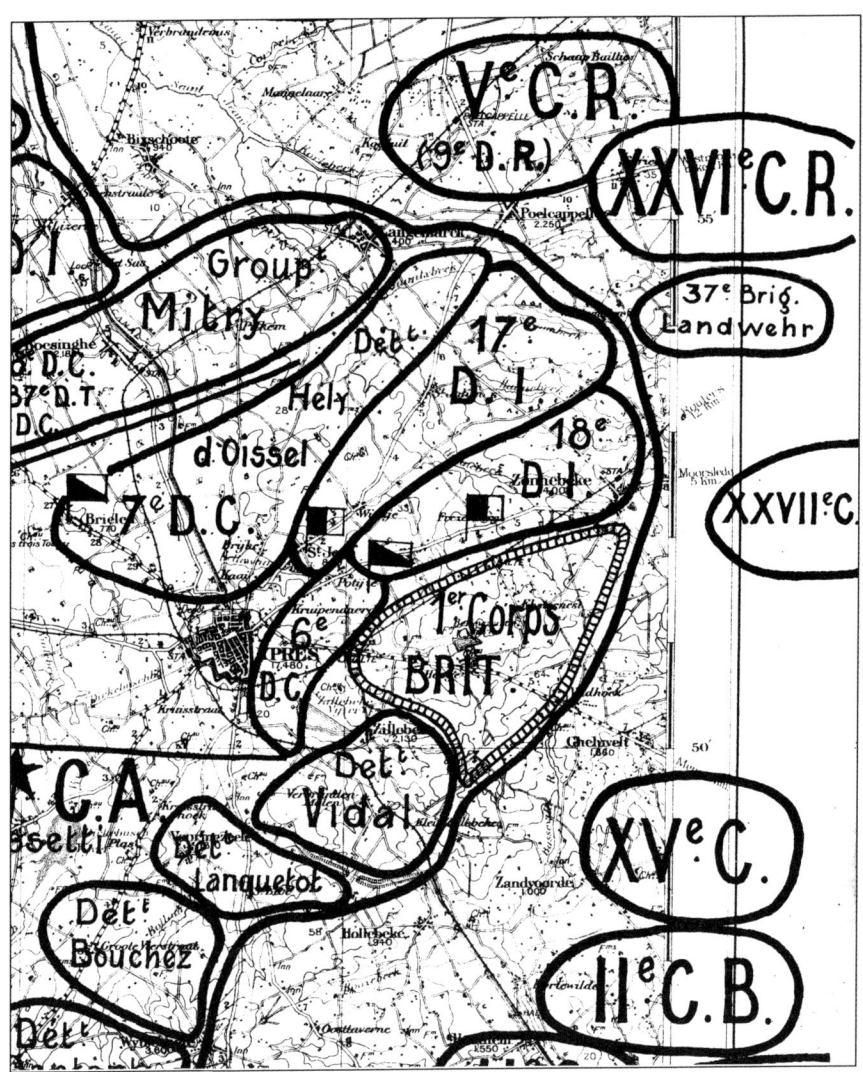

The situation on 10 November, showing the extent of the French army's dominance in the defensive battle.

substantial bombardment, the German Fourth Army succeeded in taking a bridgehead over the Yser at Dixmude by mid afternoon; and captured ground north west of Bixschoote and occupied Kortekeer Cabaret (well known to readers of *Langemarck* in this series as a scene of bitter fighting involving mainly the 1st Division on 21, 22 and 23 October) and some trenches west of Langemarck; and finally pushed the 38th Division over the Yser Canal so that the Germans were pressing up against the

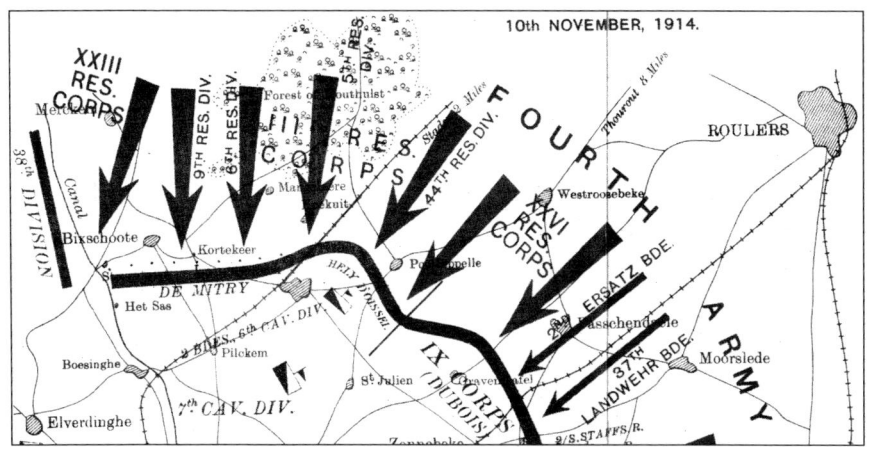

The German attack on 10 November against the French at the north of the battlefield.

eastern side of the canal south of Dixmude. All this impacted on the British, as d'Urbal, commander of French troops in Belgium (DAB), decided to recall all his troops from what had been the British sector (which did happen, with the exception of some Zouaves who were in the fighting line near Hooge). Not unreasonably, the French now felt that any major German action in Flanders would be directed against them; they were soon to be proven wrong. In fact the German intention had been for the Sixth Army to attack the British on this day as well, in particular from south of Herenthage Wood to the south of Polygon Wood, but the weather had hindered vital preparations, most notably the reconnaissance of the ground by the staffs of the new formations. In this sector it was determined to delay the attack by twenty-four hours. The failure to launch a coordinated attack, on either the 10th or the 11th, was amongst the most telling of the German errors at Ypres, for it is doubtful if the Yser-Ypres-Klein Zillebeke-Wulverghem line could have withstood such a concerted onslaught.

General Victor d'Urbal, commanding DAB. His cordial relations with Haig was a vital element in the successful defence of Ypres in 1914. He went on to command the French Tenth Army during the Battles of the Artois in 1915.

The German reliefs conducted on **9 November** were part of a much larger reorganisation of the Menin Road sector. The offensive was now to be directed by a newly formed Group Linsingen. This was based based on Headquarters II Army Corps and comprised XV Army Corps, commanded by General der Infanterie von Deimling, and the so-called Korps-Plettenberg. Plettenberg's corps was commanded by Headquarters Guard Corps, whilst, under command, were 4th Infantry Division and the composite 'Guards Division Winckler', commanded by Generalleutnant von Winckler, who had previously been commanding 2nd Guards Infantry Division. This necessitated a change in the boundaries of Army Group Fabeck, which henceforth concentrated on the sector to the west of the Comines – Ypres canal and included responsibility for Hollebeke, St Eloi, Wytschaete and Messines. Group Linsingen, deployed to the east of Army Group Fabeck, formed the southern flank of a more general Fourth Army attack and was ordered to advance towards Ypres via Hooge Chateau.

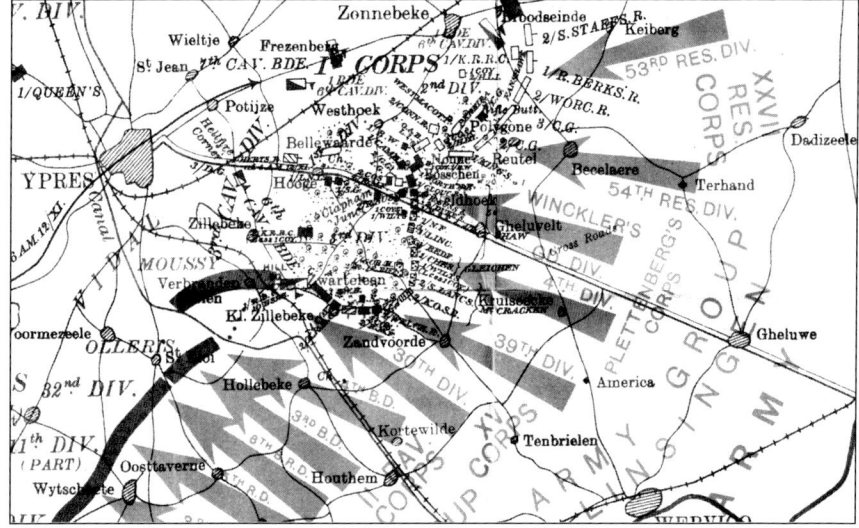

German dispositions on 10 November.

Just as the new reserve corps of Fourth Army were not comparable with the best of the active German army, so too the Guards formations, which had been fighting hard for three months along the most difficult parts of the Western Front, were only a shadow of the regiments that had originally marched away from Potsdam the previous summer. Oberstleutnant von Rieben, of Grenadier Guard Regiment 2 (Kaiser Franz) observed,

Our ranks were filled out with refugees from East Prussia, who knew nothing more of the regiment than our drill shed where they were quartered when their flight from their homeland was over.

However, we had received more officers than the Augusta Regiment [Grenadier Guard Regiment 4]. *As our commander, Oberst von Roeder, remarked as they marched slowly past one day, 'All tradition has been completely shot away!'*

Both Grenadier Guard Regiments 2 and 4 had a difficult time of it completing the relief in the line but, eventually, this was achieved and the men of both formations settled down and waited for dawn on 10 November. During a day which was devoted to orientation and observation of the ground over which their attack was to be launched, a series of orders for the operation on 11 November were issued by Guards Division Winckler and arrived at the various regimental headquarters, where they were studied, detailed orders for the forthcoming major operation were swiftly prepared and then passed down to the numerous attacking units and sub units.

1. Divisional Order for 11 November 1. Fourth Army has captured Dixmude and crossed the canal south of Dixmude in several places, taking 2,000 prisoners and six machine guns. In the area of Hollebeke numerous French soldiers have deserted to us. XIX Corps has beaten off the bitterly contested attacks of the British. A captured order is encouraging French soldiers to endure a few days longer in their trenches, by which time the attacking power of the Germans will have been reduced considerably. This order is an indication of how exhausted the enemy is already. This information is, as far as possible, to be transmitted to the front line trenches.
2. Tomorrow at 9.00 am there is to be a general assault. Should there be any sign before that time that the enemy is withdrawing then attacks are to be launched without waiting for artillery preparation and are to be driven forward with the utmost energy. All neighbouring formations will be participating in the attack.
3. Oberst Janke (Commander 7 Infantry Brigade) will assume command of the Army Group Reserve, comprising 3rd Battalion Footguard Regiment 1 and 3rd Battalion Grenadier Guard Regiment 4, at Keilberg.
4. From 7.00 am I shall be located at Oude Kruiseecke [two kilometres southeast of Gheluvelt].

A short time later the Division issued a supplementary order:

1. The infantry is to press on with the construction of their saps, in order to gain ground. It is of particular importance that 1

111

Guards Infantry Brigade gets far enough forward to permit artillery observation of the western edge of Polygon Wood and Verbeek Farm.

2. The artillery is so to deploy its guns that it can open fire at 6.30 am. The artillery is then to fire from 6.30 am to 9.00 am precisely. From 6.30 am to 8.00 am this fire is to be moderately heavy, but between 8.00 am and 9.00 am significant quantities of ammunition are to be fired.

3. At exactly 9.00 am, by synchronised watches, artillery fire is to cease. This sudden silence by our artillery is the signal for our entire forward line of infantry to launch the assault...

Chapter Five

11 November 1914:
The Battle of Nonne Bosschen

So much for the German theory. Unfortunately for the attackers there were fundamental flaws in the plan, which visualised a thrust in a northwesterly direction by 1 Guards Infantry Brigade, with Footguard Regiment 3 bypassing the southwest corner of Polygon Wood. Footguard Regiment 1's boundaries were laid down as: right Pottyn Farm, bypassing Verbeek Farm to the southwest edge of Nonne Bosschen and left skirting the northern edge of Herenthage Wood. 4 Guards Infantry Brigade was ordered to push forward more to the west. It was of course clear that this would quickly lead to a gap and although the intention was to move forward a battalion from Grenadier Guard Regiment 2, which was acting as divisional reserve to occupy the gap, the problem was that this makeshift solution simply served to obscure the weaknesses.

Herenthage Wood after the battle was over.

The attack frontage was too wide, there was insufficient strength in depth and there was a lack of the artillery necessary to provide adequate fire support. Adding to the difficulties the gunners faced was the need to support two diverging attacks and, which was worse, the location of the opposing British batteries was not known with any certainty, thus making counter battery missions wasteful and ineffective. Although strenuous efforts had been made by the infantry to familiarise themselves with what lay to their front, there was not enough time for detailed reconnaissance. So, although the general line of the British defence was fairly obvious, the precise placement of British positions, their strength and the location of their machine guns were unknown.

Despite these problems, the Guards intended to attack north of the Menin Road with all four regiments line abreast – from left to right Grenadier Guard Regiment 4, Grenadier Guard Regiment 2, Footguard Regiment 1 and Footguard Regiment 3. (See the disposition map on p. 110.) The task ahead of them was extremely difficult. There were numerous obstacles to movement, visibility was poor in some places, but not over wide stretches of the open ground which they would have to cross. The wintry weather, with squally sleet and rain, added to the unpleasantness, as did the sight and smell of unburied, rotting, corpses which littered No Man's Land from previous unsuccessful assaults. Nevertheless, preparations went ahead urgently and, in conformity with divisional orders, the forward trenches continued to be driven towards the enemy lines. In all a further fifty metres was gained overnight by the time the bombardment opened as planned, promptly at 6.30 am, lighting up the hazy morning mist. There was an immediate British reaction and there were some casualties before the attackers had even left their own trenches.

Major Schering, commanding 3rd Battalion Grenadier Guard Regiment 2 on the right, later described events on his front:

The grey dawn saw us standing in a position from which we could observe the artillery bombardment, scheduled to begin about 6.00 am. Through the roof, which had more holes than a sieve, we could watch as the smoke clouds from the explosions thickened and crept closer until they enveloped the edge of the wood. The final corrections were applied once the curtain of fire was in the correct place and then the process of softening up the positions began; the crashes as the shells exploded on and beyond the British positions were very noticeable. Through the tripod binoculars we could clearly see British soldiers here and there leaving their positions and running to the rear. We took that as a good omen, even though we knew that the hard work would begin once we were in the woods.

From the front line came a report that everything was ready for the assault. It was five minutes to nine when the harsh clatter of our machine guns began to blend with the detonation of the

*shells. I threw off my cloak and drew my sword. After briefly taking
my leave of my comrades from the artillery and von Sell, who was
also ready to go, we moved outside. All around everything was
quiet. To our front nothing was to be seen across the flat ground.
The 12th Company, to which we were going to attach ourselves,
was already moving forward in the trenches, so my staff began to
pick their way forward across a landscape which appeared to have
been turned over by rabbits. We got split up, but found each other
after fifty metres. Then at long last we were free of the confusion
of trenches and raced across the shortest gap to get to the wood
edge, which appeared to be in our hands.*

Prior to the onslaught on the 11th, the German troops in the front trenches
had been very considerably thinned out in light of the artillery
bombardment that was to precede the assault. The attack was to be against
a nine miles long front from Messines to Reutel; formations on either side
would co-operate with it. In the event, the assault only had limited success
in the Menin Road sector, the front of the newly arrived 4th and Guards
Divisions of Korps Plettenberg.

The day dawned overcast and with fog. This cleared from noon,
when the wind got up, blowing towards the enemy; it was followed by
rain, which became heavy at about 6 pm. Heavy shelling, particularly
directed against Wing's division and FitzClarence's brigade, commenced
at 6.30 am and built up from shortly before 9 am, an indicator that an
attack was on the way. One unforeseen benefit of the shelling was that
the eastern edge of the various woods along the front became an obstacle
in themselves, a mess of shattered stumps, felled trees and shell holes.
The *BOH* notes that the Germans seemed to have attacked with less
enthusiasm than on previous occasions – with the exception of those
formations new to the front.

Between Messines and the Comines Canal, the outcome of the day
was no change. The French line north of the canal was threatened, and
by noon the defenders were forced back to Verbrandenmolen and Hill
60. There were no reserves to hand – troops had been despatched to the
threatened left wing the previous day. It was only a charge by French
dismounted cavalry, at about 6.30 pm, that stabilised the situation. Lord
Cavan's force on the French left was attacked and pressurised, but the
line was left unaltered at the end of the day. On the left of the BEF line,
most of the 2nd Division had a broadly uneventful day: the line had
changed little for some time and so the defences were more robust and
established, as opposed to the continual shifting of the line on the Menin
Road. On the French front a heavy attack was made on Drie Grachten,

which was repulsed and initial success at Knocke could not be maintained.

The British Centre.

Wing's division, made up of units from II Corps, held the line from Shrewsbury Forest to the north of the Menin Road, covering Veldhoek, a front of about two miles. From south to north, the various forces were as follows: McCracken's group of fifty officers and 1,714 men; Gleichen's group, with fifty officers and 1,550 men, and Shaw's group of seventy officers and 2,638 men. Haig had also managed to hang on to a battalion of Zouaves, most of whom were now held as a reserve at Hooge. The nine hundred yards north of Veldhoek to Polygon Wood was covered by FitzClarence's force, comprising about 800 all ranks. Behind his front there were some disconnected support trenches and five 'strong points'; three in the vicinity of Veldhoek, one at Northampton Farm and one in the garden of a cottage three hundred yards south of

Brigadier General Frederick Shaw. He was wounded by a shell on 12 November, but recovered and went on to command the 13th (Western) Division at Gallipoli.

The estaminet near Hooge where General Shaw was wounded on 12 November.

Black Watch cottage; whilst all brigade and battalion HQs were prepared for defence. A staff officer subsequently said of these positions that they:

> ...were the saving of the day. The attackers blundered on them after they had broken through our line, and were taken in enfilade and broken up and driven into woods and hollows for shelter. They were a lesson in defensive tactics for all time.

The reserves were very limited – about 2,000 bayonets altogether. The 1st Division's reserve included an engineer unit of 350 men; the 2nd Division had a single weak battalion (2/Ox and Bucks LI, about 300 men); and the Corps reserve comprised four weak – or very weak –battalions, 7 Cavalry Brigade and a regiment from 6 Cavalry Brigade.

The German artillery lifted their fire at 9 am, attacking a front held by a total available force of just under 8,000 men. The attack completely failed against the southern groups of Wing's division. North of and across the Menin Road, Shaw's group was attacked by 4 Guard Brigade and FitzClarence's much smaller group (over seventy percent smaller) by 1 Guard Brigade.

Shaw's Brigade.
In this sector an uncoordinated end to the German artillery programme meant that it was impossible for the infantry to rush forward as one. Surprise was lost and the result was a disaster, as described by Leutnant von Scheele of 3rd Company Grenadier Guard Regiment 4 on the left.

> One daring lad leapt out of the trench. I blew my whistle and launched myself forward. In order not to be recognised as an officer, I was carrying a knapsack and a rifle. Right and left of me the men were going down in rows. How I myself got as far as the first line trench I do not know. It was like a miracle. I was one of the first there. The British were still firing at us, cutting us down, but some were surrendering. Only twenty-five of my men succeeded in getting into the trenches. The remainder were all shot down, the two flanking platoon mowed down by machine gun fire. About twenty men, commanded by Feldwebel Fernau, charged forward on the far side of the road with the Franz-Regiment [Grenadier Guard Regiment 2]. I pointed my revolver at the chests of two British soldiers who were trying to escape, but I could not bring myself to shoot them; they were human beings after all. Together with my twenty-five men I was completely cut off – off to the right towards the Franzers there was no link. Between them

and us there was a hedge concealing Zouaves; to the left the British were occupying the same trench as we were. There was no communication to the rear. The battalion had absolutely no idea that we had captured the trench.

The 4th Company attack on the left against 1/ Lincolns was a total failure. The interlocking arcs of fire of four machine guns, protected by barbed wire and sited behind a hedge less than fifty metres to the front, dominated all approaches. Not even the commitment of both reserve companies altered this situation as each fresh attempt was shot to pieces. The Fusilier [3rd] Battalion Grenadier Guard Regiment 2 was able to make good progress into Veldhoek Wood as far as the chateau, which was located about five hundred metres inside the wood and defended by a company of Zouaves. However, elsewhere companies began to become intermingled. 9th and 10th Companies Grenadier Guard Regiment 2 found themselves entangled with 4th Company Footguard Regiment 1 and then

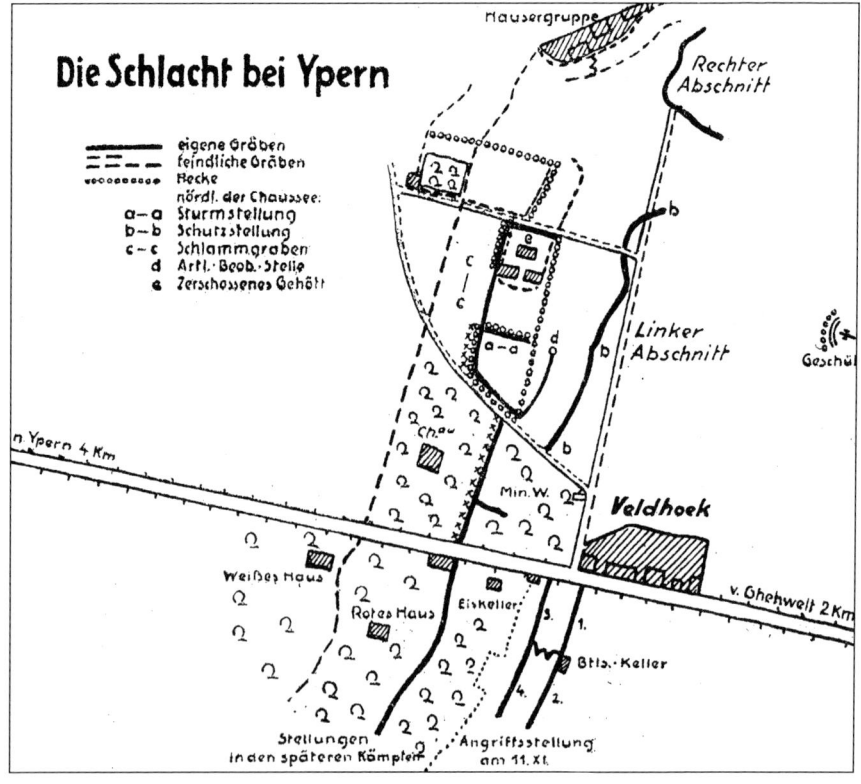

Grenadier Guard Regiment 4's locations, 11 November.

118

came under heavy fire from a combination of 2/Duke of Wellington's and 1/Scots Guards. One 3rd Battalion survivor, Feldwebelleutnant Rosenberg, later described the action.

The defenders had not suffered any casualties and were not immediately overrun, because they defended themselves desperately. However we managed to take up positions to a flank and fired into the trench, each reinforcing the other's efforts, until we had shot down the last of the defenders, who fought with great bravery to the end. Reserve Vizefeldwebel Lentz performed in an outstanding manner until he fell through [the roof of] a dugout and was seriously injured. Once we had broken the main line of resistance, we turned our attention to the individual dugouts, from which the enemy was still firing at us, and mopped them up. We were only able to take a few men prisoner.

There were five lines of trenches, one behind the other and all linked to the front line, then came a group of French [Zouaves – defending Veldhoek Chateau] and we shot them down as they tried to run off. Off to my left I witnessed the battle for an enemy machine gun. This turned into a real ding dong scrap, which was eventually decided in our favour. Once the forward enemy trenches were firmly in our hands, the advance through the thick undergrowth and the debris of fallen tree crowns went relatively swiftly, but the thickness of the vegetation made it difficult for us to observe the enemy withdrawal. Despite the fact that the majority of the junior commanders had fallen, the fusiliers pressed on determinedly with their daring advance, until they came to an impenetrable hedge and a swamp just before the chateau in the middle of the wood. Here a man brought an order to me from my commander, directing me to assume command of the company because he had been wounded.

In the line facing the attack of Grenadier Guard Regiment 4 were the centre and left flank of 1/Lincs, Shaw's right battalion, 1/NF, 4/Fusiliers and a company of Zouaves immediately south of the road and 4/Fusiliers; across the road, Grenadier Guard Regiment 2 faced 2/DoW, positioned in the woods east of Veldhoek Chateau. The elements of 4/Fusiliers nearest the road were shelled out of their positions by the artillery fire of the early morning; but nevertheless, along with the units on the right, were able to deal with the German assaults. However, the success of Grenadier Guard Regiment 2, which got into the re-entrant in the British line north of the road, meant that it could take the Fusiliers in enfilade; so that,

British dispositions on the evening of 10 November SOUTH of the Menin Road.

British dispositions on the evening of 11 November SOUTH of the Menin Road.

British dispositions on the evening of 10 November NORTH of the Menin Road.

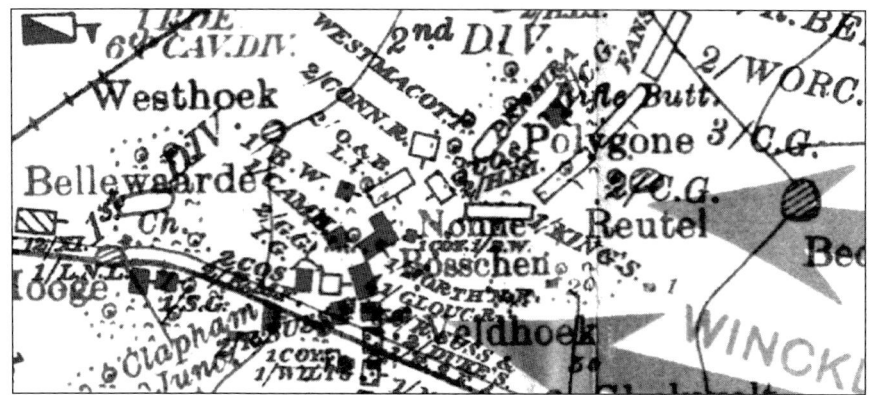

British dispositions on the evening of 11 November NORTH of the Menin Road.

attacked from the front and on the left flank (and having lost their commander, Brigadier General McMahon, recently appointed to command 10 Brigade), they – along with the Zouaves – were forced to fall back. The Germans then turned southwards towards Herenthage Wood, probably seeking to undo the British line; but a counter attack ordered by Shaw, by 1/RSF and a company of 2/Sussex, caught them in flank and drove them back. Some of 1/RSF had the strange sight of seeing the Germans on the north side of the road heading westwards whilst they were pushing eastwards. At first a body of reinforcements was sent up by Haig, but it was not used. However, reports that the Fusiliers' original line had been retaken was false; 1/RSF mistook the support

Brigadier General N McMahon. He was killed by a shell on the south side of the Menin Road and the edge of Herenthage Wood. He has no known grave.

trenches for this line, which was two hundred yards west of the original front line positions. An attack launched at 4 pm failed to regain that position. The defence had not come without cost; the Fusiliers were left with two subalterns and about a hundred men at the end of the day. But, by the end of 11 November, the line, bar a relatively small piece, had been held and the Germans rebuffed.

North of the road, 2/DoW had three companies in the line and a company in reserve. The ditch along the road was put into use as a communications trench between them and 4/Fusiliers on the south. At the eastern end of this there were two machine guns. Under the weight of the bombardment, the front line had been thinned out to a minimum; the initial German rush took the line before it could be manned and then pushed on about five hundred yards into Veldhoek Wood, 'which consisted of small oaks and chestnuts, with many rhododendron bushes in the chateau grounds'. They then hit the chateau proper, defended by a company of Zouaves and the strong point, which was positioned near the stables. Here 1st Battalion Grenadier Guard Regiment 2, which had led the attack, was halted – by these positions, fire from the rear and the very effective use of the artillery which, shell shortage or no, prevented any German reinforcements from coming forward to develop the success. The DoW's reserve company then counter attacked and drove the survivors out of the wood but were unable to retake the original trench line just beyond its eastern edge, not least because they were on their own, and therefore potentially exposed on both flanks. They dug in; a strong battalion at the start of the day, by its end they had lost seven officers out of twenty and 380 out of 820 other ranks.

This thrust was the furthest point reached that day by Grenadier Guard Regiment 2 and it came at the cost of extremely severe casualties. However, it was not quite the end of the story on this part of the front. As darkness fell on 11 November the old British front line was firmly in German hands but, in rear, the British had either denied their positions or recaptured them following hasty counter attacks. One consequence was an increase in the width of No Man's Land, which enabled men who were not too seriously wounded to make their painful way back to their start lines and thus medical care. As the true extent of the failure became known, Headquarters Guards Division was unwilling to let matter stand and, at 4.15 pm, it issued the following order:

> *Regiment Augusta* [Grenadier Guard Regiment 4], *together with Infantry Regiment 49 and supported by Regiment Franz* [Grenadier Guard Regiment 2], *is to capture the trenches to their front. 1 Guards Infantry Brigade is to remain in its current positions and support the attack of 4 Guards Infantry Brigade.*

In the event there was no chance of distributing this order to all concerned in good time and none whatever of carrying it out. Nothing came of it, and the same thing applied to a further order, released at 6.00 pm, directing Grenadier Guard Regiment 4 to launch a frontal attack at 9.00 pm with its 1st Battalion, supported by a flanking attack from north of the road by one half of 2nd Battalion. The regimental commander pointed out forcibly that the entire concept was complete folly and the order was cancelled at 7.25 pm. Quite why it was ever issued remains a mystery; it could only have been the work of a headquarters out of touch with the reality on the ground.

Footguard Regiment 1, commanded by Prince Eitel Friedrich, the second son of the Kaiser, attacking off to the right, also had a hard day. Here, too, the forward companies who rushed the British lines whilst the final shells of the bombardment were still falling managed to overrun a number of trenches, but the defenders, reacting rapidly, brought down enfilade fire which caused great slaughter amongst the skirmishing lines. 4th Company lost its company commander early on and the survivors, under Feldwebel Mazur, were thrown off course towards the so-called 'White Chateau' in Herenthage Wood. Other sub-units that managed to maintain the correct axis of advance (the majority of the Leib and 3rd Companies), then tried to press home the attack beyond the captured positions, but found themselves also under heavy fire from the right. In an attempt to avoid the worst of the fire coming from the area of Verbeek Farm, just south of Nonne Bosschen, they plunged into the cover of Nonne Bosschen; their momentum pushed out the few British troops located there, with the sole exception of a pocket of resistance in its southeast corner.

Despite severe casualties amongst the officers and NCOs, the men of Footguard Regiments 1 and 3 continued to push on. However, on arrival at the northern end of Nonne Bosschen, they discovered that there was no German gunfire coming down to their front and that, therefore, they themselves were now coming under heavy close range British gunfire. There would be no more progress in this sector that day and elsewhere confusion reigned.

So far, so good – the Germans had been halted along the Menin Road for trifling gains and Haig had nearly all his reserves in hand: but the situation to the immediate north was far less comforting. The part of the front covered by FitzClarence's group (1 (Guards) Brigade) – defended entirely by Scottish battalions (south to north: 1/Black Watch, 1/Scots Guards and 1/Camerons) – was much more open than that to the south; and the German artillery, with good observation from Reutel Ridge, had been far more effective in their shooting in the early morning. Communications between British artillery observers and their batteries were rendered useless very early on. The Black Watch had a company and half in the front line, the equivalent in reserve at Verbeek Farm, along with its HQ and that of the Camerons, and a party of forty manning the strong point at the south west corner of Polygon Wood. The Camerons,

Brigadier General FitzClarence VC, GOC 1 (Guards) Brigade, killed in action near Polygon Wood on 12 November. He has no known grave.

desperately short of officers, were organised in two half battalions of 160 men each and held about a quarter of their number in reserve. The Scots Guards were all in the front or very close to it, except for a few manning the strongpoint at Northampton Farm. 1/King's (6 Brigade), about 450 strong, held a mile long front which ran along the southern face of Polygon Wood, as far east as the Polygonbeke, but without supports or a reserve. Beyond them, the line once more angling northwards, was the composite battalion of the Coldstream (the remnants of the three battalions combined into one).

This position of the King's was crucial to the outcome of the battle; they were effectively at right angles to 1 (Guards) Brigade. Originally the line had consisted of one or two man rifle pits; but in the days preceding a continuous trench just inside the wood had been constructed and to this the men in the forward rifle pits dug connections to their own position. In addition, the German artillery fire had been chiefly directed at a supposed support line and its chief consequence had only been to force the battalion HQ to shift position.

Even at this stage of the war, the bad weather and shelling had produced dreadful conditions on what passed for roads in 1 (Guards) Brigade's area; the rides and tracks in the wood even worse. Thus hot rations rarely, if ever, got up to the men – and priority had to be given to water and limited supplies of ammunition.

Scheduled to attack this sector were the units of the German 1 Guards Brigade. Out to the right of Footguard Regiment 1 and linked up with Reserve Infantry Regiment 248, the men of Footguard Regiment 3 had spent 10 November in rather exposed, positions. Here the trenches were shallow and so they suffered a series of casualties throughout the day. These included the commanding officer of 2nd Battalion, Hauptmann von Phiseldeck, who was wounded and the adjutant 1st Battalion, Leutnant Elstermann, who was killed outright. The ground here was difficult and the regimental frontage narrow, so the commander, Oberstleutnant von Schultzendorff, decided to launch his attack on a single battalion frontage. The three waves were laid down as 1st, 2nd and Fusilier [3rd] Battalions. Despite a bold programme of patrolling during the night 10/11 November against 1/Camerons, which held this sector, little detailed information was obtained.

Nevertheless, at 9.00 am 11 November the 1st Battalion launched a vigorous attack. 2nd Company, under Oberleutnant von Marck, advanced right forward, with 3rd Company, commanded by Reserve Leutnant Henderkott, left forward. These companies easily succeeded in overrunning the lightly manned forward trenches of the Camerons and 1st Company, under Hauptmann Freiherr von Marschall, following

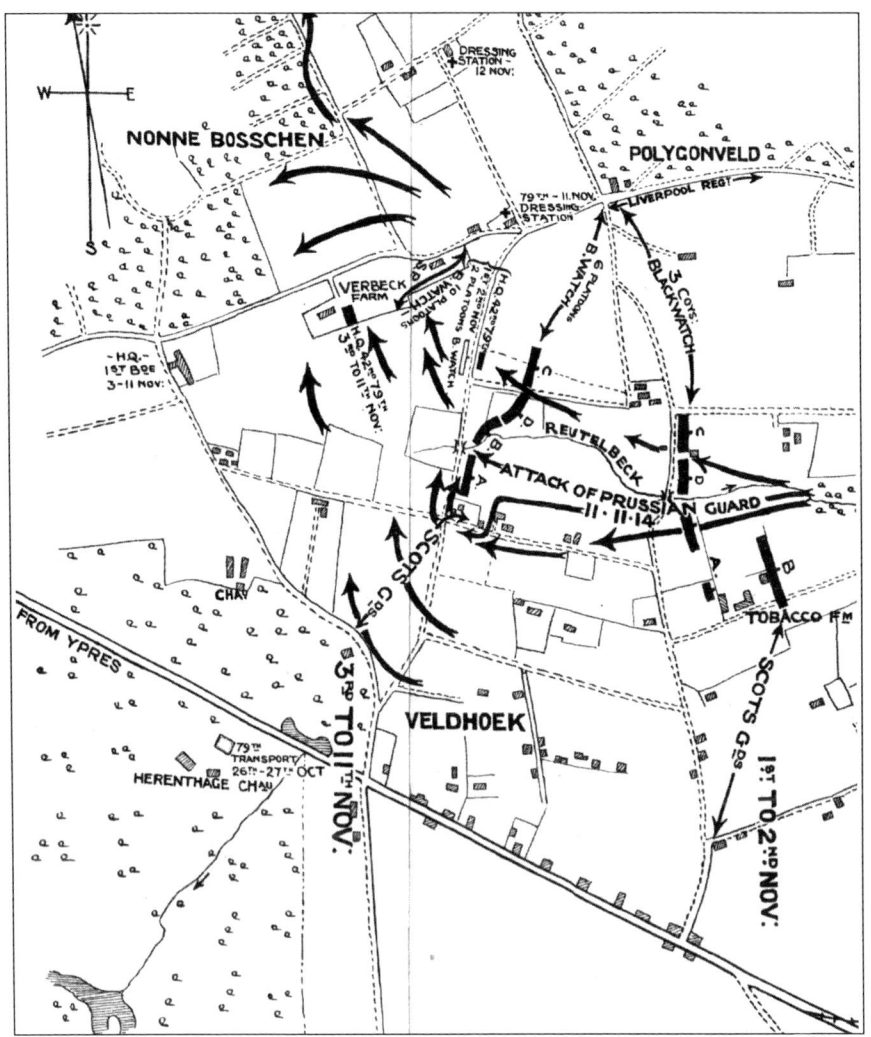

The 1st Camerons on 11 November; the letters refer to its companies. The '42nd' refers to the Black Watch, the '79th' to the Cameron Highlanders.

up the first wave very closely, also crossed No Man's Land fairly easily. It did not take the defence long to react. Intense small arms fire from 1/King's, located on the edge of Polygon Wood, cut great swathes in the ranks of Footguard Regiment 3 and all attempts to renew attacks here throughout the day were also almost all shot to a standstill in short order. There was a little progress later in the day towards Polygon Wood, but the determined defence conducted by two companies of the Black Watch, who were almost wiped out in the process, at the southwest corner of that wood, forced the remnant of this German attack into the depths of Nonne Bosschen, which was effectively undefended at that time.

The British reported later that at about 9 am, only about fifty yards from the front, a thick line of advancing Germans was seen: officers with drawn swords, the men with their rifles at the high port. They moved over the first trenches without firing, using their bayonets to deal with any defenders. The main assault was against the Scots' battalions, all of which were overwhelmed but which managed to put in a sufficient defence that the German attack began to lose cohesion. The Germans seemed to some to be advancing in massed columns; but in fact they were doing so in close waves; obstacles, such as remnants of buildings, forced these waves to bunch up occasionally, thus giving the impression of columns. FitzClarence Farm 'manned by the cooks and details [eg transport] and some men of 1/Scots Guards' was lost, but their other strong point, Northampton Farm, held out and was never taken. Once more the artillery came into its own. The observers, who had lost their communications earlier on, had gone back to alert their batteries of the imminence of an attack and the gunners were able to put down such a weight of fire that, as to the south, the Germans were not able to get adequate reinforcements forward.

The orders for 1 Guards Brigade – Foot Guard Regiment 3 to the north and Foot Guard Regiment 1 to the south, were to advance north westwards through the gap between Veldhoek and Polygon woods, the regimental boundary being the south west corner of Nonne Bosschen Wood. The gap between them and Grenadier Guard Regiment 4 just north of Veldhoek – whose orders had them striking directly westwards – was to be covered by 2nd Battalion Grenadier Guard Regiment 2 This it was unable to do because of the effectiveness of the British shelling – and the failure of the German artillery to engage successfully in any counter battery work.

To make matters worse for the Germans, Footguard Regiment 1, for whatever reason, but probably because of the fire it was under, drifted towards Verbeek Farm and then into Nonne Bosschen Wood, instead of keeping to the south of it. Meanwhile, most of Footguard Regiment 3, under withering fire from 1/King's along the southern edge of Polygon Wood, turned in to deal with it; they were unsupported by any evident activity by XXVII Reserve Corps, to the east of the wood. Not one of these men got inside the wood:

As the light improved, the men of the King's from their holes could see that what they first thought was a second attack was in reality a continuous wall of German dead and wounded, lying several deep twenty five to seventy yards away in a turnip field. The survivors either lay down and remained opposite the wood or ran to get shelter on the slope of ground towards the Reutelbeek, which prevented the Liverpool men from having a field of fire of more than a hundred and fifty to two hundred yards.

The result of this divergence between the two regiments was that a gap  of about half a mile appeared between them. All of this had occurred by about 10.15 am; which was about the same time that 2/DoW was reporting the advance of the Germans into Veldhoek woods. 1/King's now had a completely open flank on its right – 'there was nothing between it and the enemy at this point but a ruined house'.

The recently promoted Brigadier General Westmacott (5 Brigade), informed of the collapse of the line by a soldier from 1/Black Watch at his Brigade HQ at the north west corner of Polygon Wood, sent 2/Connaughts and 5 Field Company RE to form a defensive flank on the right rear of 1/King's, facing south and west. Monro, from his HQ at Potijze, instructed 2/HLI and the divisional cyclists to move forward in support and also told Colonel Pereira, commanding the Coldstream composite battalion, to let Westmacott have the 1/Coldstream part of his force, about a hundred men. Monro also moved 2/Ox & Bucks to Westhoek, to the rear of Nonne Bosschen.

Brigadier General Claude Westmacott was one of several battalion commanders who were promoted to brigade command during the battle.

FitzClarence, in his HQ trench on the edge of Glencorse Wood, was soon aware of the fate of his troops in the front line. In reply to his request for reinforcements from Landon (1st Division's HQ was still at Hooge), he was sent 1/Northants (about 200 men in total), who had only come out of the line at 2.30 am that morning. Verbeek Farm continued to hold out against the Germans – held by two sets of battalion staff and a reserve of about a hundred men of the Black Watch. Not only did the defence hold, but it was able to enfilade a hedge which ran towards Black Watch corner. Sometime after 11 am the Farm was abandoned and the defenders withdrew to FitzClarence's HQ trench, which had been turned into a strongpoint and manned by mess signallers, the signals section and stragglers. Only a few Germans entered the outbuildings; when the Farm was recaptured these were found eating rations they had found there.

Verbeek Farm marked the limit of the German advance on the left. The Black Watch strongpoint, with a platoon sized garrison, marked the limit on the right. Its rudimentary construction, a traversed trench set within the hedges (with some barbed wire inserted) of a cottage garden, was completed by 23 Field Company RE only an hour before the attack started. It was situated in a small depression and had been untouched by the German artillery; its presence was a complete surprise to the advancing Germans of Foot Guard Regiment 3. These were hit not only from the strongpoint but also from the edge of the wood and from Verbeek Farm, before its garrison withdrew; whilst an orderly advance was not made easier by the various hedge lines. The advance degenerated into one made by scattered groups.

About 200 – 300 men of both Foot Guard regiments pressed forward between the two strong points and entered Nonne Bosschen, which was bereft of defenders. Entering by its base, they emerged on its western edge and were greeted with a view of the 2nd Division's artillery lines (which ran from Bellewaarde Farm to the back of Polygon Wood). XLI Brigade and 35 Heavy Battery were only about three hundred yards from the rear of Polygon Wood and the gunners prepared to fend off attackers. The guns opened fire at point blank range, whilst everyone who could hold a rifle and was available blazed away. This included brigade HQ staff, cooks and two sections of 5 Field Company RE and some Connaughts, who were positioned on the spur by the north west corner of Polygon Wood. Attempts by the Germans to hold some sort of line failed and the survivors rushed back into the wood.

Haig had come out to the White Chateau when he first heard of the attack on the Menin Road. As the morning continued it became clear that the situation was being contained and by noon dispositions to deal with eventualities had been arranged. Landon had directed resources from his divisional reserves to provide cover in depth for his Menin Road position. 1/Northants moved through Glencorse Wood to get to 1 (Guards) Brigade's HQ, whilst 2/Ox & Bucks were ready at Westhoek. As the *BOH* puts it, 'the time had come to recover the ground that had been lost'.

Westmacott ordered Lieutenant Colonel Davies of 2/Ox & Bucks to clear Nonne Bosschen Wood; as they emerged they would be joined by 2/HLI, with the intention of retaking 1/Black Watch's original trenches, running south from Black Watch Corner. At the same time he received orders from 1 (Guards) Brigade to take part in a different counter attack, to recover the Camerons' and Scots Guards' trenches. He determined that Nonne Bosschen had to be dealt with first, with which 1st Division agreed and 1/Glosters and the Irish Guards were sent to him from the reserve at Hooge.

Without artillery support, two companies of Ox & Bucks were moved into Nonne Bosschen from the north west, sometime before 3 pm; the other two companies followed on in support. A company of 1/Northants, seeing what was going on, moved forward from Glencorse Wood from the west and 5 Field Company RE charged south across the open ground between the two woods. The artillery shelled the wood and the open ground beyond it; in which endeavour they were assisted by the German artillery. The Germans became casualties of one sort or the other almost to a man. The charge cost the Ox & Bucks minimal casualties – the total for the day was five dead and twenty-two wounded. On reaching the southern end of the wood they paused and joined up with the Northants and the sappers. After a short stop, the counter attack continued and they retook the support trenches on the left flank of 1 (Guards) Brigade. An advance to the old front line trenches was halted by the French artillery, firing from near Frezenberg, who were unaware of the way the battle had turned. Evening was falling and the weather had become foul, with heavy rain and hail; so no further move was made against the Germans.

1/Glosters was moved from the back of Glencorse Wood to fill the gap of several hundred yards between 2/DoW in the Veldhoek woods and 1/Northants, near Verbeek Farm. Units were scattered hither and thither and some time had to be taken in getting them into appropriate front, support and reserve positions. Only 1/King's had managed to stay in its original positions throughout the proceedings. The fighting had come at a cost; 1/Scots Guards was left with a battalion HQ and thirty-nine men; 1/Black Watch was reduced to a single officer; 1/Camerons had lost half its men and 5 Field Company lost three officers killed, including the CO, Major A Tyler, and Captain AEJ Collins and one wounded of its complement of six; and a quarter of its other ranks The Company was awarded seven DCMs for its actions on 11 November, a record for a small unit. Collins achieved fame when, at the age of 13, in a housematch at Clifton College in 1899, he

AEJ Collins, pictured soon after achieving his extraordinary batting score.

129

scored 628 not out. The record was only beaten in 2016 (by a 15 year-old in Bombay).

Reserve Leutnant Henderkott, commanding 3rd Company Footguard Regiment 3 and who received the Iron Cross First Class for his performance that day, wrote a detailed account of what happened on this part of the battlefield from the attackers' perspective.

During the day we had sufficient observation over the ground to our front to be able to take the correct decisions. Immediately to the front of the company was a damp meadow overlooked by the enemy. Beyond that, at a distance of about 150 metres, were individual houses, gardens and a stack of straw. The crossing of this meadow would certainly have cost heavy casualties so, during the night, I had a communication trench dug which was to spare us the necessity. The night 10/11 was very dark, the ground was mostly clay, so no noise was made and, by between 2.00 and 3.00 am, the trench was complete. During the 11th and 12th it was used by almost all advancing supports. At 7.30 am, during the artillery preparation, I stood together with Hauptmann von Hahnke of Footguard Regiment 1 at the corner of a wood and agreed the precise axis of advance. At 8.45 am, under cover of thick smoke from the heavy artillery barrage, I entered the communication trench with the 1st and 2nd Platoons of my company. At 9.00 am precisely, the 3rd Platoon went over the top, led from the front by the platoon and section commanders.

For about fifty metres they were not under fire, but then they were hit by small arms fire, which caused many casualties. Firing from the garden hedges, camouflaged by web-like festoons of grey string and daubed with clay, barely visible, were hidden machine guns, which mowed down the attacking troops. Looking back at my company I saw that those on the left flank were still pushing forward, despite being under machine gun fire. I and the troops behind me closed in on the flank of the machine guns and were able to assault and capture two of them. The crews went on firing to the last minute and several courageous men fell victim to their lead when they were within a few metres of the death-dealing weapons. As we continued to storm forward, we caught fleeting glimpses of the small gardens, noting that they had all been turned into miniature fortresses by the digging of trenches and small fire positions. We were up against tough enemies, big strapping Scotsmen – Scots Guards who, despite the lateness of the season, were fighting in their characteristic uniforms with bare knees and thighs. This caused my batman to shout, 'Leutnant! There are women there!' They fought on to the last, but soon were lying on the ground dead or seriously wounded.

However there was yet another position to the rear occupied by the enemy; a hail of deadly lead claimed more victims. It was now essential to pull together all the men who were taking cover behind garden hedges or folds in the ground and beginning to dig in and, instead, set about clearing the final section of trenches. The task was not as difficult as the first because my 3rd Platoon and 2nd Company had come up on our right and were beginning to roll up the trenches from right to left. We did the same thing from left to right and so dealt with the enemy infantry. To my left I saw other men disappear behind a hedge whilst to my front was a lengthy stretch of open meadowland leading forward into the wood. In attempting to avoid the open section and to gain the wood to our half left, we came under artillery fire, which forced us to take cover in a patch of low scrub. I still had about fifteen men with me. To our right I saw many of the men of our 2nd Company who had been cut down. The enemy artillery fire began to have an ever greater effect on us and soon some of the men with me were blown apart by direct hits, as the scrub was too low and offered insufficient cover.

When the heavy artillery fire began to ease somewhat, I attempted to find out what was to my left and right. In this, Cyclist Kalisch, who had acted as an absolutely fearless runner to me all day, distinguished himself by crawling to the left under enemy fire along what remained of a trench and establishing that there was nobody to our left but, off to the right, there were about thirty men, mostly from 2nd Company. I linked up with these men and saw that they were all united in their unshakeable determination to hold on to the position at all costs. In the meantime I failed, despite despatching runners, to make contact with those in rear, so I decided to go back myself, accompanied by two men and to seek reinforcements. We succeeded; I came across a platoon of 1st Company in the communication trench and had them guided forward by Kalisch under cover of the gathering darkness. Further on I found the commander of 10th Company and had him agree to send forward one of his platoons. With the aid of these supports the former British trench was held and consolidated.

Henderkott was wrong about his opponents. The Scots Guards did not wear kilts. The defenders must have been either Cameron Highlanders or, possibly, men of the Black Watch. Regardless of who was responsible for this precise part of the defence, the cost of this battle was enormous – for both attackers and defenders. As the fighting died down, Major von Goerne, commanding 1st Battalion Footguard Regiment 1, together with most of his men, was pinned down in No Man's Land, unable to move. He managed, however, to send a message back which underlines some of the problems the Guards faced that day: 'I am out here with 4th Company and six machine guns. I am unclear as to the situation to my front because all contact has been lost with Leib, 2nd and 3rd Companies. Where is the 2nd Battalion? Where is Footguard Regiment 3? Runners whom I have despatched to the three companies appear to have been killed. Leutnant von Busse has just been killed and Leutnant von Trotha slightly wounded in the head.'

Prinz Eitel Friedrich was quite unable to offer the necessary assistance Goerne needed. His 3rd Battalion had still not been re-subordinated to him, whilst the battalion of Grenadier Guard Regiment 2, tasked, it will be recalled, with bridging the inter-brigade gap, came under such heavy fire during its march forward that hardly any of its men reached the front line at all and those who did were completely disorganised and disorientated. There was nothing else for it; the troops caught out in the open simply had to remain in cover and wait for the dark before pulling back to their start lines. In addition, as the day wore on, increasing British pressure forced more and more of the Guardsmen back from the high water mark of their attack. All they could do was to cling to whatever cover they could and stand by to repel any British counter attacks.

This was a sensible precaution, because it seems as though Brigadier General FitzClarence, commanding 1 (Guards) Brigade had some such operation in mind, following the recapture of Nonne Bosschen by 2/ Ox & Bucks. In the event lack of reserves and the risk to the advancing troops from German enfilade flanking fire once they moved into the open ground forward of the wood ruled any such thing out. Brigadier General FitzClarence did all he could to organise counter action. He was determined to get his front line trenches back. He effectively had no Brigade left, so moved to Westmacott's HQ at the north west corner of Polygon Wood at about 5 pm. The agreed plan was that 2/Ox & Bucks would launch a surprise attack, without artillery support, at 9 pm from the area of Black Watch Corner southwards down the length of the German trenches. But it was pitch dark and raining; the attack was postponed until there should be some moonlight and was timed for 1.00 am. When FitzClarence got back to his HQ he found that Landon had given him command of 2/Grenadiers, the Irish Guards and some Royal Munster Fusiliers (RMF), a total of just under 500 men. He informed

Davies at about 11 pm that he would attack with these troops in conjunction with the Ox & Bucks.

However, Davies examined the ground before the attack, accompanied by the brigade major (the operations staff officer) of 5 Brigade. They discovered that the Germans had dug a new trench behind the old British one; thus any attack down the British line would be enfiladed, at almost point blank range, from the new German line. Besides, the ground was in an appalling state, churned up by shells and then turned into a quagmire by the torrential rain of the late afternoon. Finally, no one was completely sure where the left flank of Shaw's Group actually ended. Davies decided against the move, a decision with which Westmacott agreed. The Ox & Bucks headed back to their Nonne Bosschen position; between 2.00 and 3.00 pm they bumped into FitzClarence, leading his attack group of 2/Grenadiers and Irish Guards, formed in columns of four. The old war horse was determined to have his attack; but before they could reach their start area at Black Watch Corner, FitzClarence was mortally wounded by a bullet whilst going forward to reconnoitre. Once more the operation was cancelled. Writing subsequently about his death, Prinz Eitel Friedrich stated, 'He was an opponent before whom we dip our swords in respectful salute'.

Unteroffizier Quest, 2nd Company Footguard Regiment 1, who was one of the few men to survive the fighting unscathed, left this description of the events of the day from his perspective.

At precisely 9.00 am a whistle blast signalled the start of the attack. As one man we left our trenches at the double, charging forward hard up behind the Leib and the 4th Companies. The first assault wave protected us initially to some extent from the enemy fire. However, once we had covered one hundred metres and were hard up against the British trenches, we were greeted with lacerating machine gun fire. Many of our dear comrades sacrificed their lives for the Fatherland at this point. Because the Leib and 4th Companies had already captured the British front line trenches, we were able, together with the Leib, to clear the second trench. To begin with we were taken aback by the sight of the Scots in their extraordinary uniform of short pleated knee length skirts and thought that we must have women to our front. When it transpired that these were obstinate fighters and excellent shots, in order to protect ourselves, we had to capture the trenches out to the sides. This did not produce many prisoners.

In the meantime our ranks were thinned very considerably. Those who remained stormed forward against the third line of trenches. To have attempted to have pressed on any further would have been in vain because, on a front of twenty to thirty metres, there were only two of us left. Over to my left was my pal, Unteroffizier Göbels. We had to strain every sinew to obtain cover from view because the enemy was manning a hedge only about thirty metres away. All we could do was to press ourselves flat on the ground and attempt to scrabble away with fingers and toes as best we could. We had reasonable quantities of ammunition with us, so we laid it out in front of us so that we should be able to respond effectively in the event of a counter-attack.

Any movement from us was enough to unleash a hail of fire from the British. By now it was 1.00 pm and Göbels called across to me, 'I am going to see what the Tommies are up to'. Raising himself upright, he was hit with an enemy bullet in the head. His loss was a heavy blow to me. Now I lay completely alone, with no contact either to the right or the left. Almost simultaneously my bayonet was shot off my rifle and the weapon itself was damaged. My mess tins had already suffered similarly and bore several holes. My comrade's rifle now had to render me further good service. This unforgettable Monday afternoon seemed to stretch out to eternity. A counter attack could be expected at any moment and there were absolutely no reserves on hand. Eventually the ammunition had all been fired and slowly the longed for evening began to fall. Once it was dark I was able to crawl away from my position in order to link up once more. In the late evening I arrived back in the second trench which we had attacked and there we established a weak defensive line.

During the evening of 11 November Major von Goerne of Footguard Regiment 1 assumed command of all the troops in the area then, by combining remaining elements of his own 1st and 2nd Battalions, men from Grenadier Guard Regiment 2 and Footguard Regiment 3, he organised a thin line of resistance, supplemented by six machine guns, more or less where the original British Second Line had been. It was an extremely difficult night. Not only had the men had to endure a very hard day of battle, the winter weather was terrible. Rain came down in sheets, gathering in the hollows, shell holes and trenches and making conditions for the wounded in particular, quite appalling. First aiders worked throughout the night, but many men of both sides succumbed to their wounds before they could be helped.

Despite this, there were claims subsequently that morale had held up well, but it is sure that the loss to Footguard Regiment 1 alone of almost

800 officers and men killed, wounded or missing took its toll. Prinz Eitel Friedrich, summing up the battle of 11 November 1914, wrote, 'Ypres was the end of the peacetime regiment'. This same sentiment could of course be applied to almost every regiment of either side engaged in this desperate fighting. As a presage of things to come, the First Battle of Ypres ended in mud and ghastly conditions: hard frost, snow on the 18th, a snow storm on the 19th – six hours of it – and a snow laden landscape on the 20th. Officially the battle did not end until the 13th (for the French), the 20th (for the British) and the 30th (for the Germans).

The ruins of Veldhoek after the battle was over.

Not that the defenders knew it, but here between Veldhoek and Polygon Wood the last major attack of the First Battle of Ypres had been fought and lost by the Prussian Guards. The attacks had been pressed home with gallantry and aggression, but the battered defenders had shown themselves equal to the challenge. A small and not very significant area of ground had been captured, along with numerous British prisoners but, as has been emphasised previously, the plan was flawed, its execution deficient in many ways and the result was a splintering of the action into small group battles that favoured the defence. Nevertheless, the thrust into Nonne Bosschen could have spelt disaster for the defence had the German fire support not faltered, then failed and had not a few courageous British troops hung on while Footguard Regiments 1 and 3 were brought under direct fire over open sights by the guns of XLI Brigade and 35th Heavy Battery Royal Artillery. By such narrow margins are great battles decided and, luckily for the Allies, the Guards were checked then halted a full four kilometres from the town of Ypres.

There was more localised fighting in the area of the Menin Road, some of it severe (for example, on 13 and 14 November, around Herenthage Chateau), but the great German gamble had failed (and so, it

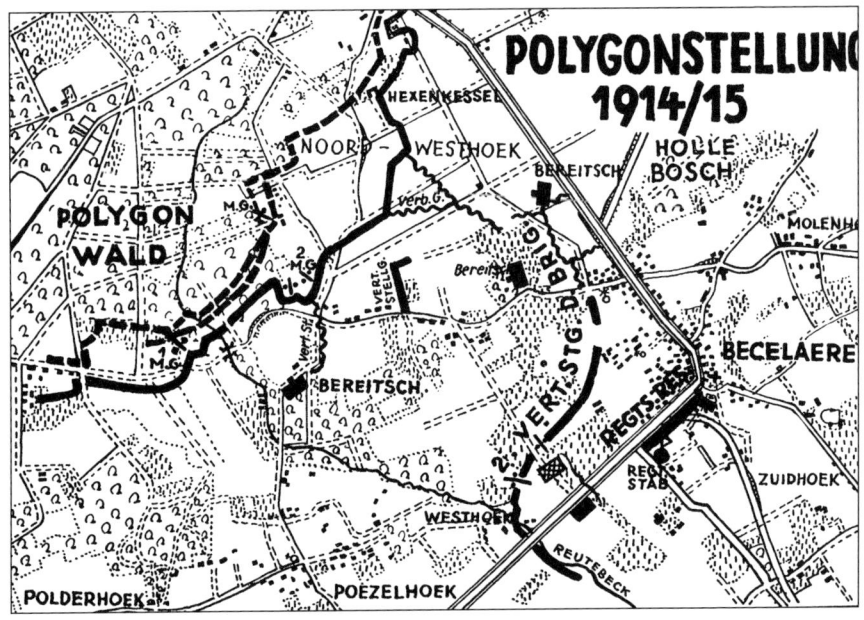

The German front line, Polygon Wood sector, in the winter of 1914/15.

has to be said, had the attempted allied breakout, launched with such high hopes on 20 October). Fiercer fighting took place further to the south, in the area of Klein Zillebeke and Hill 60. However, from 15 November onwards I Corps was gradually withdrawn from the line and the BEF was reorganised.

By 22 November all British troops were out of the Ypres Salient and the BEF now held a line from Givenchy, on the La Bassée Canal, to west of Wytschaete so, throughout the winter of 1914/15 the Ypres Salient, which later became inextricably linked with the sacrifice and exploits of the BEF, was actually an exclusively Franco-German battlefield.

Menin Road Tours Section

General Advice for Tourers:

Traditionally this has been a different section at the beginning of each of the *Battleground Europe* books; this is much less full. The series is some twenty-five years old. British motorists nowadays generally have far more experience of driving abroad and all that entails. The almost universal availability of the internet and much improved web sites (with more sophisticated search engines), from tourist office level down to individual gîtes, means that details about differing types of accommodation and other useful information is both readily available and up to date. A number of free web sites, such as that of the Western Front Association, the Great War Forum and the Long Long Trail also provide tips or provide answers to questions posed on line that usually result in very helpful responses. Since the series began the website of the CWGC has both come into existence become increasingly versatile and so the detailed cemetery section has been substantially reduced; there is a separate tour offered to the German cemetery in Menen and particular mention is made of several CWGC cemeteries, some of which will be encountered during the tours, where there are a significant number of 1914 casualties.

Some general pointers include:

• Ensure that your car insurance is fully valid (this particularly applies to comprehensive insurance); that you take out appropriate personal insurance and that you have your European Health Insurance Card. Bear in mind that even though the arrangement is reciprocal that there might well be charges in both Belgium and France that are not applicable under the NHS.

• Ensure that your vehicle is equipped with all the mandatory items: spare light bulbs; fluorescent vests for driver and all passengers (best to have them in the car rather than in the boot); breathalyzers (France – though the legal situation is fluid at the moment); warning triangles; small fire extinguishers; etc., etc. Rules change, so it would be as well to check on the AA website or equivalent for the most recent regulations. Similarly, keep up to date with regulations for the transportation of animals from the UK and back; if you are bringing a pet, the Euroshuttle is the least stressful method to get across the Channel.

• Have your passport with you. The drink drive limit is substantially less than that in the UK.

• And, of course, it is far from clear where matters will rest a year from now as regards travel requirements, so keep a close out for advisories from the AA or RAC – and check well in advance of your trip.

Menin Road 1914 Tours

The biggest advantage that tourers of the battlefields of Ypres 1914 have over their colleagues tracing events on the ground in the Salient in subsequent years is that the ground then was still largely undamaged, whilst the villages and woods were clearly recognizable. Certainly there are far fewer hedges, some small woods have disappeared, others are smaller and some are probably thicker and with more mature trees; whilst agricultural practices have changed. But there is no need to try and imagine the featureless, shattered, fouled ground of subsequent years.

For ease of navigation the modern Flemish form of the place names is usually used throughout this section – sometimes it makes more sense to follow the wartime usage; if there is any doubt about a place name in the text and its modern equivalent, the former is also given at first use. Note that there are radar traps and speed cameras all over the place in West Flanders, so it is prudent to observe all speed limits; the motorway maximum is 120 kph in Belgium and many villages and towns have areas with a 30 kph limit, especially near schools, churches and hospitals. 'Sleeping policemen' are common and can have quite a vicious bump.

A few key points.
These tours we regard as car/bike tours unless specifically stated otherwise. However, some of them are short enough to be walked by the fit and the committed. Any tour of a battlefield on foot leads to a better appreciation of the ground, but time and other factors often makes this impracticable. Not one of the tours in its entirety (and most not at all) is practicable for a coach – a minibus is probably the maximum sized vehicle and even then, with the bigger ones, there are likely to be issues. Before using a bus for a tour, therefore, we strongly urge that a reconnaissance be carried out.

In 1914 both sides were operating from very small scale maps – often 1:100,000; for example, contemporary positions are often reported in terms such as a 'quarter of an inch under the 'o' of Veldhoek'. The *BOH* and other sketch maps are good general indicators, but a certain amount of tactical military wisdom will indicate where particular positions were likely to have been.

The majority of these tours will take even regular battlefield visitors to areas that may well be new to them, covering parts of the Salient that were to see very little of the BEF after 1914 except in the later stages of the Battle of Third Ypres and from late September 1918.

Many of these tours are over minor roads – often negotiable by two passing cars only with difficulty. Obviously, cars should not block roads and entrances to farms and the like; nor should drivers move far from their car if use is made of the passing places that are a feature of some of the roads as a stopping/viewing area.

Field walking is something not to be encouraged; the nature of farming here and the type of soil are against it for one, whilst farmers tend to be less tolerant of people roaming over their land than in some other parts of the Western Front, even when there are no crops on them at the time. Generally speaking you can get close to most points because of the dense nature of the road system. If you have some special reason for wanting to get to a particular spot, then our strong advice is to ask first; on the other hand, our experience is that local farmers for the most part speak only Flemish.

The time of year of your tour is important; the tours are generally in rich agricultural areas, which brings advantages and disadvantages. There are many small, narrow roads, with minimal road signs; there are often deep ditches running alongside (hazardous especially in the winter, but also in any slippery conditions). Maize is grown widely, a problem not faced by the armies in the autumn of 1914 as it was a crop not commonly grown in Europe until the thirties, meaning that views are often blocked and some roads seem to be passing through a small Amazonian jungle, with zero visibility on either side of the road. On balance, the best touring periods are likely to be late March to mid June; and mid August to early September. However, the cultivation of cereals is far less prevalent compared to the Somme, for example, so that June and July might also be practicable. The winter months – ie mid November onwards, once the maize is gone – are also good; but beware mud from the tractors, as the harvesting of beet in particular seems to encourage a transplant of it from the fields to the roads. You will find the fields more or less clear of obstructing growth, whilst the negative side includes the greater risks on the roads themselves, the shorter daylight hours and of course adverse weather conditions and the cold.

Over the centenary years there have been some changes in facilities – for example, new car parking at Polygon Wood, near the new Black Watch Corner memorial and at its north eastern end (near the two CWGC cemeteries there). Major expansion work has been undertaken at the excellent Passchendaele Museum in Zonnebeke.

The Belgian authorities seem to have a particular way of dealing with road closures relating to utilities or perhaps road improvements or refurbishment. The overwhelming tendency is to close off a road completely – for example, whilst on an initial recce for these tours in October 2012: the Menin Road was blocked at Geluveld (a diversion for smaller vehicles only took you through the village); the Menin Gate was blocked to traffic; Beselare was blocked to heavy vehicles, with a circuitous diversion for the rest; the Dixmuide to Ypres road was blocked for several kilometres of its length; the road past the Zonnebeke Musuem was closed; Messines had been effectively cut off, we were told, for some eighteen months, at that time; and so on.

We strongly recommend that you try and lay your hands on at least the modern 1:50,000 maps that cover these tours; and a satnav set on 'view map' was invaluable during our touring. Alas, these larger scale maps are not very readily available, in our experience; the *In Flanders Fields* museum bookshop usually has some at 1:20,000 and 1:50,000, but it cannot be guaranteed that they will have them. The relevant 1:50,000 maps for this book are IEPER 27-28-36 (this one alone would suffice) and ROESELARE 19-20. These should be adequate – and are, quite frankly, easier to read than the bigger scale 1:20,000 maps. Google Earth's capabilities are also helpful for planning the visit.

The focus of this book is 1914; inevitably the routes will take you past numerous memorials and cemeteries relating to other periods of the war. Generally speaking we do not talk about these unless we are using them to assist with the navigation. As regards museums, there are several in the Salient and we mention them where applicable; if you have plenty of time or are enduring a rainy morning or afternoon, we would particularly recommend the Memorial Museum Passchendaele in Zonnebeke Chateau. It is within a five minute detour on Tour 2. Some of the museums have a philosophy that they wish to put across, some simply have an exhibit (some better labelled than others), some have trenches; each has their merits and all are worthy of a visit.

The CWGC website is now a powerful search tool. We do not include a long stand alone cemetery section (though there is a listing in the cemetery section of CWGC cemeteries with a number of 1914 burials), in part because of the website; but some cemeteries that you will pass in the relevant tour are discussed, even if only to advise that there are 1914 burials in them.

The Salient is well equipped with potential eateries; or, at least, is better in that respect than some areas of the old British front line. There is a small supermarket on the Menen Road, a few hundred metres on the left (and more or less opposite the south eastern entrance to the Town Cemetery) not far from the traffic lights and the left turn that will take you under the Menin Gate. The usual recommendations are made about

The debris of war, found near the site of Polderhoek Chateau.

'The Harvest of Iron' by the side of a field.

what kit would be useful, notably a notebook, wet weather gear and boots (plus a bag to store them in when you return to the car, thus avoiding spreading more mud than you have to inside it). Several of the churches have individually recognizable spires or towers that are invaluable for placing yourself on the battlefield. The area is, generally, in quite open countryside, often offering distant views, and so a good pair of binoculars would be an asset.

And, finally, there is the matter of munitions, which can still be found in some abundance, particularly when there has been ploughing or harvesting. Leave them alone.

Tour One:

Geluveld North and Northeast:
the German Approaches

The German cemetery at Langemark – Poelkapelle –
Westrozebeke – Passendale – Moorslede – Keiberg – Beselare

See also maps on pages 12, 14, 20 and 22.

This tour covers both the approach routes of the forces that attacked from Langemark to Geluveld and also the various ridge lines that had to be captured before the assault astride the Menin Road could be launched. Considerably more detail about this area is to be found in *Langemarck* in this series.

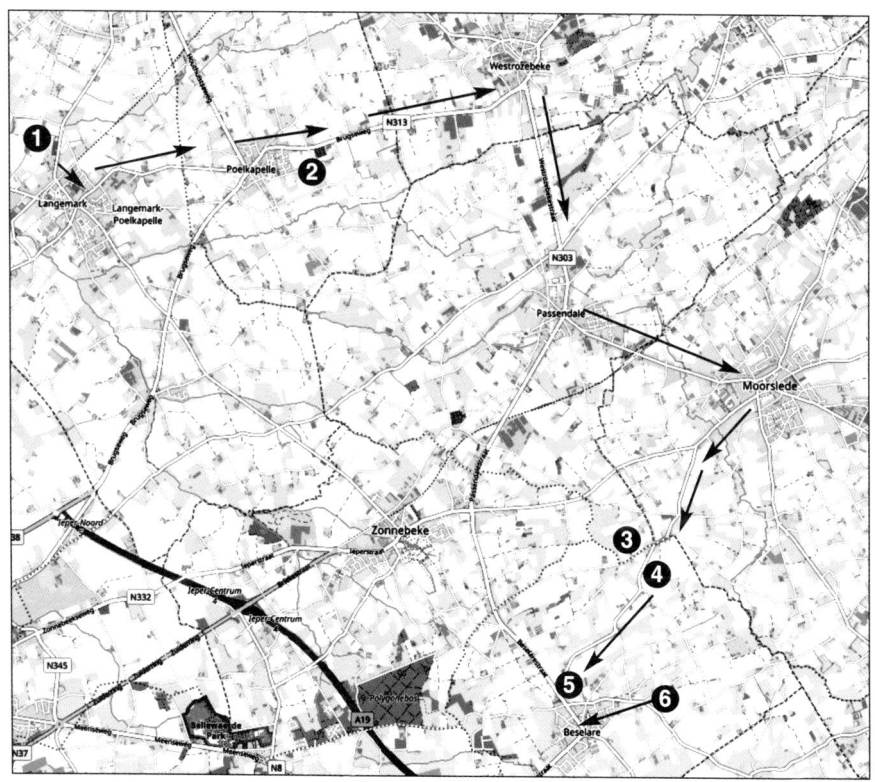

Tour MAP 1.

It begins **(1)** in the car park of the **German cemetery**, so this is an ideal opportunity to visit it and pay your respects at the graves of some who fell in the battle for the Menin Road in 1914. Because Langemarck was the focus of so much fighting throughout the war, by the time of the armistice there were numerous temporary front line cemeteries and individual burials dotted all over the area. Over the next few years the Belgian war graves authorities concentrated many of these burials in a new site located right on a former front line, as the presence of several old blockhouses within the cemetery limits testifies. A linkage between German students and the cemetery was established early in the interwar period as the *Kindermord* [Massacre of the Innocents] legend gained ground in Germany. This was underlined further when, on 10 July 1932, during the dedication of the cemetery, the President of the Association of German students was handed the key to the main gate and symbolically assumed responsibility for its care and maintenance. A speech made that day by the playwright and poet, not to mention dyed-in-the-wool Nazi, Josef Magnus Wehner, together with selected letters by students who fell in battle, were later published and printed by the tens of thousands. Its overblown language was intended to forge a link between the dead and the living as a driving force in German renewal and as a means of inspiring current and future generations to sacrifices comparable with that of the men of Langemarck 1914.

The imposing entrance is built of sandstone from the Weser Hills of North Rhine Westphalia and the hall is lined with oak panels that bear the names of the original 6,313 officers and men known at that time to be buried there. Further massive concentrations after the Second World War meant that the cemetery then housed the remains of an additional 10,000 identified soldiers and, initially, 21,000 unknowns, though many have since been identified. Of the current total of 44,296 burials, almost 25,000 are in the *Kamaradengraben* (mass grave). The names of those known (or believed) to be buried in it are recorded on sixty eight metal tablets. The individual burials are marked with stones of Belgian granite. The statues of the four grieving soldiers opposite the entrance are the work of the sculptor Professor Emil Krieger, from Munich. The design is based on a photograph of men of Reserve Infantry Regiment 238 attending the funeral of a fallen comrade in 1918.

The view through the entrance door to Langemark German Cemetery.

The mass grave in the German cemetery at Langemark.

The following names of men known to have fallen during the early battles of 1914 (and including many who fell in actions described in the two other volumes in this trilogy) is of course highly selective and biased towards officers, because the names of other ranks who were killed in action are only rarely recorded in the regimental histories. However, it is an interesting and sobering exercise to tour the cemetery and pick out the names on the tablets. It will take some time but, at the end of it, you will be left with a profound sense of the appalling cost of this war.

Kamaradengraben:

Leutnant Joseph Brenner 11th Company Bavarian Reserve Infantry Regiment 16 KIA Gheluvelt 30 October.

Hauptmann Georg Danner 3rd Company Bavarian Reserve Infantry Regiment 17 KIA Wijtschate 1 November.

Reserve Oberleutnant Adolf Eckermann 3rd Battalion Grenadier Guard Regiment 2 KIA near Veldhoek 11 November.

Oberleutnant Ernst Grimsehl 8th Company Reserve Infantry Regiment 213. KIA near Weidendrift 30 October. Known as 'Papa', Grimsehl was in his fifties when he volunteered for front line service. A physicist and technical school headmaster in civilian life, he had already been awarded an Iron Cross Second Class at the time of his death.

Hauptmann Erich Grüttner 5th Company Reserve Infantry Regiment 19 KIA southwest of Poelkapelle 10 November.

Landwehr Oberleutnant Theodor Harster 6th Company Bavarian Reserve Infantry Regiment 17 KIA Wijtschate 1 November.

Leutnant Anton Halder Bavarian Reserve Infantry Regiment 17 KIA Wijtschate 1 November.

LIST JULIUS OBERST †31.10.1914

Oberst Julius List.

Oberst Julius List Commander Bavarian Reserve Infantry Regiment 16 KIA Gheluvelt 31 October. (And so, alas, he was not to spend his time 'for all eternity' in his original resting place, as described on p 80-81.)

Reserve Leutnant Alois Otto 4th Company Reserve Infantry Regiment 19 KIA southwest of Poelkapelle 10 November.

Reserve Leutnant Friedrich Redecker Infantry Regiment 143 KIA near Herenthage Wood 5 November.

Leutnant Michael Sacherl Bavarian Reserve Infantry Regiment 17 KIA Wijtschate 1 November.

Leutnant Rudolf Schuster Bavarian Reserve Infantry Regiment 17 KIA Wijtschate 1 November.

Oberleutnant Ernst Schröder 7th Company Reserve Infantry Regiment 235 KIA rallying his men near Poelkapelle 21 October.

Leutnant Karl Freiherr [Baron] Spiegel von und zu Peckenheim Footguard Regiment 1 KIA near Veldhoek 11 November.

Vizefeldwebel Hasso Sobbe KIA near Poelkapelle 7 November. A reservist, recalled to the army on the outbreak of war, in civilian life, Sobbe was secretary to a district court in Erxleben, north of Magdeburg.

Leutnant Hermann von Zitzewitz 4th Company Reserve Infantry Regiment 234 KIA near Langemark 30 October.

Individual graves:

Hauptmann Ulrich Dabis, Commanding Officer 1st Battalion Reserve Infantry Regiment 205 KIA just east of the Ijzer 11 November. *Block A Grave 1277.*

Hauptmann Arthur Dehrmann, Commanding Officer 2nd Battalion Reserve Infantry Regiment 211 DOW received near Bikschote 23 October. *Block A Grave 2923.*

Offizierstellvertreter Max Hacker, 9th Company Bavarian Reserve Infantry Regiment 8 KIA Wijtschate 1 November. The Volksbund gives his date of death incorrectly as 31 October. *Block B Grave 13118.*

Oberleutnant Helmuth Harder Reserve Infantry Regiment 211 KIA near Bikschote 30 October. *Block A Grave 1441.*

Oberleutnant Ludwig Hieronimus, 4th Company Reserve Infantry Regiment 240 KIA near Broodseinde 22 October. *Block B Grave 13294.*

Oberstleutnant Magnus von Holleben, Commander Reserve Infantry Regiment 244 KIA at Polygon Woofd23 October. *Block B Grave 13098.*

Offizierstellvertreter Walter Huth Reserve Infantry Regiment 211 KIA near Bikschote 30 October. *Block A Grave 3351.*

Offizierstellvertreter Wilhelm Mackprang 8th Company Reserve Infantry Regiment 213 KIA near Weidendrift 30 October. *Block A Grave 2838.*

146

Leutnant Horst Münzer, Regimental Adjutant Reserve Infantry Regiment 211 KIA near Bikschote 30 October. *Block A Grave 3141.*

Feldwebelleutnant Karl Nausester Reserve Jäger Battalion 16 KIA near Steenstraat 10 November. *Block A Grave 1281.*

Hauptmann Ernst Schröter, commander 5th Company Reserve Infantry Regiment 235, KIA charging forward ahead of his men east of Langemark on 21 October. *Block B Grave 16564.*

Offizierstellvertreter Hugo Spannaus 7th Company Reserve Infantry Regiment 52 KIA near Langemark 3 November. *Block A Grave 5256.*

Leutnant Hans Voss 7th Company Reserve Infantry Regiment 52 KIA near Langemark 3 November. *Block A Grave 1811.*

From the car park turn right and drive into the centre of Langemark and then turn left at the traffic lights, signposted Poelkapelle and Roeselare. There are extensive views left and right of this road on the approaches to Poelkapelle. At the Guynemer roundabout, take the road to Westrozebeke, signposted Roeselare, Staden and Westrozebeke 4. This section of the tour is important because almost all troops involved in attacks on Langemark from the east moved along this grossly overcrowded road. Today it is a broad, high speed route, but in 1914 it was narrow and probably cobbled. March times of up to six hours for the four kilometres were common.

Exiting the town (keep right at a fork, but this is the main road still) and after several hundred yards you will arrive, on the right, at **Poelcapelle British Cemetery (2)**. This has about thirty 1914 burials, so provides an opportunity to visit, remembering to park at the first corner of the cemetery, not by the entrance, where there is no suitable space. The CWGC database can be interrogated quite simply to give you all the locations of identified 1914 burials: see the cemeteries section in this book.

Arriving at an oversized roundabout on the outskirts of Westrozebeke, turn right towards Zonnebeke, signposted to Passchendaele New Military and Tyne Cot Cemeteries. At Passendale proceed to the centre of the village and turn left after the church, signposted 11 Roeselare, 3 Moorslede. Drive southeast, crossing the line of the old Ieper – Roeselare railway and arrive at Moorslede. It was at Moorslede that General von Carlowitz (GOC XXVII Reserve Corps) issued his extraordinarily optimistic order of 20 October, informing his subordinate officers that by that evening a new line, '… Poperinghe – Dickebusch is to be secured. Orders group tonight in the town hall at Ypres'. Head towards the church and, at a roundabout before it, having passed on your right an impressive school building, complete with large chapel, turn right, signposted Dadizele, Menen and Kortrijk. After a short distance along this road turn right onto Ieperstraat, signposted Zonnebeke, Beselare and Ieper.

A little over a kilometre along this road, as the buildings of the town begin to thin out, bear left at a fork/mini roundabout by a crucifix, onto Werviksestraat, signposted Wervik and Beselare. Head up the rise for

The view from Keiberg Ridge looking west.

about 1300 metres onto the high ground of the Keiberg Ridge (entering the village the road bends quite sharply to the right and when exiting it bends left, as well as changing name to Markizaatstraat). Just before taking the left hand bend and exiting the village, there is a road that carries straight on. It is narrow and can be surprisingly busy, but stop where you can and admire the view to the west **(3)** and to Zonnebeke. As late as 27 October there were, to the west, in the valley towards Zonnebeke, British troops this far east, with men of 6 Brigade (2nd Division) occupying ground as part of a French advance; it was in this fighting that Prince Maurice of Battenberg, a grandson of Queen Victoria, was killed – he is buried in Ypres Town Cemetery.

Find a suitable spot to turn around and rejoin the main road, turning right. As soon as possible stop **(4),** cross the road and take in the view towards Beselare, which stands on the next ridge, and the approaches to the town from its east.

The view from Keiberg Ridge looking south-west.

It was here that the men of Reserve Infantry Regiments 241 and 243 of 53rd Reserve Division first came under fire on 20 October as they attempted to take and consolidate this important feature. An eyewitness from Reserve Infantry Regiment 243 later wrote:

On your feet! Double march! and the men doubled across the fields, disappearing in amongst the tall leaves of the beet fields. 'Whizz … Crack! … Crack!' Strange whirrings, interspersed with sounds like whips cracking could be heard as the enemy rifle bullets cut through the air. Ricochets buzzed overhead, the bullets deflected from their paths as they hit solid objects in the hedges. Involuntarily we ducked and weaved with every unusual sound, though the bullets themselves had long since disappeared beyond us. It became darker then, all of a sudden, came shouts of Hurra! What had happened? The first prisoners had been captured. It was men of 7th Company, under Leutnant Sellnick and Feldwebel Möller, who had succeeded in snatching a British seven man patrol and bringing it in triumphantly. Stray bullets still cracked through the air as the night wore on. Brigade ordered that the regiment was to pull back to Keiberg Mill and go firm there, so we assembled as best we could after this first clash with the enemy. We had received our baptism of fire at Keiberg Mill.

After about two and a half kilometres you will arrive at a main road, the N303, the Broodseinde road crossroads, turn left. As you head in towards the centre of the town, within a few metres you will come to another crossroads **(5)** – you will be taking the one on your right almost at the start of the next tour. The road on your left goes to what is now a suburb of Beselare, but the area retains the name of Molenhoek: the events described below took place there and in the area of this crossroad.

Men of Reserve Infantry Regiment 243 manning positions along the Becelaere-Broodseinde road, October 1914.

The car marks the crossroads at the northern end of Beselare, the scene of a rearguard action by the BEF on 20 October.

Today Beselare is a peaceful, tranquil town. On 20 October, when it was captured by elements of RIRs 245 and 246 of 54th Reserve Division, it was anything but. A Kriegsfreiwilliger of 1st Company Reserve Infantry Regiment 246 left a vivid account of his experiences here.

We pushed up close behind the withdrawing British advance guard and moved via Moelenhoek to the northern tip of Beselare, which we reached unscathed. All was deadly quiet in the village. Pressing myself against the wall of a building by the side of the road and with my rifle at the ready, I moved towards the cross roads, coming across the body of a fallen German cavalryman, whose body blocked the clean, cobbled pavement to me. Just as I was going to step over him, I noticed the single shot to his forehead. At that moment shots rang out from all sides, the shock blotting out all sight and sound to me. Cracks, whistling and roaring sounds filled the air, together with the clatter of falling roofing tiles and clouds of dust from the broken ones. There was a main British position a few hundred metres to the west and from there they had suddenly brought down a hellish rate of fire against us.

What was to be done? Answer: a swift withdrawal to the entrance to the village and take cover in a ditch. Just then a group of soldiers rushed up from Molenhoek, urged on by shouts from the tall figure of Oberst Roschmann in their midst. In quick time we pushed back into Beselare, beyond the cross roads and into a field of tobacco which adjoined the village. There we dug in as quickly as possible. The 3rd Battalion, moving in column with 300 metre intervals, followed this advance party along the line of track which ran southwest about 600 metres east of Molenhoek towards

The magnificent parish church in Beselare.

Beselare Church early in the war.

Beselare church. The battalion had tried in vain to make contact with General[Leutnant] *von* Reinhardt [Commander 107 Reserve Infantry Brigade, killed in action 22 October], *so the advance was continued without fresh orders through the southern portion of Beselare, as far as the southwest exit, which was under heavy enemy artillery fire and was still unoccupied by our troops.*

The tour ends at Beselare church **(6)**, a couple of hundred metres down the road; it would be sensible to turn left immediately after the church and when the main road bends to the right. There is plenty of parking by the church and there is parking opposite it as well. This marks the end of this tour.

Tour Two:

The Eastern Approaches and the Northern Battlefield

Beselare – Reutel – Circuit of Polygon Wood – De Veldhoek – Reutel – Vijverbos – Geluveld

See also maps on pages 14, 20, 22, 26, 27, 31, 42, 43, 76, 83 and 92.

In common with the other tours, this one aims to allow the visitor to get a grasp of the nature of the terrain fought over for the best part of a month in October-November 1914. Reference to the various maps in the main body of the text will allow the visitor to follow at least some of the numerous actions that took place during this period.

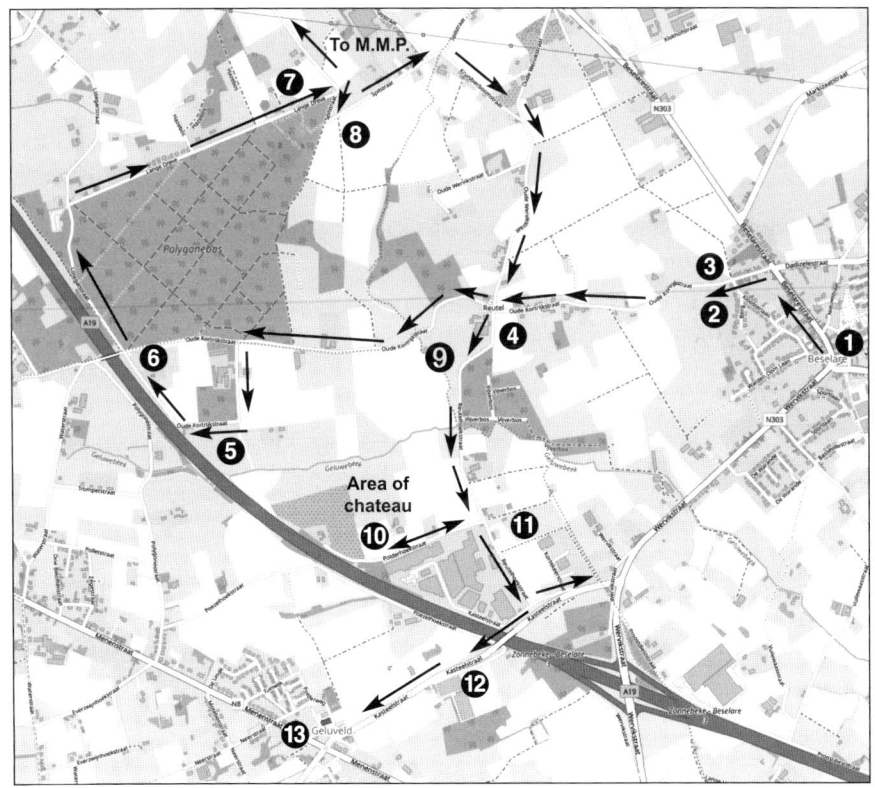

The eastern approaches and the northern battlefield.

153

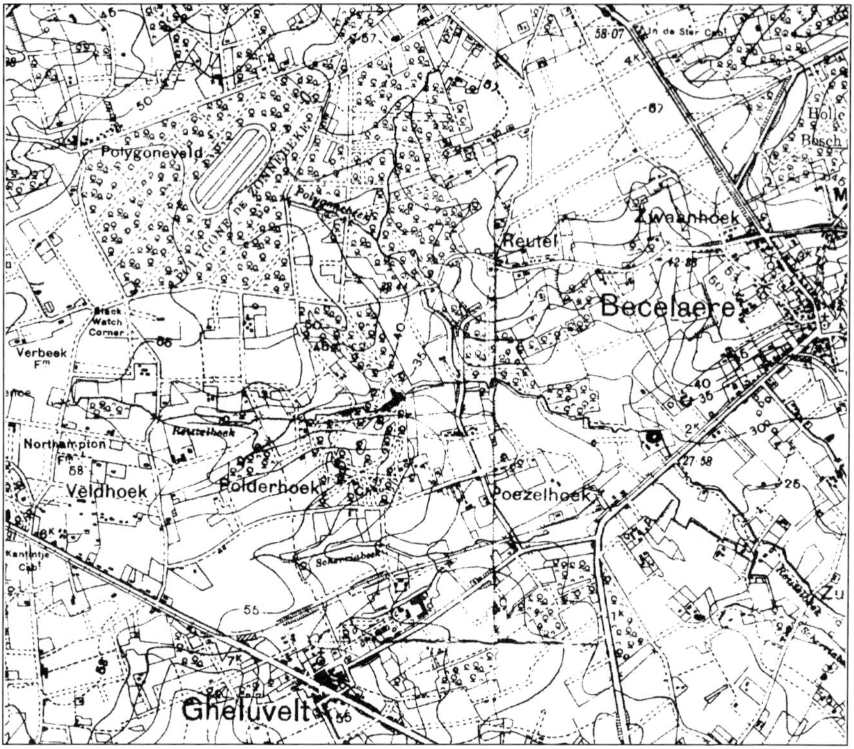

A map of the same area as it was at the time of the outbreak of the war.

This tour begins at Beselare church **(1)** and is definitely unsuitable for coaches, unless there has been a full check of the route previously. Before moving off, take time to look at the gravestone mounted on a plinth by the west end of the church. Take the main road northeast towards Zonnebeke and Passendale. After a few hundred yards, coming towards the end of the built up area, turn left and head towards Reutel at what is in effect a crossroads, though the road that you will take (Oude Kortrijk Straat) is relatively narrow. Beware, the turn is partially obscured by buildings and is

The original gravestone of Leutnant Friedrich Gaede (1893-1918), who was killed by a shell near Molenhoek, has been erected on a plinth outside the church. Originally buried in Beselare German Cemetery, he was transferred to Menen, L3137.

154

A funeral in the German cemetery in Molenhoek in Spring 1915.

A street (modern day Wervikstraat) scene in German controlled and as yet relatively undamaged Beselare, 1915.

By the end of the Third Battle of Ypres, Beselare had been erased from the map, with only the church, top centre, vaguely recognisable.

Top of church tower in Geluveld   Mast at west end of Geluveld   Road to Reutel

The view from the edge of Beselare, looking to the south-west.

The Reutel Road   Polygon Wood

View west from the edge of Beselare.

on to a narrow road. Stop **(2)** after about 250 yards at the edge of Beselare, where a rough track leads off to the right – there is street parking or, if occupied, there is usually space on the side road on the left. Walk up this track a to a bench by the village cemetery **(3)** to get a good outlook to the west. This provides excellent views over the fiercely disputed fields northeast of the Reutel crossroads where many of the early battles on 21 and 22 October took place. German casualties were truly horrific here. Such was the inexperience of those involved that, lacking any understanding of fire and movement and minor tactics, they hurled themselves forward in disorganised masses, only to be cut down by the British defenders. Several battalion and company commanders were killed, including Major Strelin, commanding officer 3rd Battalion Reserve Infantry Regiment 247, conspicuous in a light coloured coat, as he tried to force a way forward to the south of Reutel itself. When the Feldwebel of 5th Company Reserve Infantry Regiment 245 called the roll that night back at Beselare only thirty six men were still on their feet, having begun the day with a strength well over 200. This is also the area where the 2/Wilts had such a torrid time on 21 October.

Continue to the crossroads by the De Reutel pub **(4)**. Beware! This area can at times have a peculiar traffic arrangement (and in the autumn of 2018 there were major road works, meaning the roads in the area were closed to through traffic). Because this is a popular area for a day out in the summer and the roads are narrow, especially towards the Menin Road, there may be some form of one way system in place. Especial care has to be taken at these crossroads.

Temporary burials beside the Sunken Road, Reutel.

Proceed straight on, signposted De Akkerwinde. This is probably the sunken road of Reutel, which appears in several descriptions of the fighting. There are excellent views of the terrain as the road descends, including to the left past Vijverbos and out towards Polygon Wood on the right as you cross the Reutelbeek. Drive along the south side of Polygon Wood then look for a minor, but tarmaced, road to the left, about 300 yards from the eastern edge of the wood. This is Oude Kortrijk Straat. Passing a large set of buildings on the right, certainly a farm at some stage, the road turns sharply right; proceed straight ahead at this point and find a convenient place to stop **(5)**. A track leads on down to the Reutelbeek, but views can be had over some of the ground over which the Worcesters charged on 31 October.

View across the A19 motorway to the area of the Worcesters' attack (right flank); Geluveld Church was used as a guiding point.

Geluveld Church

Return to the road and continue along to the left; as the wooded area clears to open country, there is an opportunity as you turn right to run parallel with the motorway to observe the ground where the 31 October charge of the Worcesters began as they manoeuvred into an assault position for the counter-attack on Geluveld Chateau. Imagination is required, because the local topography was altered considerably when the new road was built. As you head alongside the motorway, off to your right is the forward edge of Polygon Wood, defended by the King's Regiment on 11 November. Note that this was a reverse slope position, which worked in favour of the defence, ruling out, as it did, directly observed artillery fire. Stop **(6)** by the impressive Black Watch Memorial, dedicated in 2014. Its position is an acknowledgement to Black Watch Corner, whose location was either here or at another junction just over the motorway bridge – trench maps seem to favour one or the other. It was in this area, at the corner of Polygon Wood, that 2/Worcesters assembled for their desperate counter-attack on Geluveld, heading in the general direction of the church tower there.

The Memorial to the Black Watch, dedicated in May 2014.

Go straight across at the junction next to the motorway bridge and Black Watch Corner and begin a clockwise circuit of Polygon Wood, initially along Lotergatstraat and then turn right onto Langedreve at the

Men of Reserve Infantry Regiment 246 manning positions in Polygon Wood, November 1914.

café on the northwest tip of the wood. There is now an opportunity to visit Polygon Wood and Buttes New British Cemetery, in the latter of which there are a few identified 1914 burials. You have to use the parking facilities **(7)** provided right at the north eastern end of Polygon Wood; whilst a new path from there has been created into Polygon Wood and the Buttes cemetery and memorials.

[**Note – possible diversion.** This would be a good time to visit the *Memorial Museum Passchendaele* in Zonnebeke. Come out of the car park and turn left and then take the turning on the left at the crossroads. Follow this (narrow, again!) road until you reach a crossroads on the outskirts of the village. Turn right and at the T junction turn left; the car park for the Museum is reached after a few metres, on the right. Note that the car park is quite small; however, should this be the case, there is usually street parking in the village centre. This museum is, in our opinion, first class and well worth a visit. It has the advantage of providing toilets and there are eateries nearby as well as the possibility of buying the necessaries for a picnic.]

At the northeast tip of Polygon Wood go hard right then left (there is space to park at this bend on the right hand side, off a track), bringing you on to Spilstraat. A few metres further, on the right, there is an opportunity to walk up a rough track a short distance from which point there are extensive

Recent landscaping has opened up the 5th (Australian) Division's memorial on the Butte in Polygon Wood.

The view across to Geluveld.

views **(8)**. About two hundred metres further on there is parking space on your left, and from here it is possible to see across to both Beselare and Gheluveld.

Go past a left turn (Plasstraat) and then turn right sixty metres further on, where there is a house with a red roof off on the right, onto Kruisbierboomstraat. On reaching a T junction, turn right on to Oude Wervikstraat. Off to the left of the road as you run into Reutel was where some of the most intense early fighting occurred, including that involving 2/Wilts. Beselare church can be seen off to the left as you near the Reutel crossroads **(4)**. Go straight on at the Reutel crossroads; but beware of

A German photograph of late 1914 of Beselare from Reutel.

any traffic restrictions. Proceed with caution. This can be a surprisingly busy road, it is narrow and there are a couple of blind bends.

As the road bears right, Vijverbos is on your left. There are a couple of parking spaces for a light vehicle here on the right (just about the only ones on this narrow road) **(9)**, from which there are good views back across the Reutelbeek and forward to Polygon Wood; whilst a parking space (on the right) at the bottom of the rise offers views across to Geluveld and Polderhoek.

Geluveld Church   **The Reutelbeek**

View to the south from the eastern edge of Vijverboss, known to the British during the war as Juniper Wood.

Continue on and cross the Reutelbeek, which was no great obstacle to troops on foot. As you emerge into open ground you can see, on the right, light industrial buildings, currently marked Deslee, with a redbrick house with two white garage doors. If you turn right here on Polderhoekstraat, you can drive out and back to visit part of the site of Polderhoek Chateau's grounds **(10)**, which were stormed unsuccessfully no fewer than five times on 21 October by men of Reserve Infantry Regiment 245. The chateau itself was in the fields to the right, about 150 to 200 metres east of the new buildings at the end of this road.

The road is a dead end, but there is plenty of room to turn a light

By the end of 1917 the area around Polderhoek Chateau was reduced to this.

161

Reutel   Vijverbos

Reutel and Vijverbos Wood, taken from near the site of Polderhoek Chateau.

vehicle. If you walk around here there are good views towards Beselare, Polygon Wood and Geluveld and the chateau gardens. Return to the main road from Reutel (on the far side of the road at the junction you will be in the area of Poezelhoek **(11)**) and turn right. At a T junction with the embankment to the motorway bridge to your front, turn left to a junction then take a hard climbing turn to the right to cross over the motorway to Geluveld. The chateau grounds are clearly visible to the right once you have crossed the motorway; should you wish to peer through the entrance to view the rebuilt chateau, there is ample parking if you take the sharp turning on the left **(12)** and it is only a short walk from there. The chateau is private property. However, note that a visit to the chateau is included in a later tour.

Arriving in Geluveld, turn right into the square in front of the church and park **(13)**: this is the last stop of the tour.

The Menin Road at Gheluvelt after the battle.

162

Tour Three:

The Kruiseke Defences

Geluveld Church – Nachtegaal – Oude Kruiseke – Doornkapel –
Kruiseke – Eastern edge of Kruiseke – Kruiseke Church
Additional Tour: *A drive down the Menin Road to Ypres.*

See also maps on pages 14, 20, 22, 42, 43, 51, 56, 60, 61, 67, 71 and 74.

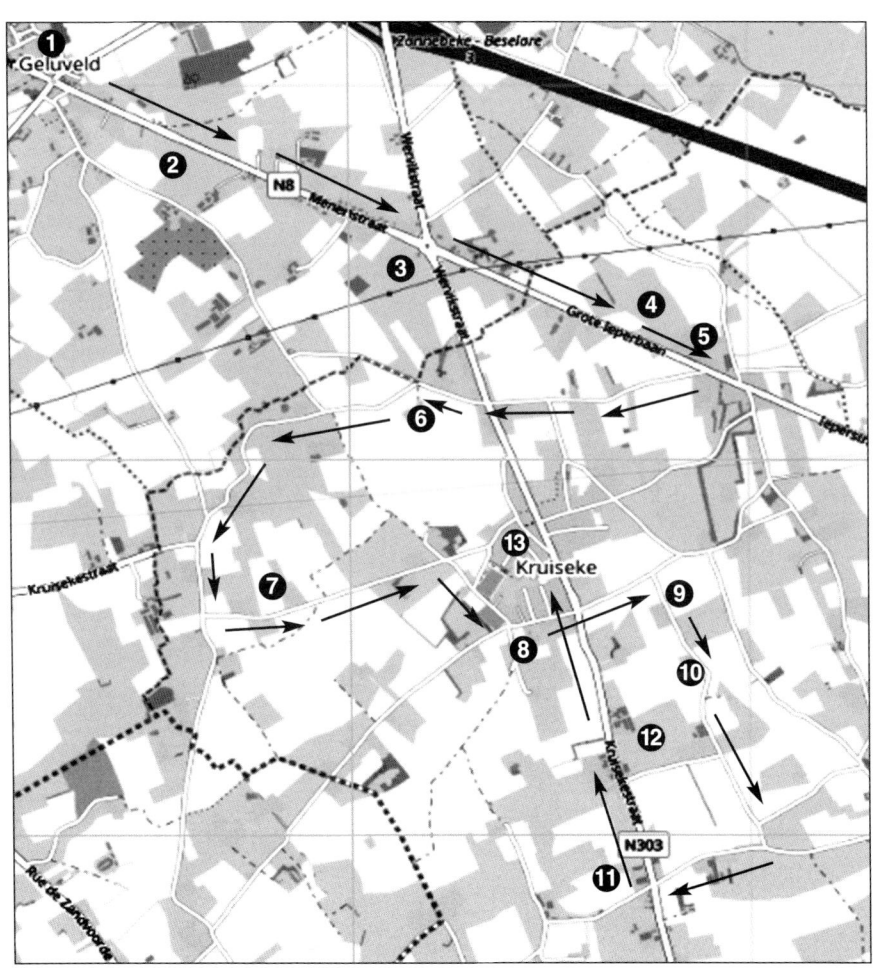

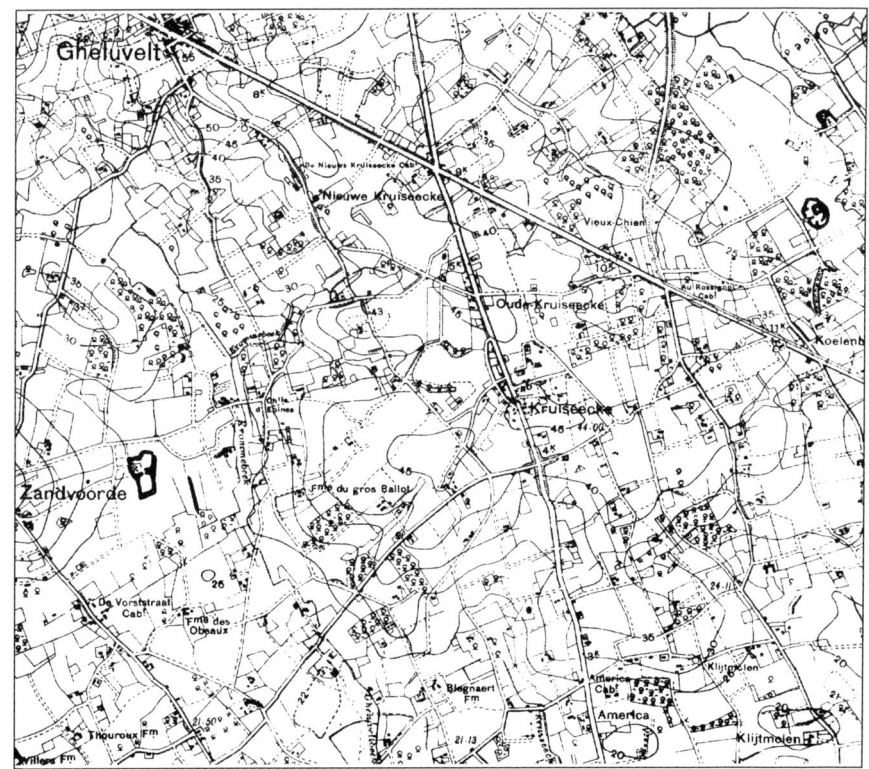

The same area on a contemporary map.

This tour, which begins at the church in Geluveld **(1)**, is effectively an anti-clockwise tour around Kruiseke and covers the ground fought over on 25/26 October when a twenty four hour battle ended with German troops in possession of Kruiseke and the British defenders pushed back to positions near Geluveld.

Turn left onto the Menin Road; note how the road rises and then dips down, providing clear views over the country and clearly illustrating the tactical significance of the village's position. As you come out of the built up area you will pass the site of the eight kilometre marker stone **(2)**. On the opposite side of the road and some metres into the field there was a windmill in 1914.

Drive straight on past the roundabout that marks the former crossroads at Nieuwe Kruiseke, the setting for the famous painting of the 2nd Green Howards **(3)**. There is an Esso filling station on the left here. Shortly after this was the nine kilometre marker stone, frequently referred to in various accounts. The hamlet of Vieux Chien was off to your left **(4)**. Continue on up a rise then, once the ground has begun to drop away once more, turn hard right at Nachtegaal **(5)**, near which was Rossignol Cabaret, onto

164

The 2/Green Howards at the Gheluvelt Crossroads.

Oude Ieperstraat (there are some older industrial buildings at this point). Driving along this road one can appreciate the gently sloping plateau to the east and north of Kruiseke, which adds to the understanding of Capper's decision as regards the defence arrangements of the Kruiseke Salient. The crossroads where the Beselare – Werwik main road meets this minor road is Oude Kruiseke.

Continue straight across the main road onto Doornkapellestraat. Follow this road; at a junction you will keep to the left. It should be possible to stop (with care and with courtesy to other users) **(6)** in the drive leading up to some agricultural buildings. In the fields ahead of you at this point, looking down the road on the right of the junction and in the direction of Geluveld, and to the right of that road, Captain J Brooke of the Gordons won his posthumous VC. It also provides an opportunity to take in the

A view over the fields, north east of Kruiseke and south of the Menin Road.

The spire of Kruiseke Church

German view of the British position before Geluveld, particularly south of the Menin Road, which you can appreciate better if you walk down the left hand road a short distance and then look west..

Pass Oude Komenstraat, Blokstraat and Kruisekestraat on your right and turn left at the next T junction, along Nieuw Zoetendaalstraat, stopping by a large building on the left (which seems to be some sort of craft centre) **(7)**; there is space for parking which will not obstruct other users. By walking back down the road you will get spectacular views from the north (via west) to the south and, on a clear day, will be able to see, among others, the church towers or spires of Geluveld, Zandvoorde, Wytschaete, Zillebeke and Messines; and beyond them, Kemmel Hill.

Continue towards Kruiseke, turning right into Hogebossenstraat. Follow this road through an area of sports pitches on your left to a junction with Vossaardestraat **(8)** It is possible to find a parking spot here and will give you some idea of the forward positions that Capper fixed for the 7th Division, overlooking the Germans in Wervik.

There has always been controversy about the line that Capper selected, especially the siting of his trenches under direct German observation. Indeed there is a strong view that Kruiseke should have been given up and the line pulled back – presumably to the one adopted after the village fell, in front of Geluveld. There are a number of problems with this view; one is that the British and French were still expecting to attack the Germans further north (from the area of Zonnebeke northwards) – one such attack took place on 27 October; and it was not until almost the very end of the month that offensive actions by the allies were finally abandoned. In this situation, the Kruiseke position was of great significance. It should be noted, also, that the Kruiseke position to the east took advantage of the plateau and thus there was space to avoid having defensive works on a forward slope.

Turn left and cross the Beselare – Wervik road. Continue along this road, noting the area where the defensive positions were located just to the east of Kruiseke and take the first right, Klijtbossstraat, on your right, noting the views down towards Wervik **(9)**. At a left, right kink in the road there are excellent views across to the Messines Ridge **(10)** – opportunities should always be taken to place the various 'areas' of the extensive battlefield that was First Ypres.

Ignore the first turning on the right; at the T junction turn right and this will bring you out on the main road, the N303, at the tiny hamlet of Amerika **(11)**, which is where John Eden (killed on 17 October whilst serving with the 12th Lancers) was originally buried before he was moved to Larch Wood Cemetery after the war.

Turn right onto Kruisekestraat; Find a convenient place to stop and look at the views to the north west **(12)** and the forward defences there of the 7th Division. The tour finishes in the middle of the village by the church in Kruiseke **(13)**. There is a possibility of parking in front of the church, but your best bet would probably be to park on the street.

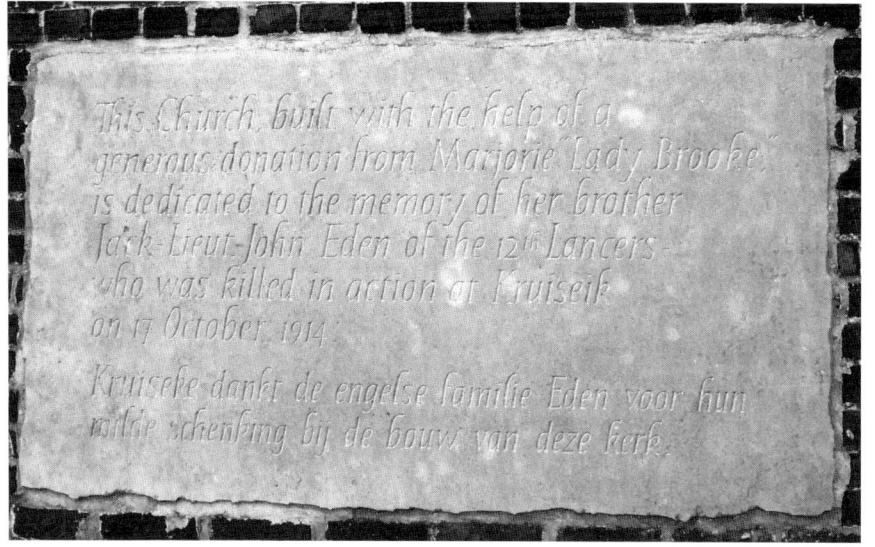

The memorial plaque to John (Jack) Eden on the wall of Kruiseke Church.

View the plaque on the church, explaining that part of the cost of the reconstruction was met by Lady Brooke in memory of her brother, John Eden, who died at Amerika in the early, cavalry dominated, stage of the 1914 battles. They were the siblings of Sir Anthony Eden, Prime Minister during the Suez Crisis of 1956 and for most of the Second World War the British Foreign Secretary.

A drive down the Menin Road to Ypres.
This drive can be done at any stage, but needs to start on the Menin Road before Geluveld to get the full benefit.

Drive through Geluveld. Its chateau was one of five significant ones that straddled the Menin Road before the war, only two of which were rebuilt afterwards. North of the Menin Road there was Polderhoek Chateau (not rebuilt) and Geluveld Chateau (rebuilt to its former splendour). At Veldhoek (which is all but absorbed in a linear development with Geluveld), Veldhoek Chateau – which in fact had only recently (1911-1913) been rebuilt after a catastrophic fire – was on the right and was not rebuilt, nor was Herenthage Chateau, further down the road on the left in the wooded area.

After the amusement park on the right you will come to what is now the Hooge Chateau hotel; the fine pre-war chateau was not rebuilt on its old site and instead this much more modest construction, closer to the Menin Road, was put up. It is possible to go in and have a meal or a drink there, and the opportunity can be taken to take a walk around the

The Menin Road in 1917.

recreated trench system, the bunkers and craters, tastefully turned into a small lake by Baron Gaston de Vinck.

Baron Hervé de Vinck, Gaston's grandson, shared some photographs and an account of the family's connection with Hooge Chateau with us (see also the photographs on page 89). The chateau has a long history; the original, early eighteenth century chateau was burnt down during the turbulent period of the 1789 French Revolution and was rebuilt on a somewhat larger scale. Gaston was a keen patron of the arts, particularly of painters and musicians; the construction of the 1896 annexe, on the west side of the chateau, was designed to provide them with living quarters and working space, chiefly in the Orangery. This building, with its three large windows, was where the staffs of the 1st and 2nd Divisions were meeting when it was struck by a shell on 31 October.

The photograph of the Chateau ruins at the end of the war was turned into a postcard; this version was sent by Gaston to his son, who was then at college in Ghent. He is pictured (on the left, with walking stick and smoking a pipe) on the wreck of a British tank on his estate; Hervé was subsequently told that it was blown up as part of the clearance operations. The family tombs were in the crypt of Zillebeke church; ironically, the destruction of the building, particularly the tower, and the consequent wreckage, served to protect the crypt and they survived the war untouched. The new chateau was built in 1919 and 1920. Gaston had hoped to rebuild it on its former location, but by this stage he was old (born in 1855), ill (he died in 1927) and the compensation that he got would not allow it. The paving in front of the chateau was made by using some of the prefabricated concrete blocks that the Germans used in the construction of pillboxes, until this was found to be inadequate against prolonged shelling by heavy guns; other war material was also used – for example, the curious metal 'tubes'/bollards that border the crater-lake.

168

Hooge Chateau after the war. The lake is in the distance, now a feature of the 'Alton Towers' style park. (Baron Hervé de Vinck)

Gaston de Vinck (left) sitting on a wrecked British tank, which is next to a plank track. Note the new building going up on the left. (Baron Hervé de Vinck)

The mound indicates the site of Zillebeke Church, under which the de Vinck family tombs emerged unscathed. (Baron Hervé de Vinck)

The new chateau, built in 1919-1920. (Baron Hervé de Vinck)

The Hill 62 Museum has a fine collection of head gear, much of which would have been worn during the battle (albeit, in the case of the Germans, usually with canvas covers).

The 'Shrine', near Hell Fire Corner.

Immediately to the west there is the excellent Hooge Crater Museum and café and opposite them is Hooge Crater Cemetery.

Continue towards Ypres and after several hundred metres there is a left turn to Sanctuary Wood Cemetery and to the oldest trench museum in the Salient at Hill 62. Return to the Menin Road and onwards towards Ypres; Birr Cross Roads Cemetery is on your left after some five hundred metres – there is parking on the right hand side of the road, your direction of travel. At the Hell Fire Corner roundabout (known as 'Halte' during the battle), continue along the Menin Road; an entrance to Ypres Town Cemetery is on the road on the right, more or less opposite a supermarket that is set back on the left and with a set of traffic lights and the right turn to the Menin gate in sight. There is street parking available here, but it is often filled and you might have to resign yourself to a walk through the cemetery from the entrance to the Extension (see below). There is a number of burials immediately through the somewhat battered green gate, straight ahead and to your left. The others, grouped just beyond the Extension, can be visited at the same time as you visit it. Over 120 of the 136 identified graves date from the battle; from the beginning of November these are almost exclusively officers. Continue down the Menin Road and at the traffic lights turn right.

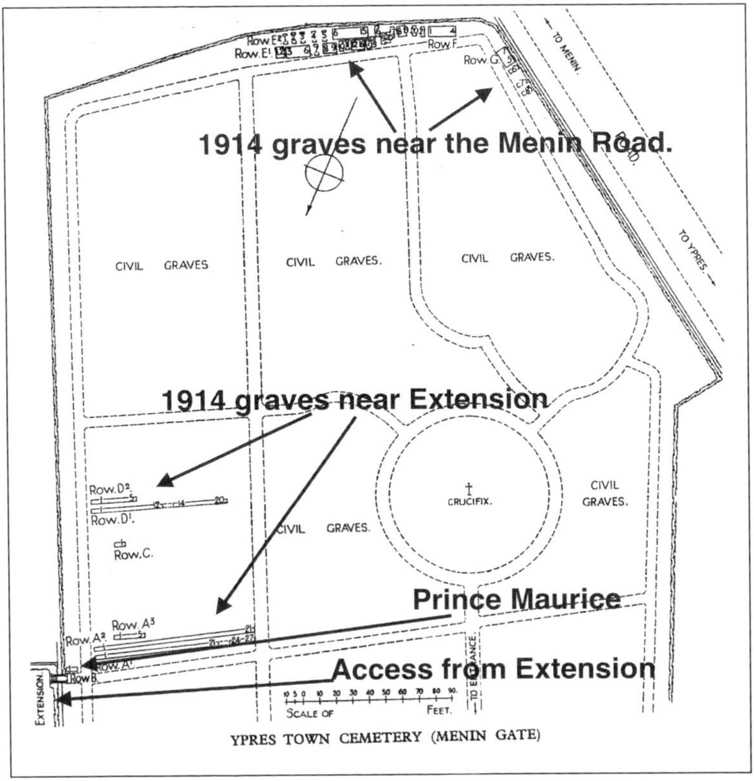
1914 graves near the Menin Road.
1914 graves near Extension
Prince Maurice
Access from Extension
CIVIL GRAVES
CIVIL GRAVES.
CIVIL GRAVES.
CIVIL GRAVES.
CIVIL GRAVES.
CRUCIFIX.
Row.D².
Row.D¹.
Row.C.
Row.A³
Row.A².
Row.A¹
Row.B.
Row.E²
Row.E¹
Row.F
Row.G.
TO MENIN.
TO YPRES.
TO ENTRANCE.
EXTENSION.
SCALE OF FEET.
YPRES TOWN CEMETERY (MENIN GATE)

Ypres Town Cemetery.

Ypres Town Cemetery Extension is accessed via a path coming off Zonnebeekseweg, about 300 metres after the turn and on your right. There are 129 known casualties buried here from the period of the battle and its intermediate aftermath, including a few from the shelling of Hooge Chateau on 31 October. Most of these casualties are in Plot II, with only a dozen or so who date from after the early days of November in Plot III. There is a set of stairs to the

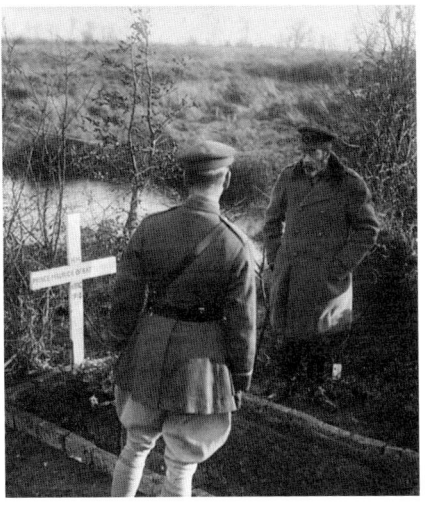

King George V visiting the grave of his cousin in 1921.

Prince Maurice of Battenberg's headstone.

The Menin Gate.

right of the Cross of Sacrifice that give access to the Town Cemetery proper and to the group of graves at this end of it. You will almost straight away hit on the isolated grave of Prince Maurice of Battenberg, which his cousin, George V, visited very shortly after the Armistice was signed. The rest of the graves in this part of the Town Cemetery are over to the right (south) of it.

Turn around at a convenient point and drive into Ypres through the Menin Gate. The great majority of the fatal casualties of First Ypres are commemorated on its walls; coming from Ypres, the first name on the first column of names on the north side is that of Brigadier General C FitzClarence VC.

COMMANDS AND STAFF
V.C. BRIGADIER GENERAL C. FITZCLARENCE.

FitzClarence VC, commemorated on the Menin Gate.

Tour Four:

Geluveld southeast

Geluveld Church – Zandvoorde – Doornkapel –
Motebos – Geluveld

Please see maps on pages 61, 67, 71, 74, 76, 83 and 99.

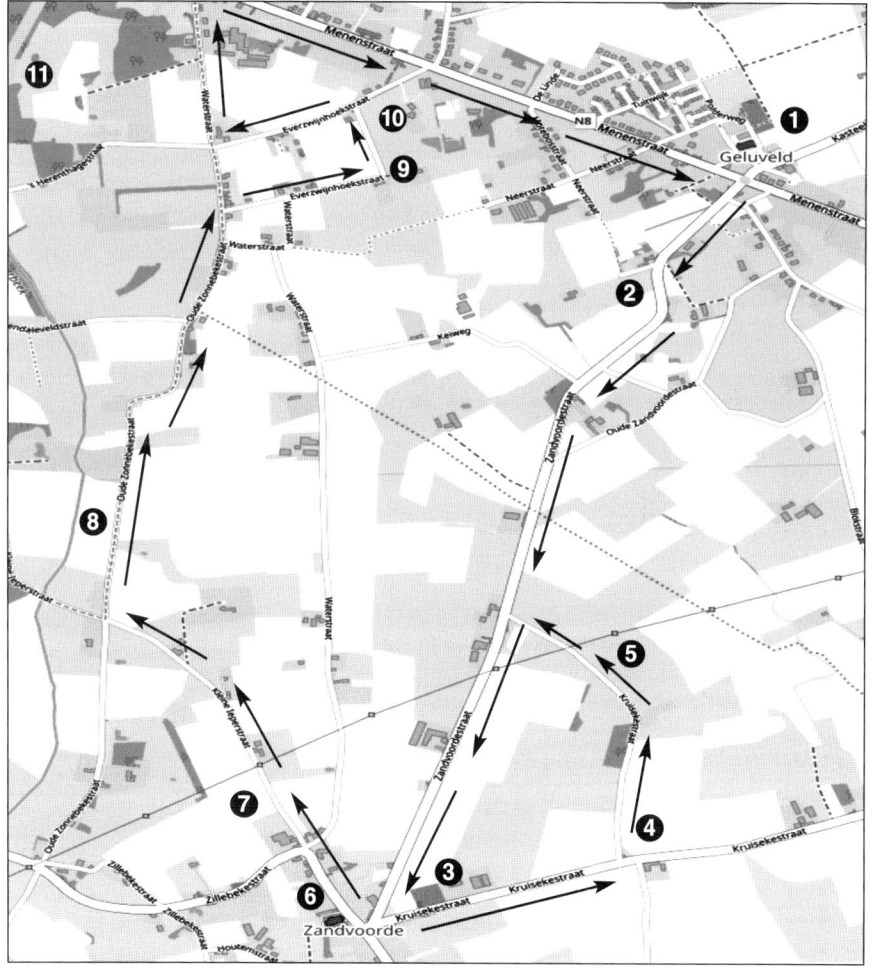

Geluveld southeast.

A memorial erected by Infantry Regiment 105, which claimed the honour of capturing Gheluvelt, to its dead of 1914. Originally placed in the square, it was destroyed in later fighting during the war.

Leave the square outside Geluveld church **(1)**, turn right and go straight across the Menin Road onto Zandvoordestraat. Just as you exit the village, there are very good views off to the right **(2)**; it is possible to stop at the edge of the village at the start of a private road, but space is tight and so be aware of other road users – this private road can be surprisingly busy. From here you can look south over Zandvoorde and beyond and, by walking down the main road a few metres, look over to the right and the site of some very bitter fighting on 31 October and 1 November south of the Menin Road towards Veldhoek and from then on what turned out to be the final peak of the fighting, on 11 November.

'Gloria Finis' Captain J Brooke VC.

Drive to Zandvoorde and turn left at a T junction onto Kruisekestraat, also signposted to Zantvoorde (sic) British Cemetery. Stop at the cemetery **(3)**. Besides the opportunity to visit the grave of Captain Brooke VC (VI E 2), there are 102 other 1914 burials in this concentration cemetery, including those in a

TO THE MEMORY OF
THESE 32 SOLDIERS
OF THE BRITISH EMPIRE
WHO FELL IN 1914
AND 1915 AND WERE
BURIED AT THE TIME
IN KRUISEECKE GERMAN
CEMETERY AND IN
WERVICQ ROAD GERMAN
CEMETERY COMINES
BUT WHOSE GRAVES
ARE NOW LOST

THEIR GLORY
SHALL NOT BE BLOTTED OUT

Zantvoorde British Cemetery, Special Memorial. The majority of those commemorated died during First Ypres.

Special Memorial area in Zantvoorde British Cemetery.

View of the area of the British position south of Geluveld.

special memorial area for thirty or so men whose locations were lost in later fighting although they had been buried by the Germans. Go to the back wall of the cemetery and a whole length of the southern side of the Menin Road is opened before you, from Veldhoek to Kruiseke and beyond. When you return to the road, keeping to the left of the entrance portico, note the views south to Ten Brielen and Wervik, indicated by their church spires; and if you look to the east it is possible to make out the tower of Kruiseke church.

View south east from Zantvoorde British Cemetery.

Continue along the road and take the first left, Krusiekestraat, **(4)**, a narrow road that heads north. It was in this area that the 2nd RWF suffered such horrendous losses in the course of the capture of Zandvoorde – see *Messines 1914* in this series of books. As the road rises, look to your right and you will observe the significance of the Kruiseke Ridge. After some farm buildings on your right the road bends to the left. Circumstances allowing, it is worth getting out here **(5)** to see yet another view of the British positions south of the Menin Road and the country across which the attacking Germans had to advance. We cannot emphasise enough how important an appreciation of the ground is to an understanding of the development of this battle.

RWF Memorial, next to the church in Zandvoorde.

At the junction turn left and head once more down into Zandvoorde; at the junction turn right and at the next junction turn right again. However, ahead of you at this junction there is a place to park, and it would be as well to make use of this. Visit the imposing church **(6)**, which is usually open. In the right (north) aisle there is a fine stained class window, dedicated to the memory of two officers and four troopers of the

Zandvoorde in October 1914, still under British occupation.

The memorial window in Zandvoorde Church.

Zandvoorde in mid 1916. A light railway, train and human cargo; note the sandbagged building on the left.

10th Hussars who were killed near the church on 26 October. The Turnor family paid for it; Lieutenant Christopher Turnor was one of those killed. He is buried outside the church on the north (right) side, along with Captain Rose and two of the troopers.

Carry on out of the village. At a left angled bend, with signs to Ieper and Zillebeke, go straight on (Kleine Ieperstraat), signed Gasthuis Bossen; however, beware another road coming in at this point from your right.

As you proceed look to your left, with good views in particular of the distinctive spire of the church at Hollebeke (7). At a crossroads after a little short of a kilometre, turn right on to the seemingly ubiquitous Waterstraat.

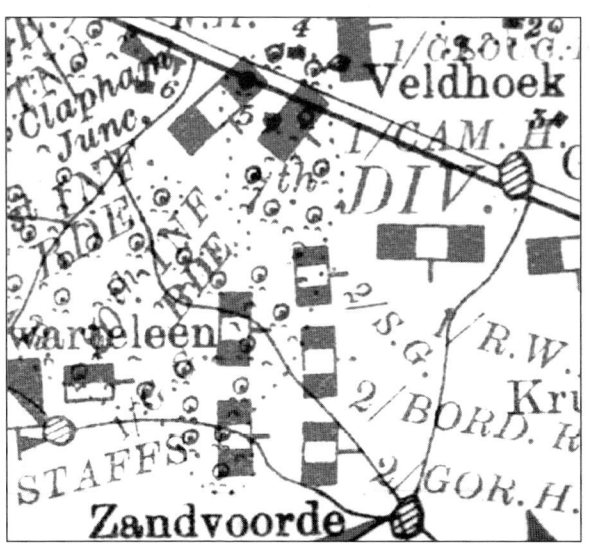

Map showing positions of 2/Scots Guards, 2/Border and 2/Gordons in the Waterstraat area, evening 26 October.

This area is where there were defensive positions and in depth defences lower down, just east of the Bassevillebeek (which is off to the left, more or less parallel with this road) **(8)**. Continue north, passing a road to the left then one to the right and take the next right turn onto Everzwijnhoekstraat, after about one and a half kilometres. There are good views ahead **(9)** on this road towards Geluveld and the Menin Road area and Zandvoorde across to the right – there is a suitable place to stop to do this by some houses on the left.

Just before the road turns sharply left, pause by a redbrick house with a high hedge and numerous trees **(10)**. This area is where a section of guns of 116th Battery Royal Artillery was captured by Oberleutnant Lentz of 3rd Company Infantry Regiment 143 during the afternoon of 2 November. They had been placed there because of the excellent fields of fire the position offered over targets south of the Menin Road. In his later account of the events of the day, Generalleutnant von Altrock, commander 60 Infantry Brigade, wrote,

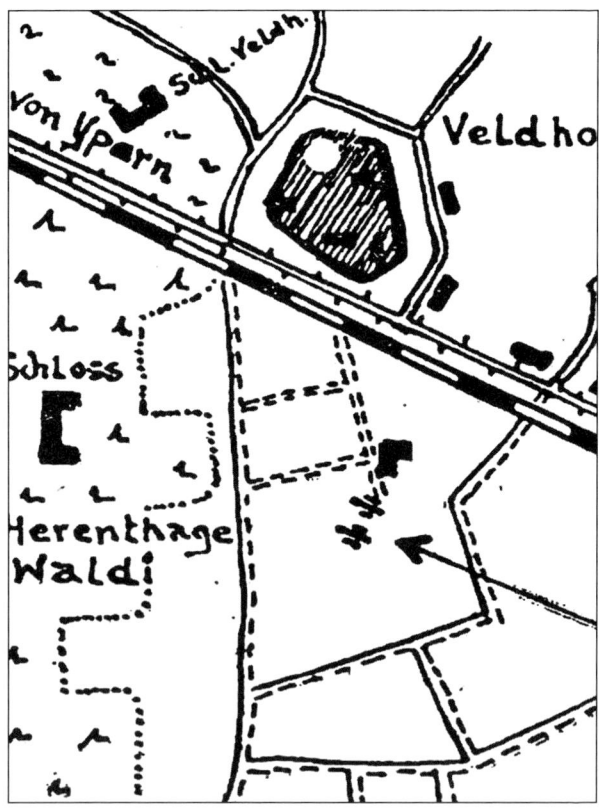

Location of the guns captured by 3rd Company Infantry Regiment 143 on 2 November.

178

During the afternoon of 2 November, Infantry Regiment 99 captured British trenches in front of Veldhoek, taking 400 prisoners, including ten officers of the 'Rifles, Buffs, Coldstreams and Guards Regiments' [sic.]. *A French attack threatened from the right, but General von Altrock directed artillery fire against it. Reinforcement was requested from Headquarters XV Corps. Infantry Regiment 143, Reserve Hussar Regiment 8 and two companies of engineers were despatched and were sent into action. Infantry Regiment 143 advanced south of the Geluveld – Veldhoek road and succeeded in capturing two British guns, together with their crews. These were the only ones taken by XV Corps on the Ypres front.* [In fact these were the only guns captured at all from the British during the battle.]

The guns were later put on display in Strasburg, before being claimed as trophies by the regiment and placed in their barracks.

Scots Guards enjoying hot cocoa, probably in the shelter of Herenthage Wood, 27 October.

Follow the road round to the left – we are in the vicinity of Herenthage Wood **(11)**. At the junction **EITHER** turn left on to Waterstraat; we think it is worthwhile to retrace your route and see the ground from the opposite direction (you will pass, on your right and almost immediately, an information panel about Tower Hamlets, located nearby and which earned great notoriety during Third Ypres). Just follow the route in reverse and the tour ends at Geluveld Church. By looking ahead and to the right you

Early German trenches in Herenthage Wood.

can appreciate the wooded country – for example the sprawling mass of Shrewsbury Forest on the right – in the midst of which the battle ground to a halt.

OR you can turn right, heading north; to the left of the road there were defensive positions on 10 November and, running north-south to the east of the road was the start line of Grenadier Guard Regiment 4 (Queen Augusta) on 11 November. Back at the Menin Road, turn right towards Geluveld and the tour finishes at the church there **(1)**.

Tour Five:

(Walk/Drive) The 11th November: Veldhoek and the Woods battlefield

Car Park Nonnebossen – Black Watch Corner – Reutelbeek –
Veldhoek – Menen Road – Site of Fitz Clarence Farm –
Circuit of Nonnebossen. Extension to north side of
Nonnebossen via Polygon Wood

Please see maps on pages 104, 108, 110, 118, 120, 121, 125 and 136.

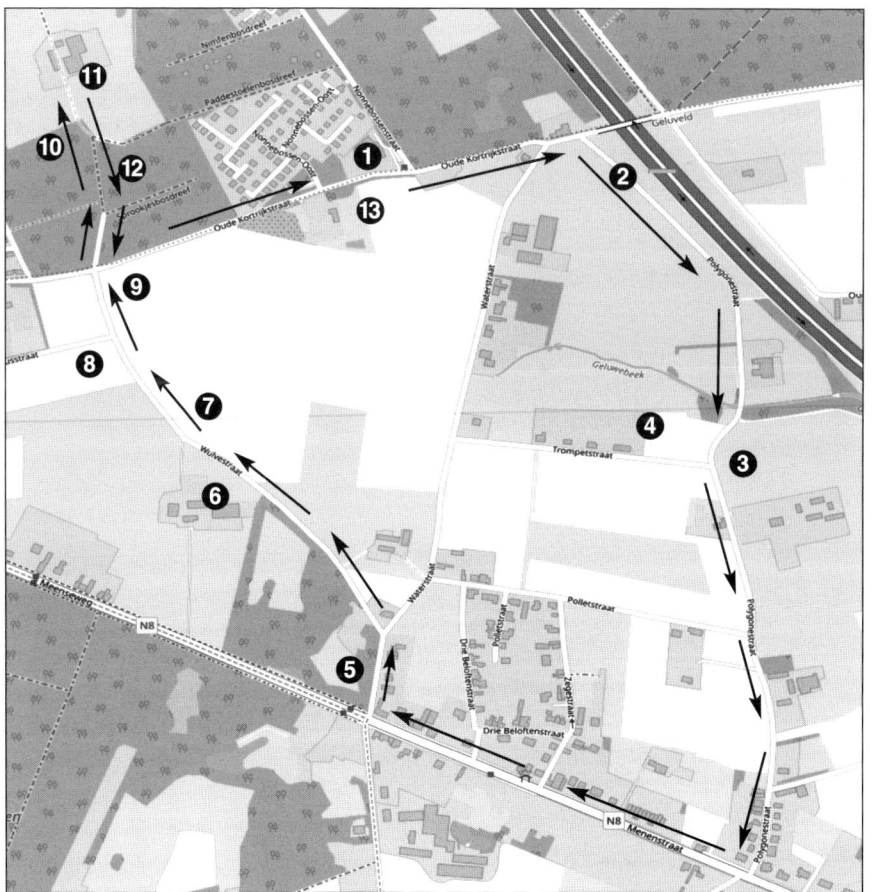

Veldhoek and the Woods battlefield.

This walk, which can also be driven, covers much of the battlefield of 11 November north of Veldhoek. It is split into two parts (the second part should be driven). Park your car in the car park by Nonnebossen, at its eastern end **(1)**, and head east along the road towards Black Watch Corner along Oude Kortrijk Straat. Just before the motorway bridge turn right onto Polygonstraat, which runs parallel to the motorway on its southern side. There are good views **(2)** to the left along the southern edge of Polygon Wood. Drop down over the Reutelbeek, which was no obstacle to movement on foot in this area. The road then ascends slightly; stop at a T junction **(3)**. Look along the line of the road on the right; about a hundred metres along it, now more or less buried under the road or the buildings to the right of it, is the site of Northampton Farm **(4)**, one of several farms in the immediate area that were transformed into strong points and proved their worth during the attack of 11 November. Continue straight ahead, where there are views over to Geluveld church here and the 11 November start line of Footguard Regiments 3 and 1.

Northampton Farm was approximately in the area between the second and third post on the right of the road.

Continue straight on and enter the built up part of Veldhoek, turning right along the Menin Road and follow it for about 600 metres; there are two right turns before you come to a third, right at the end of the built up area; this right turn is Waterstraat **(5)** – a continuation of the one that you encountered in Tour 4. The grounds of Veldhoek Chateau were on the left. This is the assault sector of 3rd Battalion Grenadier Guard Regiment 2 'Kaiser Franz'. Somewhere very near to this point, or just off to the west, Reserve Oberleutnant Adolf Eckermann was killed. His temporary burial was concentrated later to Langemark and he lies in the *Kamaradengrab* there.

After a little short of 150 metres take a left fork onto Wulvestraat. As you emerge into open ground, Veldhoek Chateau occupied much of the ground that now has a farm and associated buildings on it; there is an

Agricultural buildings now stand on the site of Veldhoek Chateau. Rebuilt after a major fire burnt it down in 1911, it was not long before it was destroyed once more.

explanatory plaque on the side of the road **(6)**. Just beyond this, on the right, in 1914 there was a track with a cluster of buildings; on some trench maps, especially those after the start of 1916, this is described as FitzC[or with a small 'c']larence Farm **(7)**. A short distance further on a narrow road **(8)** leads up to Clapham Junction on the Menin Road and close to the five kilometre marker. That area was used by various divisions as an advanced headquarters; whilst Haig came past here during his famous 'ride up the

Minor road to Clapham Junction

Glencorse Wood

Early trench maps describe this location as FitzClarence Farm

The road from Veldhoek Chateau up to Glencorse Wood.

Looking south west from the same location.

Geluveld Church

Approximate site of FitzClarence Farm on later trench maps

Site of Veldhoek Chateau

Glencorse Wood   Nonnebossen Wood   Verbeek Farm   Polygon Wood

Menin Road' on 31 October. Depending on the crops, it is possible to get reasonable views to the east, and certainly towards Verbeek Farm **(13)** (another of the strong points), Veldhoek Chateau and Geluveld.

Continue to the end of this road; on the right at the outbreak of the war there was a building (presumably agricultural and possibly a farm) **(9)** that is also marked on trench maps, particularly the early ones, as FitzClarence Farm – and there is an information panel here now. Continue to the cross roads then head straight across into what the British called Glencorse Wood, along Sprookjesbosdreef – a somewhat bumpy road, passing holiday chalets. At a road junction, find somewhere safe to park **(10)**. At the end of a section of high, close mesh fencing walk first straight on to the drive into a house and a sign which translates as 'Private Road; keep the entrance clear'. Look forward, past the house **(11)** to where the British gun lines were on the southern edge of Westhoek (for some time in the early days of the war this area was also called Eskernest). Return to the junction and the Captain Brodie memorial is about twenty five metres further on, on the right **(12)**. Brodie has no known grave and is commemorated on the Menin Gate.

Car drivers have to return to the main road the way they entered the wood, but walkers can continue past the memorial to a further T junction,

Captain Brodie, 1st Camerons, memorial.

TO THE
GLORY OF GOD
AND
IN MEMORY OF
EWEN JAMES BRODIE
CAPTAIN
1ST BATT QUEENS OWN
CAMERON HIGHLANDERS
WHO WAS KILLED AT THE
FIRST BATTLE OF YPRES
11TH NOV. 1914.
BURIED NEAR THIS SPOT.

Detail of Captain Brodie's plaque.

184

reached after about 350 metres. [Note that the continuation tour, by car, from this junction on, will take you over this ground.] Turning left, move to the edge of Nonnebossen and once more there are good views over the area where the Royal Artillery prevented any further forward movement by the Prussian Guards on 11 November. Retrace your steps, carry straight on past the junction and you will emerge at the car park. If you walk to the road and look right, the approximate site of Verbeek Farm, another strongpoint, **(13)** is on the other side of the road where a replacement farm has been built more or less on the original site.

Part Two

Extension to north side of Nonnebossen
via Polygon Wood.

From the car park turn left and cross over the A19 motorway, taking the left turn immediately afterwards. Follow the road on the west side of Polygon Wood; at the junction with a road on the right – the entrance to the café here is off the road on the right), go straight ahead (being very cautious while doing so). In this vicinity, on the edge of Polygon Wood,

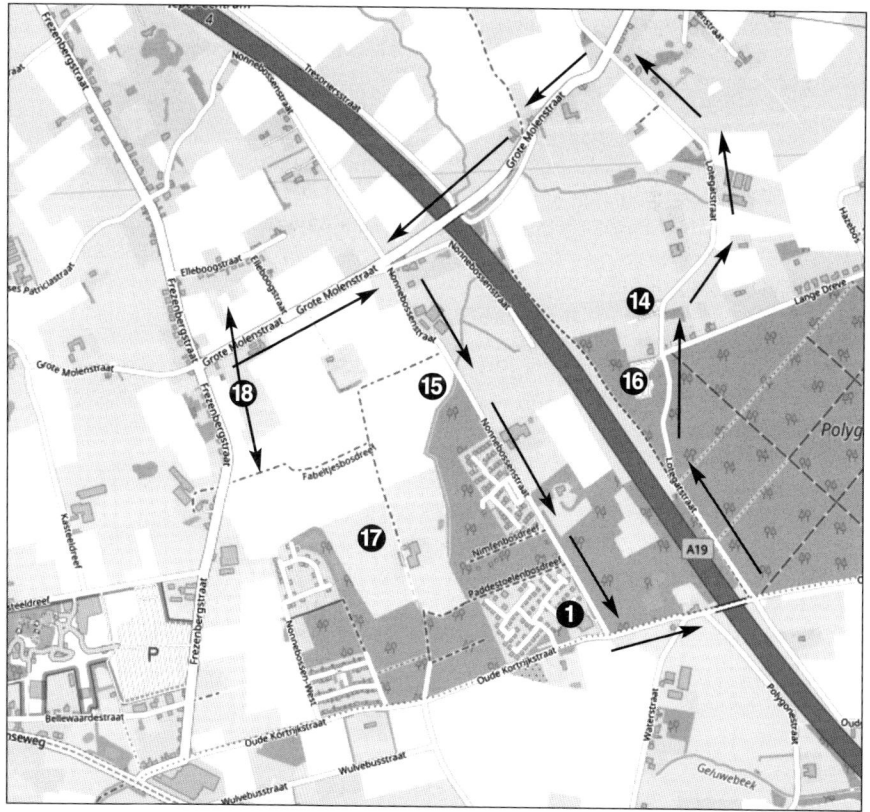

Men of Reserve Infantry Regiment 246 manning positions in Polygon Wood, November 1914.

was 5 Field Company RE, to which Captain Collins was attached. It was from here that they were launched into a counter attack on the Germans who were caught up in Nonneboschen (as then written) on 11 November. Members of the Company won a total of seven DCMs that day, a record for a small unit. The development of 'The Brother-in-Arms Park', which you will see almost immediately on the left, is the work of the café proprietor. At this end of Polygon Wood there were several brigade headquarters stationed here at one time or the other during the battle **(14)**.

Continue along this road, appreciating the distant views, including the spires of Ypres. At a crossroads, turn left (again, be careful, as this can be a busy traffic area). Cross over the A19 once more and almost immediately take a sharp left hand turn. The road then bends sharply to the right. Proceed towards the edge of the woods, where there is parking space **(15)**.

If you move around here you will find good views across the motorway towards Polygon Wood **(16)**; to the farm that is at the end of the track near Captain Brodie's memorial **(17)**, and up to Westhoek Ridge **(18)**, along which a number of British guns were arrayed.

You continue along Nonnebossenstraat, and pass the car park; the tour ends here.

Westhoek (Eskernest) Ridge.

Tour Six:

The Gheluvelt defences – a walking tour, with a car tour option

Please see maps on pages 60, 61, 67, 71, 74, 76, 83, 88, 92 and 99.

Geluveld has expanded considerably, especially along the Menin Road; there is ribbon development along much of the length of the road between it and the Veldhoek area, and from its eastern end towards the so-called Gheluvelt cross roads, certainly much more than there was in 1914. The

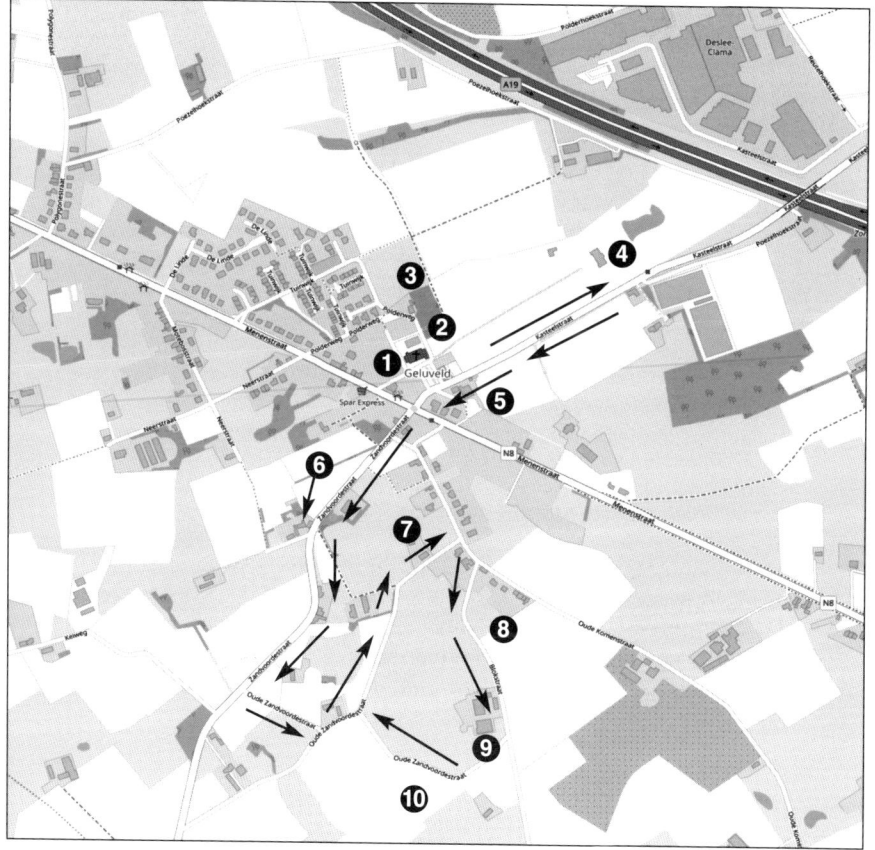

The Geluveld defences - a walking tour

The square in Geluveld photographed in 1915.

fighting actually in the village was so confused that little useful can be said about it in touring terms; but a walk around its immediate vicinity is well worthwhile.

Park by the church in Geluveld **(1)**. Walk to the north end of it (the tower end – how fortunate to have such a distinctive one, visible from so much of the battlefield!) and nearby are the gates and drive leading to the chateau **(2)**, which give good views of the grounds and of the rebuilt house. Unusually for many of the chateaux that figure in accounts of the Great War, the grounds are of the same dimensions (the drive appears to follow the same route, for example) and the chateau of more or less the same size, though of a slightly different design. The chateau was occupied by the Keingiaert family for over two hundred years (1737-1965) and this lengthy tenure possibly explains why there were so keen to return and to rebuild. The chatelaine, Léonie, soon returned to this village after the

Geluveld Chateau taken from the gates near the east end of the parish church.

Armistice, which had had a population of over 1700 before the war. She became Belgium's first woman mayor, established a brickyard to speed up the rebuilding in the area – not only the chateau, but the church, farms and homes for the returning refugees; and was finally able to return to her chateau when it was completed in 1929. There is an explanatory board on the other side of the road from the gates.

Continue around the back of the church and enter the adjacent communal cemetery; views into the chateau are obstructed by vegetation **(3)**. In the new section of the cemetery, at the western end, there are views across to Polygon Wood and to the area of Poelderhoek Chateau; but, like so much about this northern side of the Menin Road battlefield, the motorway makes the reconstruction of events on the ground difficult. At the chateau side of the cemetery there is a (potentially rather muddy) track leading west that will give you good views of the approach of the Worcesters on the 31st and is, indeed an option, as the path connects to the second part of this tour (see below, p. 195)

Now walk back through the car park and down alongside the length of the chateau grounds. The road was probably more sunken then than now, but looking across to the right front of the road gives some idea of the dispositions of the British defenders; whilst as the battle developed the road itself became part of the defensive line. Be aware that this road can be quite busy. The chateau and chateau grounds **(4)** are not open to the public, but we have been able to enter without being challenged by what appeared to be staff members and been able to take a photograph of the new chateau. The key here is not to push your luck and not to wander about the place more than strictly necessary – ie no more than a few feet up the drive – to get a decent photograph of the new building.

Gheluvelt Chateau before the war.

189

Gheluvelt Chateau before the War (from the rear of the building).

Geluveld Chateau today.

Gheluvelt Chateau, the Worcesters and the SWB. As well as depicting accurately individuals, the Chateau itself is a fair reproduction. The figures are in the approximate area where the drive sweeps around in front of the house.

Gheluvelt Chateau in the autumn of 1917.

Walk back up Kasteelstraat and then take the road to the left (inaccessible to cars that are not those of residents), opposite the car park. At the end of it **(5)** there is a replacement of the original windmill (itself in need of much restoration work now) and memorials to the South Wales Borderers and the Worcesters (the latter moved here to a more appropriate spot than that of the original position at Herenthage). It is easy to scramble up to the mound on which the mill stands and gives some satisfactory, if not complete, views over the north eastern approaches to

South Wales Borderers Memorial, with the Windmill behind, with detail of inscription.

191

the village, more or less the direction from which the assaults of the reinforced 54th Reserve Division came in continuous succession from 28 – 31 October. There is also a clear view north, along the eastern side of the road that led to Polderhoek.

[*This next stage can be done by car, but stopping places are practically non existent and a lot more will be gained by walking rather than driving.*]

Retrace your steps and cross the Menin Road, noting how, to the east, the road rises gradually and then dips downwards. Proceed down what is a post war road towards Zandvoorde; as you exit from the housing area, there is a private road on the right and it should be possible to stop here briefly. There are good views south **(6)** to the British line that was held immediately after the fighting at Kruiseke, the fall of Zandvoorde on and after 31 October. You can also see the ground over which Infantry Regiment 143 attacked to capture the section of guns on 2

2/Worcesters' Memorial, erected by 'a man of Worcester' and an association of disabled Belgian soldiers.

View from the Gheluveld 'windmill mound' looking to the north, over the motorway and to Polderhoek. Poezelhoek and beyond. The South Wales Borderers held a line to the right of the road on 31 October.

Approximate location of the British guns captured by IR 143 on 2 November. It is indicative that these were the only British guns lost at First Ypres.

November, including where the guns themselves were positioned. Continue along the road as it bends left and right and then take the narrow road on the left soon after a small farm and a (modern) calvary, both also on the left. After about 250 metres (the road has a distinct left kink in it), at a T junction turn left, heading back up towards the Menin Road and an area called Motebos, on Oude Zanvoordestraat. There are a couple of knolls in this area on the left **(7)** and straight ahead as you proceed along this road, up to a T junction, indicating strong defensive positions held by the British in the days leading up to 31 October. The knoll on the left was occupied by A Company 1/Queen's and elements of 2/KRRC and the one of the right, near a farm with a distinct silo, was held by D Company; whilst the re-entrant in between was manned by B and C Companies 1/Queen's – a naturally strong position.

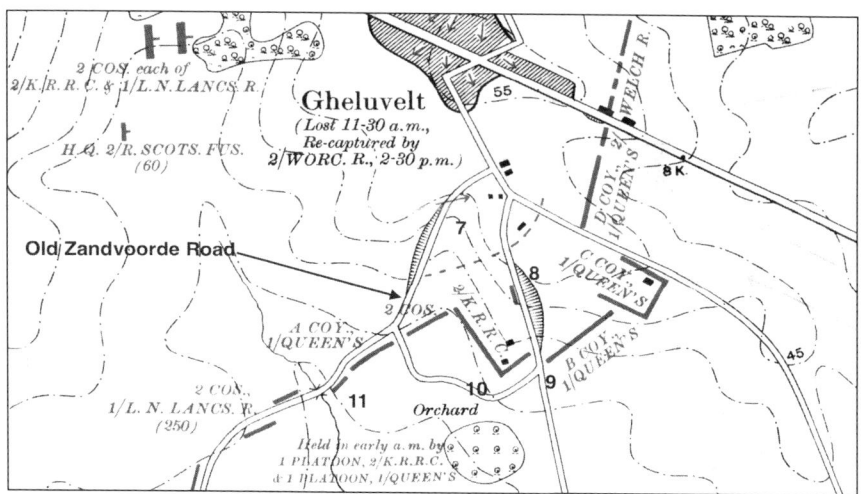

Detail of the 31 October defences in the area.

At the T junction turn right on Oudekomenstraat and within about sixty metres take the first turning right, Bokstraat. After a short distance and a left bend in the road, there is space to stop for a while (this space is designed as a passing point and is not for parking) **(8)**. There are excellent views to the east, towards Kruiseke, to the south and to the south west, with many of the now familiar church spires visible on a clear day. Just above this spot there was the mill found in narratives of the fighting. Note how it is impossible to see much of the Menin Road, let alone what was going on on the far side of it.

After some four hundred metres, by a farm and a large concreted area for various clamps, turn right on Oude Zandvoordestraat **(9)**. Just to the left at this junction were men of 1/Queen's. Soon after you turn left, in the field on the left, there was an orchard **(10)**, that was held by a couple of platoons until the morning of the 31st. Take your time to look around here, looking back up to the British positions south of the Menin Road and to the west; as well as the German lines of attack. Proceed to a T junction and then turn left (it is a sobering thought that this was the main road in 1914 between Geluveld and Zandvoorde). British troops lined this road to the south for several hundred yards. Almost immediately turn right, which brings you back to the junction with the (new) road back to Geluveld, where this tour ends.

View from the area of the Orchard towards the 'knolls' and the Menin Road.

Tour Extension – *The charge of the 2nd Worcesters*
Finally, there is an opportunity at the end of this tour to get an excellent view of the entirety of the Worcesters' attack, crops allowing. Drive down towards the motorway and very shortly after the Chateau entrance take the sharp turning to the right **(11)**, which will take you past some sports fields. At the T junction turn left and follow this narrow road up the hill; there is a sharp bend to the left **(12)** – gated access comes off the road, straight ahead, which more or less coincides with what was an entrance to Polderhoek Chateau and then stop, as practicable, by an explanatory panel **(13)**. It is important that you get off the road as much as possible, because this is a surprisingly busy road for its size. There are spots to get off the road but beware 'soft' verges.

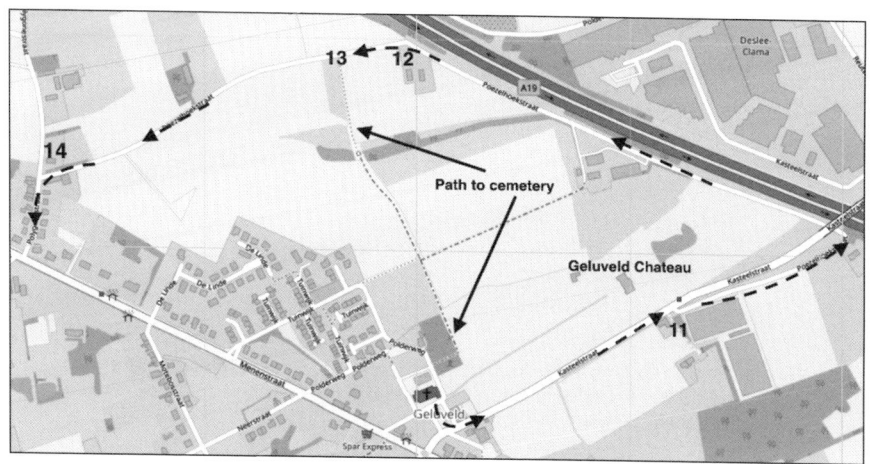

Map to view the attack of 2/Worcesters. See also map p. 92.

There is a well maintained footpath, mentioned earlier in this tour, that will bring you out by the cemetery in Geluveld. Indeed it is an option to add this stage to the walking tour; but driving does save time, which may well be precious.

Polderhoek Chateau before the war. Although the chateau itself does not appear very large, the chateau grounds were extensive, with beautiful lawns, flowers and shrubs.

View across to Polygon Wood. The right flank marker for 2/Worcesters was Geluveld Church. It was only when the men got here that they could see below to the chateau grounds.

The Chateau grounds   Path to the communal cemetery   Church

View over Geluveld looking south.

Once you get clear of the tree plantation on the far (north) side of the road there are good views to the north and the area of the start line of 2/Worcesters. Similarly, you can get good views across to the church in Geluveld and, at least in winter, glimpses of the chateau below.

As has been pointed out, the Germans professed themselves to be completely in control of Gheluvelt early on and there is minimal reference to any sort of British activity after they had achieved this. The British, on the other hand, are quite adamant that they had retaken the village and were there until the early evening of the 31st. Everyone will have to agree to differ, as the primary evidence seems so contradictory. The point is that the 'believed' result was as important as what actually happened in the confusion of the battle. So far as the British were concerned, on this desperate day of fighting when things truly hung in the balance, with disruption through casualties at the highest levels of the British command structure, when Haig deemed it expedient to ride up the Menin Road, possibly as a calming influence, the line was held. Almost immediately, it would seem, the charge of 2/Worcesters was seen to epitomise the endurance of numerous units or parts of units during the day. More than that, it has come to be <u>the</u> example, taken from numerous others and possibly only facing competition in its dominance in the narrative of the battle from the London Scottish at Messines. In this sense, the confused facts of the charge become of little consequence compared to the known impact of it on the BEF (and, in due course, the British public) at this key time in the war; and what the BEF (and the British public) made of it in the months to come. On the other hand, what actually did happen will remain of great interest to military historians for years to come.

From here it is easy to proceed to the Menin Road and your next destination. Alternatively, at **(14)** you can turn right and the road will bring you out on the west side of the motorway, in the area of Black Watch Corner.

Cemeteries Section:

Menen German Cemetery and Short Notes on Relevant CWGC Cemeteries

A visit to the German cemetery at Menen
From Geluveld drive towards Menen, passing through Koelenberg and Geluwe, both of which saw action in October 1914. At Menen follow the bypass signs 'Alle Richtingen', which avoid the town centre and exit on the road to Kortrijk (the N8); about a kilometre after the road passes over the motorway there is a turning on the left. The cemetery is badly signed from the main road, though just before it on the left is a house which appears to be what the polite circles of yesteryear called a 'house of ill repute' – at evening time lit up in a shocking pink – and there is a church with a short green topped tower nearby. Look for a modest sign on the LEFT of the road in pale blue that indicates the turn to the cemetery 'Menen Deutscher Soldatenfriedhof'. This is Henri Debrabanderstraat.

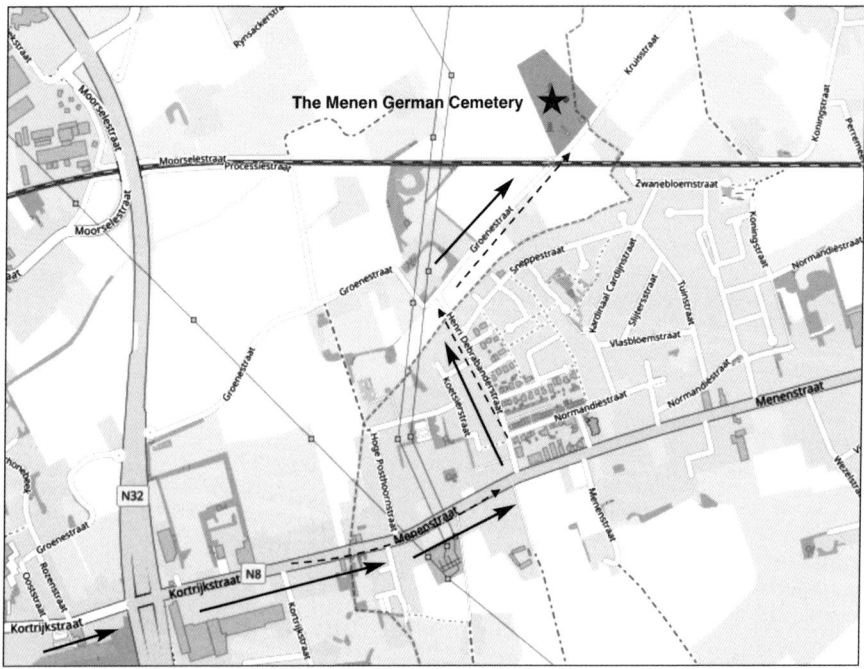

Location map for the German cemetery.

Drive past the houses to a T junction, which is once more signed to the cemetery (Groenestraat) and turn right; cross the railway line and the cemetery is a hundred metres beyond that on the left. There is a parking space just by the entrance.

The horrendous total of German soldiers buried at Menen: 47,864 of them.

Although apparently modest in size, with 47,864 burials, this cemetery has the dubious distinction of being the largest of the German Great War burial places. In the early post war years 6,340 men were buried here then, following the Second World War and a major policy of rationalisation in Belgium, between 1955 and 1959, the *Volksbund* concentrated all the graves of forty nine cemeteries in southern Flanders here. At the same time the entrance and the memorial chapel were built. These buildings in sandstone from the Weser Hills of North Rhine Westphalia are the work of the then chief architect of the *Volksbund*, Robert Tischler (1885 – 1959).

Robert Tischler (second from left), the architect of the German cemetery in Menen.

The octagonal shape of the memorial chapel was inspired by the design of Byzantine burial chambers and this theme is continued in the interior by the use of lions sculpted by Fritz Schmoll around a central pillar and mosaics by Franz Grau, which show biblical scenes: golden angels; the Tree of Knowledge from the Garden of Eden; and the New Jerusalem are all represented - the last two symbolising Alpha and Omega, the beginning and end of human history, strung out between the Fall and Redemption, between Heaven and Earth. Often this iconography features Jacob's Ladder from the Book of Genesis in the Old Testament, but here the angels alone serve the purpose, conveying the idea of the transition from Earth to Heaven by soldiers whose sacrifice is repaid by resurrection.

Until the 1970s simple wooden grave markers were used, but these were then replaced by permanent stone grave markers laid flat and interspersed with crosses made of black volcanic lava. The majority of burials are from later in the war, but this place houses the final resting places of many who fell in autumn 1914.Your attention is drawn to the graves of the men in the following list, who are representative of all those killed during the fierce battles along the Menin Road and down towards the Messines Ridge. Note there is usually a simple laminated sheet guide to the Block system in the small reception room; please do not take it away!

The German cemetery at Menen prior to its reorganisation to its present condition.

200

Menen German Cemetery. All but a handful of the burials are of known casualties.

Hauptmann Karl Sattig 1st Company Reserve Infantry Regiment 19 KIA southwest of Poelcappelle 10 November. *Block A Grave 60.*

Major Hermann Helmes Bavarian Reserve Infantry Regiment 17 KIA Wytschaete 1 November. *Block A Grave 379.*

Oberstleutnant Anton Deboi Commander Bavarian Reserve Infantry Regiment 5 KIA Wytschaete 15 Nov 14. *Block A Grave 3383.*

Oberleutnant Hermann von Busse 1st Battalion Footguard Regiment 1KIA near Veldhoek 11 November. *Block B Grave 414.*

Oberstleutnant Magnus von Holleben Commander Reserve Infantry Regiment 244 KIA east of Polygon Wood 22 October. The date of his death is wrongly recorded by the German *Volksbund* as 20 October. *Block B Grave 13098.*

Oberleutnant Gebhardt Meßbauer 1st Company Reserve Infantry Regiment 247 KIA Vieux Chien 29 October. *Block C Grave 120.*

Hauptmann Theodor Probst 6th Battery Reserve Field Artillery Regiment 54 KIA near Poezelhoek 4 November. *Block D Grave 153.*

Hauptmann Alfred Stockmeyer 9th Company Reserve Infantry Regiment 246. Born in Göppingen, near Stuttgart, 19 November 1872, he was forty one years old when he was KIA Reutel 21 October. *Block D Grave 2334.*

Reserve Leutnant Ernst Körner 5th Battery Reserve Field Artillery Regiment 54. Born in Stuttgart 13 February 1893, he was twenty-one years old when he was KIA at Poezelhoek 3/4 November. *Block D Grave 2564.*

201

Major Karl Horn 1st Battalion Reserve Infantry Regiment 19 KIA southwest of Poelcappelle 10 November. *Block D Grave 3541.*

Major Hans Strelin 3rd Battalion Reserve Infantry Regiment 246 KIA Reutel 21 October. *Block D Grave 2891.*

Leutnant Wolfgang Schumann 2nd Battalion Infantry Regiment 136 KIA near Zandvoorde 30 October. *Block F Grave 1605.*

Leutnant Hans Kaphengst Reserve Field Artillery Regiment 51 KIA near Veldhoek 8 November. His date of death is wrongly stated by the *Volksbund* to be 9 November. *Block F Grave 1692.*

Leutnant Hans Kaphengst.

Offiziertellvertreter Adolf Heß 3rd Battalion Reserve Infantry Regiment 213 KIA at Weidendrift 30 October. *Block F Grave 2125.*

Oberstleutnant Friedrich Linker Infantry Regiment 143 KIA near Veldhoek 8 November. *Block G Grave 1725.*

Leutnant Georg Fillweber Bavarian Reserve Infantry Regiment 17 KIA Wytschaete 1 November. *Block G Grave 2155.*

Reserve Lt Ernst Hoffmann 11th Company Infantry Regiment 143 KIA near Veldhoek 3 November. *Block G Grave 2293.*

Hauptmann Friedrich Schöler 1st Battalion Reserve Infantry Regiment 236 KIA Langemarck 21 October. *Block H Grave 12.*

Offizierstellvertreter Albert Bauerschmidt Footguard Regiment 3 KIA near Veldhoek 11 November. *Block I Grave 911.*

Musketier Arthur Waldmeyer, Oboe player with the band of Infantry Regiment 143 KIA near Veldhoek 9 November. *Block I Grave 995.*

Unteroffizier Alfred Gläser Machine Gun Company Infantry Regiment 105 KIA Gheluvelt 31 October. *Block I Grave 1019.*

Major Max Jordan 3rd Battalion Reserve Infantry Regiment 248 DOW at Kortrijk 29 October, having been wounded near Vieux Chien two days previously. *Block K Grave 3245.*

Musketier Wilhelm Keilholz 10th Company Infantry Regiment 143 KIA near Veldhoek 8 November. *Block L Grave 443.*

Oberleutnant Gerhard Arnold Reserve Infantry Regiment 245 KIA 1 November near Polderhoek Chateau. *Block N Grave 1871.*

Major Julius Graf [Count] von Zech auf Neuhofen 1st Battalion Bavarian Reserve Infantry Regiment 16 and former Governor of the German colony of Togo. KIA by a shot to the head while crossing the Kruiseecke – Becelaere Road 29 October. *Block N Grave 1947.*

Oberstleutnant Hermann Johannes Garten 3rd Battalion Reserve Infantry Regiment 242 KIA Kruiseecke 25 October. *Block N Grave 2031.*

The Chapel in the German cemetery at Menen.

Oberstleutnant Max Hammer Reserve Infantry Regiment 242 KIA near
Kruisecke 26 October. *Block N Grave 2032.*
Hauptmann Ludwig Obermann 2nd Battalion Reserve Infantry Regiment
247 KIA near Vieux Chien 29 October. *Block N Grave 2593.*
Oberleutnant Karl von Dobbeler 2nd Battalion Footguard Regiment 1 KIA
near Veldhoek 11 November. *Block O Grave 1249.*

If you choose to return to Geluveld via Werwik, Amerika and Kruiseke you
will be able to gain an impression of the terrain over which units and
formations of the Bavarian cavalry division operated during early – mid
October.

British Cemeteries
There are a number of CWGC cemeteries in the area with identified British
burials from the period, a selected list of which follows below.

To find such burials on the CWGC, go to the cemeteries section and
select the cemetery that you wish to investigate. The page will tell you
how many identified casualties there are. Click on 'Find these records'.
On the new page there is a 'Relevance' box; from the drop down menu
select 'date of death'. From here you can find the ones buried in the
particular cemetery in the given period. A similar approach using the War
Dead search facility and inserting Belgium and, say, 15 October to 25
November, will list all those buried or commemorated in Belgium within
those dates, in this case over 10,500 casualties.

Obviously by far the majority of the fatalities are commemorated on
the **Menin Gate** – over 7,000 of them from the arrival of British troops in
the area in October to the (albeit temporary) departure of the BEF from
the Salient towards the end of November. Even though it is not according

to the criterion, some of the casualties from the fighting in the area covered by this book are commemorated on the Ploegsteert Memorial to the Missing.

The cemeteries with ten or more identified casualties from this period include:

Bedford House has around fifty casualties buried in it from the Battle; these are mainly to be found in Enclosure 4, with a couple in Enclosure 6. Enclosure 6 was opened to deal with the bodies that were being found in the thirties (and was used for the casualties of the Second World War in the area).

Bedford House Cemetery.

Hooge Crater Cemetery and Chapel.

There are a dozen named casualties in **Birr Cross Roads**. Although there are likely to be a significant number of burials of men killed at First Ypres in **Buttes New British**, in fact there are only four who are identified and fit the dates. Amongst these is Lieutenant Horace Grimston of the ill-fated 2/Wilts, who was killed on 21 October 1914 and is now buried in XXII C 15. **Hooge Crater** has seventeen identified casualties of the period, including Lieutenant Colonel H Cadogan of the Royal Welsh Fusiliers (IXA L 11) and Captain Lord Richard Wellesley, Grenadier Guards (XVI B 11). In **Perth Cemetery (China Wall)** there are 165 identified casualties, including those on Special memorials. Note that these special memorials (marked with a 'Duhallow' stone – an example of which is in the foreground) were erected when a soldier was known to have been buried in a particular cemetery but whose body could not be recovered after the war – either because the cemetery was destroyed (usually) or because the body could not be found, for example.

Special Memorials Section, Perth Cemetery (China Wall).

Poelcapelle British, a large post war concentration cemetery, has about thirty casualties. All twenty-one British casualties in **Poperinge Communal Cemetery** are from this period; there is a row of eight officers in Plot 1, Row B, against the south wall. Nearby is **Poperinghe (sic) Old Military Cemetery**. The relevant plot is to the rear left of this unusually laid out cemetery – Plot 1, Rows L and M; there are about 140 casualties

Poelcapelle British Cemetery.

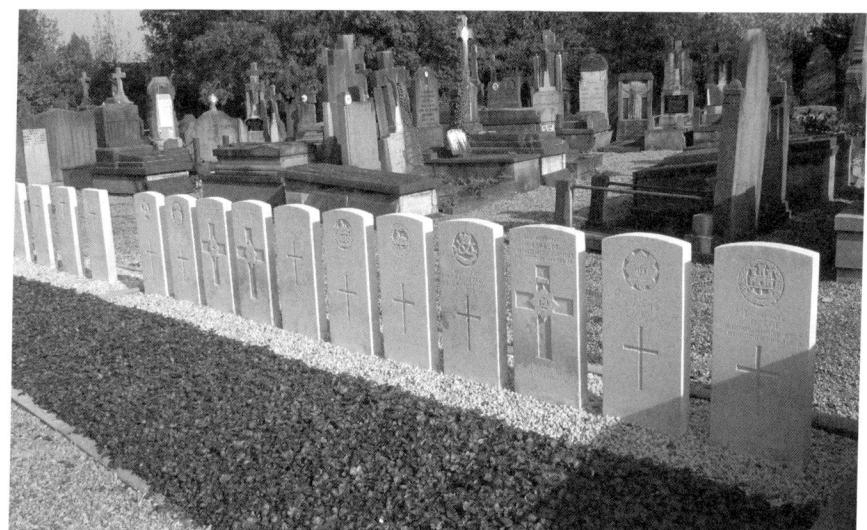

One of the rows of British graves in Poperinge Communal Cemetery.

from this period. It has an almost hidden entrance; it is more or less on the opposite side of the street from the Communal Cemetery (NOT to be mixed up with the modern one, on the eastern outskirts of the town).

There are some sixty identified casualties in **Sanctuary Wood Cemetery**. In **Tyne Cot** there are seventy-seven identified casualties from mid October to end November 1914. In **Ypres Town Cemetery** there are 122 identified casualties of First Ypres – these are to be found in two groupings: by the eastern entrance on the Menin Road or near the Extension (of these latter, Prince Maurice of Battenberg is on his own). See cemetery plan, p. 171. A visitor would be advised to visit the eastern burials first and then drive or walk around to the entrance to the cemetery

206

Plot I, Rows L and M in Poperinghe (sic) Old Military Cemetery.

Tyne Cot.

Ypres Town Cemetery.

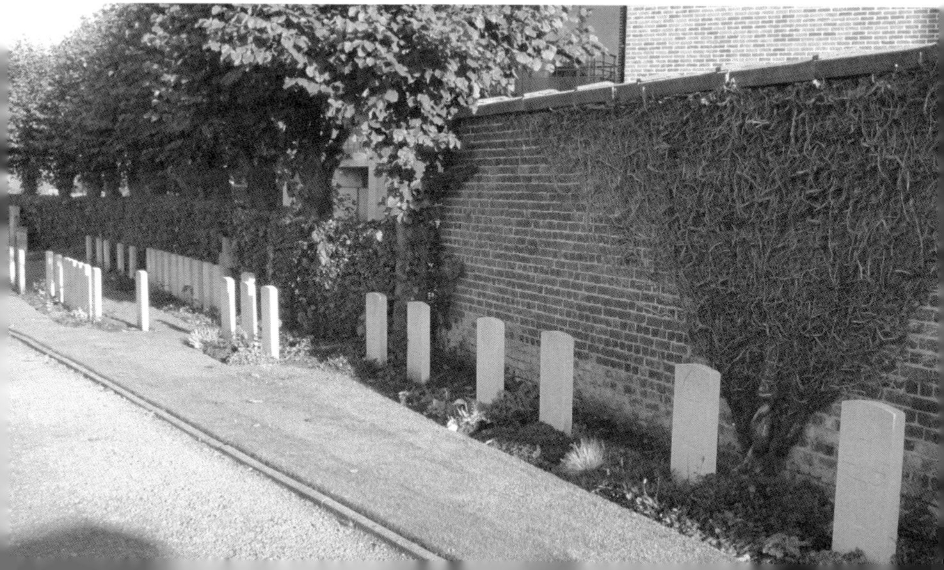

via the Extension (parking appears to be relatively easy here); otherwise it is a long, somewhat circuitous, walk through this vast cemetery. In **Ypres Town Cemetery Extension**, which is best accessed from Zonnebeekseweg, 129 of the identified burials are from First Ypres. There is access to the Town Cemetery at the right rear of the Extension and nearby will be found the majority of those buried there. Amongst those buried in the extension are several of the casualties from the shelling of Hooge Chateau on 31 October – for example Colonel Kerr, who was on the staff of the 1st Division. In **Zantvoorde British Cemetery** (notice the use of 't' instead of 'd') there are about a hundred or so commemorations from the period (some are Special Memorials), including JAO Brooke VC, 2/Gordons and Lieutenant Colonel B Pell, who was commanding 2/Queen's when he was killed on 4 November.

The Menin Road 1914:
Skeleton Order of Battle of the
German Army

All formations came under the overall command of the German Fourth Army of Generaloberst Duke Albrecht of Württemberg, whose headquarters was established at Gent.

Initial Attacks:
XXVII Reserve Corps
53rd Reserve Division
105 Reserve Infantry Brigade (Reserve Infantry Regiments 241 & 242)
106 Res Infantry Brigade (Reserve Infantry Regiments 243 & 244)
54th Reserve Division
107 Reserve Infantry Brigade (Reserve Infantry Regiments 245 & 246)
108 Reserve Infantry Brigade (Reserve Infantry Regiments 247 & 248)
Reserve Jäger Battalions 25 & 26

From 29 October
Bavarian Reserve Infantry Regiment 16
Landwehr Detachment Waxmann
Elements of XV Corps:
30th Infantry Division
60 Infantry Brigade (Infantry Regiments 99 & 143)
85 Infantry Brigade (Infantry Regiment 103)
N.B Infantry Regiment 136, part of this brigade, operated primarily further south with 39th Infantry Division

From 8 November
Ad hoc Guards Division Winckler (Winckler was normally Commander 2nd Guards Infantry Division)
1 Guards Infantry Brigade (Footguard Regiments 1 & 3)
4 Guards Infantry Brigade (Grenadier Guard Regiments 2 &4)

Select Bibliography

Anglesey, The Marquess of, *A History of the British Cavalry 1816 – 1919:* Vol 7, *The Curragh Incident and the Western Front, 1914*, 1996

Anon ('By a Regimental Committee'), *Historical Records of the Queen's Own Cameron Highlanders*, Vol 3, 1931

Anon: *Ypres 1914*, Battery Press, n.d.

Atkinson, CH, *The Seventh Division 1914 – 1918*, 1927

Atkinson, CH, *The History of the South Wales Borderers 1914 – 1918*, 1931

Bickersteth, JB, *History of the Sixth Cavalry Brigade 1914 – 1918*, 1920

Craster, JM (ed), *Fifteen Rounds a Minute*, 1976

Edmonds, JE: *Military Operations France and Belgium Vols 1 and 2.* Macmillan and Co., 1922 and 1929

Ewart, W (et al), *The Scots Guards in the Great War 1914 -1918*, 1925

Hamilton, Lord E, *The First Seven Divisions*, 1916

Hare, S, *The Annals of the King's Royal Rifle Corps*, Vol V: *The Great War*, 1932

Hyndson, *From Mons to the First Battle of Ypres*, 1932

Jourdain, HFN and Fraser, E: *The Connaught Rangers Volume I.* Naval & Military Press, n.d.

Kipling, R, *The Irish Guards in the Great War* Vols I and II, 1923

Mockler-Ferryman, AF (comp and ed), The Oxfordshire and Buckinghamshire Light Infantry Chronicle 1914 – 1915, n.d.

Ponsonby, Sir F, *The Grenadier Guards in the Great War of 1914 – 1918*, Vol I, 1920

Ross-of-Bladensburg, Sir J, *The Coldstream Guards 1914 – 1918*, 1928

Sheffield, G and Bourne, J (eds), *Douglas Haig: War Diaries and Letters 1914 – 1918*, 2005

Sheldon, J: *The German Army in Ypres, 1914.* Pen and Sword, 2010

Stacke, H Fitz M, *The Worcestershire Regiment in the Great War*, 1928

Ward, CH Dudley, *Regimental Records of the Royal Welch Fusiliers*, Vol III, 1928

Wauchope, AG, *A History of the Black Watch (Royal Highlanders) in the Great War, 1914 – 1918*, Vol One, 1925

Wylly, HC, *History of the Queen's Royal (West Surrey) Regiment in the Great War*

Wylly, HC, *The Loyal North Lancashire Regiment*, Vol II 1914 – 1919, 1933

Wyrall, E, *The History of the Second Division*, N&M reprint, n.d.

Index